WHAT IF
THERE WAS

NO
CONGRESS

WHAT IF
THERE WAS
NO
CONGRESS

PRIYAM GANDHI-MODY

RUPA

Published by
Rupa Publications India Pvt. Ltd 2024
7/16, Ansari Road, Daryaganj
New Delhi 110002

Sales centres:
Bengaluru Chennai
Hyderabad Jaipur Kathmandu
Kolkata Mumbai Prayagraj

P-ISBN: 978-93-5702-893-6
E-ISBN: 978-93-5702-949-0

First impression 2024

10 9 8 7 6 5 4 2 3 1

The moral right of the author has been asserted.

Printed in India

To Maha Shakti

For you are omnipresent and omnipotent
I am but only a means to an end that
you have already envisaged
I remain in eternal, servile gratitude

CONTENTS

INTRODUCTION

In the Winter Session of Parliament in February 2022, Prime Minister (PM) Modi posed a question, 'What if there was no Congress in India?'[1] This was a question that forced the intellectual community, historians and the social media armies of India to delve into seeking answers, some with the intent to support the PM's thoughts, some to oppose and the rest to troll.

It is no secret that in 1948, on the day of his assassination, Mohandas Karamchand Gandhi called for disbandment of the Congress via what seems to be the last letter written by the Mahatma and is believed to be his last will and testament. To Gandhi, the Congress, as it was in 1948, had 'outlived its use'.[2] He believed that the Congress's role in Indian independence had been one of a propaganda machine and that it was time for the party to convert itself into a non-political organization called Lok Sevak Sangh.[3] Indeed, the Congress had played a crucial role in the Indian freedom struggle; however, its leadership also made some missteps that resulted in the Balkanization of undivided India. Before any more damage could be done, he gave out his orders. However, were the orders too late? Had they come 15 years earlier, perhaps we would have had an undivided India, a peaceful Kashmir and the Mahatma himself with us for many more years.

It is not often when the minds of two of the greatest leaders to serve India, born seven decades apart, intersect to meet at a common thought. However, when they do, it becomes the duty of

---

[1]'If There Was No Congress...': PM Modi Attacks Grand Old Party in Rajya Sabha', *The Times of India*, 8 February 2022, https://tinyurl.com/mr37zfwj. Accessed on 5 June 2023.
[2]Gandhi, M.K., 'His Last Will and Testament', *Harijan*, 15 February 1948, https://tinyurl.com/5w4uvabs. Accessed on 5 May 2023.
[3]Ibid.

intellectuals to carefully and deeply study the merits of those ideas and arrive at reasons why such a consensus may have reached in the minds of both.

To understand why the Mahatma may have left behind this final guiding light (fully forgotten by claimants of his political legacy, only to be revisited by PM Modi decades later), I have set out on an endeavour to understand the circumstances and undercurrents around the time of Indian independence that followed hundreds of years of colonial rule. I have made a sincere attempt to understand the methods of working of the Congress party in its current state to analyse why Gandhi's final words seem to indeed be prophetic. History must be told, retold and retold again in order for the lessons learned from the mistakes of the past, solutions to the challenges and achievements to stay relevant for the current generation. Through my book, I hope to revisit some of the events that took place over the last 80 years but continue to shape the politics of today's India.

For this, I have attempted to study material from several books, original speeches, recorded debates and interviews. As I sought to study relationships between the leaders of each time period over the last 80 years, I was compelled to ask myself: what direction would independent India have taken had Jawaharlal Nehru not been the first PM? What if we had a leader like Narendra Modi as our first PM in 1948 instead? And if there were new political organizations that may have taken birth after the disbandment of the old Congress, which of those would have found popular support? What if Subhas Chandra Bose had lived beyond Independence—how would his leadership have shaped India? Had Sardar Vallabhbhai Patel not been repeatedly sidelined for the top job, how would he have shaped the course of independent India?

In order to make the research more concise, I have attempted to study historical events from four lenses, that is, pressing issues which continue to stay crucial even today: Partition, territorial integrity, economic policy and governance. Each lens makes one section, at the beginning of which I have laid out a background of events that took place immediately preceding and succeeding

Independence. These have formed the basis of policy-making over the last 75 years and continue to dominate political dialogue even today.

I see no better time to bring out this book than now, when the country has completed 75 years of Independence, and a chunk of the country has begun to seriously question if we have fulfilled the true meaning of independence. In order to reach the milestone of India achieving the status of a developed country in the next 25 years, laid out by PM Modi in his Independence Day speech of 2022,[4] it is absolutely critical to evaluate successes and failures of our policies in order to separate historical facts from the noise generated by blame games and chest thumping by political parties. India has had a long-standing tendency of sanitizing its history to suit political narratives. This must stop. The present generation of Indians must be presented with raw, unbiased, unfiltered, historically accurate information, so that it can use its own judgement to develop opinions. We owe this to tomorrow's India, at the very least.

---

[4]Modi, Narendra, 'PM Narendra Modi's 76th Independence Day Speech from Red Fort', *YouTube*, 15 August 2022, https://tinyurl.com/2fwdcynp. Accessed on 4 October 2023.

SECTION I

PARTITION

1

PARTITION: PART I

On 15 August 1947, when the long-desired independence came to India, the country was simultaneously divided into three parts: mainland India and East plus West Pakistan. Everything about running two wedges through India, cutting it from the core, remains painful and bloody. Many argue that Partition remains possibly the bloodiest exodus in global history, with communities being uprooted from their homes, resulting in loss of lives. Millions were killed; precious human lives were lost. And yet, we still do not know much about the circumstances and events leading up to Partition. We do know now that it was only a select few men from the Indian political leadership who made the decision to divide the country. However, we still do not fully understand why they made such a painful choice. Several lingering questions remain: who takes accountability and ownership of the violence? What are the lessons learned? In the years leading up to the fateful day, what were some of the important alerting events that catalysed and cemented the inevitability of Partition? Do our colonizers recognize their heinous role in perpetrating this massacre to further their own interests? And finally, could it all have been avoided?

We need to dig for honest answers to these questions as they will provide incredible learning for us—a learning that will help us avoid a repetition of missteps and, thus, avert a similar ghastly event in the future.

Several theories have made rounds—some blame Nehru and the rest of the Congress leadership for underestimating Jinnah's ambitions, some blame Jinnah for choosing to pursue his ambition at the high cost of morality and millions of human lives, and others blame the British. The truth, in my opinion, lies in all three of the above, combined with the lack of deftness in Nehru's political dealings, the Congress's lack of geopolitical acumen and the desperation for independence at any cost, however bloody it may be. The aforementioned truths snowballed into a rather dangerous situation with the incapability of the Congress leadership in 1947 to resist and defeat radical, violent and communal acts unleashed by Jinnah's All-India Muslim League, egged on by the faithful support of the outgoing British Indian government that was desperate to keep a slice of its colony.

PRE-INDEPENDENCE CONGRESS AND ITS PERSONALITIES

The Indian National Congress (INC) was founded in 1885 by a retired British Civil Service officer, a Scotsman, Allan Octavian Hume, and widely believed to have been supported by the British to mitigate anti-British sentiments in India at the time.[1] By creating a political outfit to voice grievances and increase participation of the Indian people in the country's governance, the British provided angry Indians with an outlet. Since the Congress at the time of founding was run with the full involvement of the British Indian government, the organization ensured that Indians were kept on a leash and that any overt, inconvenient gestures against the Raj were snuffed out. At that time, it was merely a debating society with educated Indians who wanted to be more involved in conversations around governance. After 1920, Gandhi changed that by involving women, peasants and the ordinary Indian in the party, much to his credit, even though this did not reflect in his personal life. His wife Kasturba always walked a few steps behind him, fully letting him be the star of the show.[2]

It was in 1915 that Gandhi returned to India from South Africa

---

[1]Bhardwaj, Deeksha, 'AO Hume, "Father" of Indian National Congress Who Was Distrusted by British & Indians', *The Print*, 6 June 2019, https://tinyurl.com/3j4xjmr3. Accessed on 4 October 2023.

[2]Dalrymple, William and Anita Anand, 'Mahatma Gandhi', *Empire*, 20 September 2022, https://tinyurl.com/mr3msxuj. Accessed on 4 October 2023.

at the request of his mentor Gopal Krishna Gokhale,[3] who was worried about the revolutionary, violent turn that factions within the Congress, like Lala Lajpat Rai's and Bhagat Singh's, were adopting against the Raj. Gandhi, with his non-violent approach, had succeeded in resisting a British pass law that had discriminated against Indians in South Africa. Already hailed a hero, he had navigated his way to the top leadership position of the Congress in a very short period of time.

Gandhi was born to an upper-middle-class trader in Gujarat. He was married to Kasturba at the age of 13, after which he went to Britain to get his law degree. His upbringing in a Hindu family ensured that he abstained from consuming meat while studying in Britain, making him explore the streets of the city to find vegetarian food. In the late 1880s, there were very few vegetarian restaurants in London due to the insignificant number of folks who ate a vegetarian meal. Often, at a vegetarian restaurant in London in the 1880s, one would only find lone travellers and odd, hippie characters who stood out from the mainstream population with their choice of a vegetarian diet in a predominantly meat-eating culture. It is in one of these vegetarian restaurants that he encountered some Edwardian, mystic, spiritual women from an occult, unorthodox world, who also seemed to have left an impressionable imprint on his personality in his formative, late-teen years. During his restaurant visits, he befriended theosophists like Madam Blavatsky and Annie Besant. Blavatsky claimed to have received instruction in occult knowledge from masters in the Himalayas and radiant astro-figures whom she called Mahatmas and believed them to be immortal beings. As a mark of her friendship with Gandhi, she began to call him Mahatma, and, in fact, it is from her that Gandhi's title of Mahatma seems to have originated which of course was later officially bestowed upon him by Rabindranath Tagore. He stayed friends with them even after he moved to South Africa, having

---

[3]Gokhale, Sunil, 'Gopal Krishna Gokhale's Repeated Requests Brought Mahatma Gandhi Back to India', *The Economic Times*, 6 January 2015, https://tinyurl.com/ysnzcdxx. Accessed on 4 October 2023.

been called to the Bar at the age of 21 for a legal case. So Gandhi, essentially this small, skinny man, had a mix of his Hindu traditional upbringing cocktailed with experiences in the courtrooms of Great Britain and influence of his friendships with mystics who called him Mahatma.[4] When he returned to India and became Mahatma Gandhi in a loincloth, a combination of all of the abovementioned life experiences and choices were evident in his personality.[5]

Jawaharlal Motilal Nehru, on the other hand, hailed from an aristocrat Kashmiri Brahmin family. His father Motilal Nehru was a prosperous lawyer, and, at home in Allahabad (now Prayagraj), Jawaharlal was brought up in great luxury and with English influence. In fact, the atmosphere that he was raised in was one that any other cultivated English gentleman would also be subject to in his childhood. Their residence was always filled with mostly English guests but also frequented by Hindus and Muslims alike. So much was the social activity in the Nehru household that it is believed that Motilal Nehru ran three separate kitchens to cater to everyone's tastes.[6] With a slew of British tutors, Jawaharlal became fluent in English, although he made only little progress in Hindi and Sanskrit. At the age of 15, he was shipped off to Harrow, and at the age of 22, when he returned to India as a Cambridge-educated lawyer, he was soaked in British tastes and preferences. To demonstrate how even his food palette was rather British than Indian, there is a popular anecdote from the year 1956 that surprised the Americans during his visit to their country. When President Dwight D. Eisenhower had the White House and State Department ascertain his food preferences prior to his visit to the United States (US) as the PM of India, they were rather surprised to learn that the leader of the 'world's largest Hindu country' and his daughter Indira, who was to accompany him, preferred beef (filet mignon to be specific) along with an occasional scotch (all in

---

[4]Dalrymple, William and Anita Anand, 'Mahatma Gandhi', *Empire*, 20 September 2022, https://tinyurl.com/mr3msxuj. Accessed on 4 October 2023.
[5]Ibid.
[6]Mosley, Leonard, *The Last Days of the British Raj*, Harcourt, Brace & World, Inc., New York, 1961, p. 74

private of course) versus the more traditional and expected Indian vegetarian meal with a non-alcoholic beverage.[7] After Cambridge and his return to India, Jawaharlal threw himself into Indian politics and aligned himself with the machinations of the Congress Party. His father was one of the early foreign-educated Indians (Cambridge) and a force to be reckoned with in the Congress of the day (he had been Congress president twice—in 1919 and 1928). It was during his 1928 presidency that he led the Nehru resolution to accept dominion status for India, which was subsequently passed. When time came to pass on the reigns of the Congress presidency the following year in 1929, Motilal lobbied Gandhi into making Jawaharlal the president. As a matter of fact, since 1927, he had been pressing Gandhi to give Jawaharlal the reigns of the Congress, but the latter thought that the time was not suitable then.[8] In 1928, too, Motilal had renewed his efforts for his son, but the Congress leaders insisted that Motilal be the president instead, which was what ended up happening. In 1929, however, when Jawaharlal's name finally came up for presidency, the two other contenders were Gandhi and Sardar Vallabhbhai Patel. Jawaharlal won three votes, Patel won five and Gandhi won ten. On being declared elected, Gandhi resigned and pushed for Jawaharlal to lead.[9] This was the first but not the last time when Sardar Vallabhbhai Patel had to yield power to Jawaharlal on Gandhi's behest. The second time was in 1936, just a year before the general elections were scheduled in India. Despite coming to a consensus that the party would vote in Patel, on the eve of the presidentship elections, Gandhi summoned Patel and pleaded with him to withdraw his candidacy and support Jawaharlal's instead.[10] The third time was in

---

[7]Riedel, Bruce, *JFK's Forgotten Crisis: Tibet, the CIA, and the Sino-Indian War*, HarperCollins India, Noida, 2015, p. 8.

[8]Mukherjee, Rudrangshu, *Nehru & Bose: Parallel Lives*, Penguin Books, New Delhi, 2015, pp. 66–7.

[9]Sitaramaya, B. Pattabhi, *The History of the Indian National Congress*, Vol. 1, Padma Publications, 1946, p. 347.

[10]Mosley, Leonard, *The Last Days of the British Raj*, Harcourt, Brace & World, Inc., New York, 1961, p. 77.

1946, when the negotiations for Independence had begun to bear fruit. The outgoing president Maulana Azad proposed Jawaharlal's name instead. Patel was sure that Gandhi favoured his election this time around—he had waited a long time for this moment, after all. Gandhi had clearly indicated in previous conversations with Patel that he would be favourable to having Patel as the president. However, when the time came, Gandhi gave him no support, and Patel was sidelined once again for a role—the most important of them—he had wanted.

Sardar Vallabhbhai Patel from Bombay (now Mumbai) was the strongman of the party, renowned for dealing matters with an iron fist, so much so that he didn't even bother to wear a velvet glove over it most times. Unlike Jawaharlal's socialist ideologies, Patel was a middle-of-the-road capitalist. He hammered agreements and discussions with sheer force and the weight of numbers. A true follower of Gandhi at heart, despite being a man with deep personal ambitions, he allowed himself to be superseded thrice by Nehru whom he thought was a temperamental dreamer. He kept the Congress going with regular infusions of money from the big Hindu millionaires. He was adept at carrying out the frequent groundwork that was required to run a political party—the purging and oiling needed to keep the party funded, its members satisfied and motivated—the kind of work that Nehru could have never been able to soil his hands with. Speaking only Gujarati and English and usually getting his hands dirty on the job, Patel was considered a non-intellectual and a non-idealist.[11] The Congress, then, took more pride in the scholastic achievements of its leaders than it did in their mass connect—just like it does today. Had mass connect been the gold standard of promoting its leadership, there's little doubt that Sardar Patel would have been an out and out frontrunner. There have been no lessons learnt there—even today, the Congress party prefers to promote members with scholastic qualifications over those who have strong people connect.

To gain context, it is important to understand that the

---

[11]Ibid.

constitution of the pre-Independence Congress vis-à-vis the Congress of today. Both share the flavour of optical secularism and the dynastic leadership. However, they do differ in one case: pre-Independence Congress had members from diverse ideologies, for anyone with a serious desire to fight for the cause of Indian Independence aligned themselves with either the Congress or the Muslim League, the less popular but only other relevant national party. In other words, for most Hindus, the only political party of choice to join in order to participate in the freedom struggle against the Raj was the Congress. With time, two distinct groups emerged within the Congress, specifically post Gandhi's takeover— the nationalists and the revolutionaries. Nationalists, as they called themselves, were those who followed Gandhian principles and rallied behind his teachings, giving impetus to his movements. Revolutionaries, on the other hand, did not believe that only non-violent efforts and Gandhian principles would get India its freedom. They organized mass movements inspired by teachings of Hindu legends like Swami Vivekanand, Chhatrapati Shivaji Maharaj and Sri Aurobindo Ghosh. Closer to Independence, it was Subhas Chandra Bose who seemed to lead this group within the Congress. Frustrated with Gandhi's partiality to Nehru due to his lineage, despite the latter being weaker in merit, Bose left the Congress and organized the armed Indian freedom struggle. There is great debate today about whether it was Bose's armed struggle or Nehru–Gandhi's non-violent one that led us to Independence. Perhaps the events we cover through this section may contribute to it further. There were several other notable leaders like Maulana Abdul Kalam Azad, C. Rajagopalachari, Baldev Singh and Khan Abdul Ghaffar Khan who associated themselves with the Congress either directly or as an ally. Dr B.R. Ambedkar, who emerged as a Dalit leader, was keen to rally the Dalits together and create a third front. The third front would further split Indians on the basis of caste. When Gandhi got wind of Ambedkar's intentions to create a separate party for the Dalits, he fasted for the causes that were important to the community. Gandhi's fast demotivated Ambedkar to create a new political party and assured him that Gandhi would stand by the Dalit community's needs. Thus, despite his personal reservations towards Gandhian philosophies, Ambedkar remained with the Congress.

Another crucial character in this mix at the time was Muhammad Ali Jinnah. Born to a lower middle-class Shia Muslim family of the Khoja community, Jinnah's father was a boatman who used to ferry passengers up and down the Sind.[12] Jinnah, a young, brilliant boy, was provided an opportunity by a British acquaintance of his father to further his legal studies in London. At the age of 16, just like Gandhi, Jinnah went to law school in Britain and, in fact, due to his extraordinary intellect, became the youngest Indian to be called to the bar at the age of 19.[13] Jinnah was sharp, precise, blessed with rapier wit, a natural performer and believed that he was born to achieve greatness. He was truly secular and fully embraced Western culture; enjoying his alcohol and meat, including pork.[14] On returning to India, he worked for a British law firm, accumulating wealth, upgrading his lifestyle and becoming a connoisseur of fine suits, silk ties and court shoes.[15] Jinnah's political career at the age of 30 began with the Congress too, a few years after which he joined the Muslim League. His main aim during this time was to bring about Hindu–Muslim unity and coordinate the drives of both parties towards the common goal of Indian independence. Until 1920, he kept rising in the hierarchy of the Congress Party, after which his rise in the ranks abruptly stopped due to the arrival of the new rising star—Gandhi.[16] He even took part in the civil disobedience movement but saw how 'peaceful' demonstrators

---

[12]Dalrymple, William and Anita Anand, 'Muhammad Ali Jinnah', *Empire*, 25 October 2022, https://tinyurl.com/juewk78b. Accessed on 9 November 2023.

[13]Ibid.

[14]Parthasarathy, G., 'Reimagining Pakistan Talks about How Jinnah Gave Clerics Free Hand in Political Mobilization', *India Today*, 6 May 2018, https://tinyurl.com/5zpwuunt. Accessed on 9 November 2023.

[15]Dalrymple, William and Anita Anand, 'Muhammad Ali Jinnah', *Empire*, 25 October 2022, https://tinyurl.com/juewk78b. Accessed on 9 November 2023.

[16]Ibid.

indulged in destruction and violence. Jinnah became convinced that Gandhi's ways were not realistic and neither was Gandhi. This is not popular knowledge but he grew to detest Gandhi precisely because of how the latter tied Hinduism to politics.[17] Jinnah believed that for a society like India, bringing religion into politics would be akin to opening Pandora's Box. And then, along came Gandhi, preaching predominantly Hindu concepts such as *satyagraha*, *ahimsa*, speaking about *varna*s, observing strikes in the name of prayer meets at ashrams, being called Mahatma and Bapu, dressed in a *dhoti*, clearly trying to unite the much-divided Hindu society with their common religion. Most disturbing to the Indian minorities of the time, and especially to Jinnah, was when Gandhi described British-free India as '*ramrajya*'.[18] It is this insecurity that drove Jinnah to build in minority rights in whatever new India was to be cut out. The thinking obviously was that if it really was the Hindu paradise that Gandhi and the Congress wanted, then where would the quarter of the population—the Muslims—fit in?

NEHRU–GANDHI AND JINNAH

In the years between 1914 and 1920, Jinnah and Gandhi, who had remarkably similar backgrounds, had personal clashes that cemented the enmity that ended up eventually dividing the Indian subcontinent. There is a famous party that took place in 1914 for Gandhi when he stopped over in London after returning from South Africa, in which Jinnah was also present. It is believed that this is where the two gentlemen first met and had a conversation, presumably on Indian politics. Two years later, they met once again, this time at a party thrown by Gokhale at Jinnah's house in Bombay, and here is where the first signs of sparks began to surface. At this party, where Jinnah was the host, Gandhi took the stage at one point and said of Jinnah, 'I am so pleased to see that not only is a

---

[17]Ibid.
[18]Ibid.

Muslim part of the Congress but that he is in charge of this branch of it.'[19] Jinnah found these remarks rather condescending because not only was he Gandhi's senior, he had also been able to make quite a bit of progress in fighting the British in court and in making a name for himself. But Gandhi completely minimized him to being just a 'Muslim' than recounting any of his other remarkable achievements.[20]

Once again, at the Nagpur session of the Congress in 1920, Jinnah tried to make an agitated plea referring to Gandhi as Mr Gandhi instead of Mahatma but was quickly heckled and shut down by Gandhi's supporters in the audience. For thin-skinned Jinnah, being interrupted by his junior colleague's supporters was too much of an insult to take in.[21] He then began to fade out of the Congress, although he did remain involved on and off until as late as 1928. He quickly realized that in front of the godly status that Gandhi had begun to acquire among the party members and supporters due to his focus on Hindu revivalism, his own secular thoughts stood no chance. Famously, in as late as 1924, he said, 'Foreign rule and its continuance is primarily due to the fact that the people of India, Hindus and Muslims, are not united and do not sufficiently trust each other.'[22] Soon after, he left for England to practise law before the Privy Council and amassed great wealth as a successful barrister. He had a house in Hempstead Heath and a thriving social life. He did dabble in stocks on the London Exchange and some real estate business, but his heart lay in Indian politics of the time.[23] In 1933, Liaquat

---

[19]Ibid.

[20]Ibid.

[21]Ibid.

[22]Allana, G., 'Jinnah's Speech at the Annual Session of the Muslim League, May 1924', Pakistan Movement Historical Documents, Department of International Relations, University of Karachi, Karachi, 1969.

[23]Dalrymple, William and Anita Anand, 'Muhammad Ali Jinnah', Empire, 25 October 2022, https://tinyurl.com/juewk78b. Accessed on 9 November 2023; Sarila, Narendra Singh, The Shadow of the Great Game: The Untold Story of India's Partition, HarperCollins India, Noida, 2009.

Ali Khan, another Muslim Leaguer and a long-time fan, met him at his house while the latter was on his honeymoon. During their conversation, Khan described to Jinnah the sorry state of the Muslim League and pleaded with him to come and lead it. Jinnah responded by asking Khan to see if he could muster sufficient support for his leadership. Forty-eight hours after returning to India, Khan cabled a single word to Jinnah—'Come'. However, it wasn't until 1935 that he sold his assets in London and returned to India. During his stint in Britain, Jinnah grew increasingly arrogant and self-serving. Many, including Nehru, believed that he possibly even took up the League leadership to get back at the Congress that had deprived him of what he believed was deservingly his. Maybe he did, maybe he didn't—there was no way to read Jinnah's mind—but one of the gravest errors the Congress leadership made was to underestimate his intentions and abilities. It is this misjudgement of Jinnah's character that led Nehru to make mistakes while dealing with him in the years 1939–48. Several people had several opinions of Jinnah, but the one thing that everyone seemed to concur with was that Jinnah had a fragile ego and he liked to win, at any cost, famously by trapping his opponents in details.

Between mid-1920s and mid-1930s, Jinnah's personal affairs made news, which included a close friendship with Sarojini Naidu who was all praise for him[24] (she incidentally was the Congress's first female president with Gandhi's support) and then with a second marriage at the age of 40. Rattanbai (Ruttie) Petit was all of 17 and a daughter of one of Jinnah's Parsi business associates. The couple eloped, and it was only when news of her having converted to Islamic faith was published in *The Times of India* that her father got to know of the marriage.[25] The couple had a daughter together and, shortly after, their marriage came to an end. Not too long

---

[24]Raghavan, TCA, 'Who's Afraid of Muhammad Ali Jinnah?', *Open Magazine*, 10 May 2018, https://tinyurl.com/5hfz99ey. Accessed on 9 November 2023.

[25]Dalrymple, William and Anita Anand, 'Muhammad Ali Jinnah', *Empire*, 25 October 2022, https://tinyurl.com/juewk78b. Accessed on 9 November 2023.

after that, in 1928, she was found dead in a hotel room in Bombay's Taj Mahal Hotel.[26]

At the same time, Ramsay MacDonald, a Labour Party leader with whom Jinnah had a good rapport, became the PM of Great Britain. Jinnah immediately wrote to him, suggesting that Britain should commit to transferring governance to India under dominion status. He advised the PM that this would deflate the Congress, which was gunning for Independence. He also recommended that His Majesty's Government (HMG) convene a round-table conference with participation of British and Indian leaders to discuss India's future constitutional advances.[27] In a private reply, PM MacDonald agreed that dominion status for India should be the goal.[28] Jinnah felt heard and inspired. It was at one of these round-table conferences that he took note of Sir Sultan Muhammad Shah, Agha Khan III, founder of the All-India Muslim League. He noticed how, by cooperating with the British, Khan was able to not only further his own interests but also the interests of the Khoja sect—a sect both belonged to and whose members were successful in setting up business establishments and shops throughout the Empire. Agha Khan was recognized as a prominent voice of the Indian Muslims, and, thus, it was to him that Jinnah went to seek sponsorship for a conservative seat in the House of Commons. (By 1935, MacDonald had been replaced by the conservative contender Stanley Baldwin and Jinnah had already been rejected for a Labour seat.) While the exercise did not succeed, it is believed that Jinnah was able to make strong relationships with several influential members of the Conservative Party, including but not limited to future PM Winston Churchill.

---

[26]'How Jinnah Lost His Love, and Political Relevance', *The Times of India*, 28 June 2015, https://tinyurl.com/4jynxbyr. Accessed on 9 November 2023.
[27]Sarila, Narendra Singh, *The Shadow of the Great Game: The Untold Story of India's Partition*, HarperCollins India, Noida, 2009, p. 86.
[28]Ibid.

THE GREAT CONGRESS BLUNDER OF 1939

While Jinnah had been busy making connections in England and furthering his personal ambitions, the Congress party had succeeded in getting the Government of India Act passed by the British legislature in 1935. This Act provided for self-government at the provincial level and a bicameral legislature at the centre, in which 11 British provinces as well as 350 princely states would get representation. In simpler words, this made way for Indian political parties to contest elections and begin to self-govern if they secured an electoral majority. Subsequent to the passing of the Act, the provincial elections were held in 1937—the first general elections in India. It is believed that Britain's intent was to install a conservative government at the centre that would be able to accommodate essential British interests while, at the same time, promote unity in the country and make sure that India makes steady progress towards dominion status.[29]

Before going to the polls, the Congress decided that it needed a dynamic leader to take them into the all-crucial year. For most of the party, there was one obvious choice—Patel. He, too, was eager to lead. He had all the resources and wielded enough influence over the party machinery to have swung enough support for himself. However, on the eve of the elections, Gandhi called Patel and pleaded with him to withdraw his candidacy and support Nehru instead. Patel reluctantly agreed, despite having no admiration or liking for Nehru.[30] Although Patel and Nehru were both staunch followers of Gandhi, their views were starkly opposite as far as Indian independence and how the country should be run once freedom was won was concerned.

Jinnah had also returned from London by then. He started to immediately reorganize the Muslim League. When he took over the party as the chief, it had hardly any district cells. There

---

[29]Sarila, Narendra Singh, *The Shadow of the Great Game: The Untold Story of India's Partition*, HarperCollins India, Noida, 2009, p. 36.

[30]Mosley, Leonard, *The Last Days of the British Raj*, Harcourt, Brace & World, Inc., New York, 1961, p. 77.

was no coordination with other important Muslim leaders either. Jinnah constituted the party's central and provincial boards and began to spread the message of the Muslim League on ground. He also made allies with other powerful Muslim voices. Despite his efforts, the Muslim League only won 108 out of the 485 seats reserved for Muslims in the British provinces.[31] In other words, these results were clearly indicative of the fact that in 1937, the Muslim League did not represent even a quarter of the Muslims of India. The Congress, on the other hand, won handsomely and formed governments in eight out of the 11 provinces.

In the story of India's freedom struggle, this was perhaps the closest our leaders had come to Independence through constitutional means. Once the Indian parties had control over provinces, it would have been almost impossible for the British to oust them without causing much international uproar and domestic revolt. Some historians believe that this unprecedented victory of the Congress unsettled the Muslims across the country and had an axiomatic effect, drawing members to the League in large numbers, which, in a way, contributed to the recovery of the Muslim League in 1938–39.[32] The Congress victory also began to worry the British and alerted them to the possibility of it dominating at the centre in the all-India federal legislature. Since the Muslim League hadn't even won one-fourth of the seats reserved for Muslims, there was a chance that even if half of the Muslim leaders outside the League formed alliances with the Congress, the Congress would achieve majority in the Lower House too. In the Lower House of the bicameral federal legislature, one-third of the seats were reserved for Muslims and an equal number for the nominees of the rulers of the princely states.

It is understood that the then British PM Winston Churchill sent intermediaries to India to persuade the princes to stay out

---

[31]Sarila, Narendra Singh, *The Shadow of the Great Game: The Untold Story of India's Partition*, HarperCollins India, Noida, 2009, p. 90.
[32]Ibid.

of the federal legislature.[33] This endeavour was quietly supported by the officers of the Indian political service who dealt with the princes. Eventually, the princely states refused to join as intended by Britain. Had the princely states joined the all-India federation, a great momentum would have come to the idea of a unitary India. But due to Churchill's aggressive efforts, the federal legislature remained a no-go. These efforts were supplemented by Jinnah who was shaken by the overwhelming Congress victory. He proposed to the then acting viceroy that the British should keep the centre as it was now and that they should make friends with Muslims by protecting them in the Congress's provinces. If they did that, Muslims would protect them at the centre.[34] Although Jinnah's party had no way to control a Congress majority in the Lower House without the help of Muslim allies outside of the League's umbrella, this episode is one of the first ones to mark the policy of 'mutual support' between Jinnah and the British government, which, of course, eventually had far-reaching consequences and was a major contributing factor of the partition of India.

ᔆ

It would have been wise at this point for the Congress led by Nehru to let the importance of this momentous event sink in, settle down and establish strong, stable governments in the eight provinces they now controlled. It would have also greatly benefitted the party to reach out to the princely states and make alliances by convincing them to join the all-India federation. The atmosphere in the country had changed, and this was being viewed as an important step in Gandhi's peaceful independence movement of India. However, Nehru failed to feel the pulse and act swiftly to counter British tactics aimed at sabotaging a solid plan that had the potential to give the Congress the all-important control at the centre.

---

[33]Ibid. 36.

[34]Wolpert, Stanley, *Jinnah of Pakistan*, 9th ed., Oxford University Press, London, 2002p. 170–1. This meeting between Jinnah and the Viceroy took place on 16 August 1938 in Shimla, as also confirmed in document F/1095 in the National Archives of Pakistan.

Shockingly, in 1939, the Congress made one of the gravest mistakes in the history of the Indian freedom struggle and gave up all their electoral gains by resigning from the governments in all eight provinces. This was, in Jinnah's words, 'a Himalayan blunder'.[35] As V.P. Menon mentioned in his book *The Transfer of Power in India*:

> By resigning, the Congress Party showed a lamentable political wisdom. There was little chance of its being put out of office: the British Government would surely have hesitated to incur the odium of dismissing Ministries, which had the overwhelming support of the people. Nor could it have resisted a unanimous demand for a change at the Centre ... In any case it is clear that but for the resignation of the Congress Ministries, Jinnah and the Muslim League would have never attained the position they did.[36]

Indeed, on taking a closer look at the events that led to the 1939 resignations and those that immediately followed, one cannot resist from concluding that during the years between 1939 and 1947, the Congress's mishandling of various events conspiring simultaneously or in fast succession led to a snowball effect, which eventually ended in the partition of India.

SUPPORT FOR BRITISH WORLD WAR II EFFORTS

Why was this blunder made? What were the events leading up to this manic mess and who was responsible?

World War II began in 1939. So helpful and supportive was Gandhi to the War efforts of the Allies during World War I that he was truly Britain's 'chief recruiting officer' for the War efforts in India, the primary source for human resource to fight in the

---

[35]Sarila, Narendra Singh, *The Shadow of the Great Game: The Untold Story of India's Partition*, HarperCollins India, Noida, 2009, p. 38.
[36]Menon, V.P., *The Transfer of Power in India*, Longmans, Green and Co., London, 1957, p. 52.

British Army.[37] And so, naturally, he was the first Indian leader that the viceroy at the time, Lord Linlithgrow, reached out to for consultation after the start of World War II. At their meeting, which took place in Shimla on 4 September 1939, Gandhi is said to have explained in moving terms the depth of his affection for England and how the idea of an enemy defacing the British was intolerable to him. In the same meeting, Gandhi assured the Viceroy that he was absolutely willing to help with the recruitment of Indians into the army, as he had done during World War I as well.[38] In the following days, Congress leadership held several meetings in Wardha, the location of Gandhi's ashram in western India. Nehru and Bose were the two prominent voices against Gandhi's offer to support the War effort, albeit for contrasting reasons. Subhas Chandra Bose was the Congress president a year ago, in 1938. He opposed Gandhi's offer to help the British because he didn't think that cooperating with the British would persuade the latter into granting India freedom. They had seen this before. After fully cooperating with the British in the War efforts, once World War I had ended, the British had tightened their control over the freedom movement.[39] He did not want to see history repeat itself. Nehru, on the other hand, wanted to oppose lending a helping hand to the British because PM Arthur Neville Chamberlain's government, just a year ago, had strangulated the Socialist International, an international political organization consisting of political parties seeking to establish democratic socialism.[40] Prime Minister Chamberlain's government also seemed to have been in connivance with Francisco Franco's takeover of Spain to appease Hitler—a geopolitical move Nehru didn't support. The Socialist International had various members in Europe whose company Nehru rather enjoyed and kept. He was

---

[37]Dalrymple, William and Anita Anand, 'Mahatma Gandhi', *Empire*, 20 September 2022, https://tinyurl.com/mr3msxuj. Accessed on 4 October 2023.

[38]MSS/EUR F 118/8, Vol. V, Oriental and Indian Collection, British Library, London, p. 96.

[39]Sarila, Narendra Singh, *The Shadow of the Great Game: The Untold Story of India's Partition*, HarperCollins India, Noida, 2009, p. 40.

[40]Ibid.

angry at PM Chamberlain for squeezing his friends and wanted to avenge the insult to them.[41] So strong was Bose's and Nehru's stance that Gandhi simply could not rally the Congress leadership behind his own intent to unconditionally support the British War effort unless they specifically guaranteed India freedom at the end of the War.

Simultaneously, Jinnah was holding consultations with Linlithgrow and promising him unconditional support of Muslims through the War. Gandhi sought multiple meetings with Linlithgrow to put across the party's point of view but in vain. Determined to prevent failure of talks and a break in the Anglo-Congress relationship, Gandhi met Linlithgrow with a plan to help Britain and bypass the obstacles created by some of his Congress colleagues (a fact that he hid from the party leadership).[42] However, Gandhi's offer was met with no reciprocation because, by now, the British trusted Jinnah as a more reliable ally. Despite that, Gandhi made his best effort not to let his party colleagues obstruct the War effort until the Cripps Mission of 1942, in which Britain had sneakily concealed the embryo of the creation of Pakistan.

Unimpressed by Gandhi, Linlithgrow asked his new pal, Jinnah, for his opinion on the Congress's demand for the British to declare their post-War objectives in India and on the expansion of the Viceroy's Executive Council to accommodate political parties. Jinnah replied firmly that he would refuse to reach an agreement with the Congress concerning the structure of the new republic of India to be formed unless the plan of creating a united India was abandoned and effective protection was given to the Muslim minorities in the provinces to preserve their rights and interests. In conversations, he convinced Linlithgrow that Muslim support can help provide them with a means to win a war. He also iterated that the Congress was out to destroy the British and Muslims as well as that the Muslim areas should be

---

[41]Ibid. 39.
[42]MSS/EUR F 115/8, Vol. IV, Oriental and Indian Collection, British Library, London, p. 161 (a) to (k).

separated from Hindu India and run by Muslims in collaboration with Great Britain.[43] From then on, 'Muslim objection' became a comfortable excuse for the British to deflect the demands of the Congress as well as critics of the Labour Party back home. Based on Jinnah's remarks, Linlithgrow issued a statement promising that after the War, consultations with representatives of various communities, parties and interests in British India, including the Indian princes, will be held to secure their cooperation to renew efforts to ensure satisfactory inclusion of all groups in the government.[44] This statement was as far as it could get from the Congress's demand, and the party considered it another attempt of the British to be deceitful. They did not expect to compete with the Muslim League for federal inclusion.

On 23 October, in a rage, the Congress governments in the provinces suddenly decided to quit. Linlithgrow extended an olive branch by offering to expand the Viceroy's Executive Council to include political leaders. The Congress, instead of holding onto their positions of power in the provinces while also making way into the Viceroy's Executive Council (which they eventually ended up doing in 1945), quit anyway. This came as a watershed moment in the Indo-British relationship because the latter interpreted it as unwillingness of the Congress to support them during their life-and-death struggle against the Axis powers.

This break in the British–Congress trust presented an opportunity for Jinnah to grow closer to the British and offer unconditional support. It is now understood that Nehru was taking the council of Sir Stafford Cripps, a Labour Party politician, to 'stand firm and not recede by an inch from the position he had taken (on the declaration of British interests in India post War)'.[45] This mistake of the Congress to step down from their position of power and

---

[43]MSS/EUR F 115/8, Vol. V, Oriental and Indian Collection, British Library, London, pp. 100–2.

[44]Menon, V.P., *The Transfer of Power in India*, Longmans, Green and Co., London, 1957, p. 66.

[45]MSS/EUR/125/8, Vol. IV, Viceroy to Secretary of State, 26 October 1939, Oriental and Indian Collection, British Library, London.

reject an inclusion in the Viceroy's Executive Council at the time, allowing an opportunist like Jinnah to gain momentum, is looked at as one of Nehru's biggest mistakes in the decade leading up to the doomed Partition. Could it have been that Cripps was misleading Nehru all along? For when he did make his first offer on behalf of HMG in 1942, it certainly included the idea of Pakistan hidden in it. On further introspection, it does seem that Cripps may have exploited Nehru's naivety and misled him, urging him to commit this 'Himalayan Blunder' by wrongly egging him on to stay firm on an unreasonable position.

Nehru had Gandhi's ear; Bose didn't, despite being the Congress president. Following the dramatic resignations, tension between Gandhi and Bose reached such an intolerable level due to Gandhi's stepfatherly treatment towards Bose that he quit the Congress in April 1939, to be succeeded by Nehru–Gandhi-backed Dr Rajendra Prasad. In 1940, Bose formed his own organization, the Forward Bloc. The Forward Bloc engaged in armed resistance with the British, a strategy that is widely believed to perhaps have contributed more to demoralize the British and break their will to remain in India than the Congress party's non-cooperation movement.

STRATEGIC IMPORTANCE OF THE NORTH-WEST FRONTIER PROVINCE

Just a few months after the mass resignations, the Viceroy met Jinnah on 13 January and requested him to install a Muslim League unit in the North-West Frontier Province (NWFP), the very crucial province that the Congress had achieved majority in and walked out of in 1939. It stretched from the Pamirs in the north to the Arabian Sea in the south. It was indeed the most important land boundary of India. It was the only land frontier through which India could be invaded by strength because further north and east, the Himalayan wall, stretching from Afghanistan to Burma (now Myanmar), protected it. To further explain India's vulnerability vis-à-vis this boundary is the moving fact that over 30 major invasions of India have taken place from this direction over the last 2,000 years.

The NWFP was perhaps the most sensitive and crucial region for the vast British Empire because Russia's frontier lay within a few hundred miles of India. It was here that the best officers of the British Indian Army were posted. The British had strategically developed the frontier over several decades. They had fought three wars and incorporated parts of Afghanistan into the province and Baluchistan which lay just to the south of it. They had also built a formidable railway network through the Khyber and Bolan passes, helped the Hindu Kashmiri Dogra-Rajput ruler to extend his rule all the way to Sinkiang (then an independent nation; present-day Xinjiang) border, and constructed a road from Gilgit in Hunza in northern Kashmir through the 13,000-feet-high Mintaka Pass in the Karakoram mountains to Kashgar in Sinkiang and posted agents there to monitor Russian activities across the border in Uzbekistan and the Pamirs. In addition, they bribed and threatened the Shahs of Persia to keep the areas of India's western approaches from Russian influence. The NWFP also served as a base for the British Empire to move freely in South Asia and also keep control of the oil wells in the Middle East. A memorandum from the Mountbatten Papers in 1948, after creating Pakistan, perfectly encapsulates the importance of this region to British interests:

> The Indus Valley, western Punjab and Baluchistan are vital to any strategic plans for the defence of the all important Muslim belt the oil supplies of the Middle East. If one looks upon this area as a strategic wall (against Soviet expansionism) the five most important bricks in the wall are: Turkey, Iran, Iraq, Afghanistan and Pakistan. Only through the open ocean port of Karachi could the opponents of the Soviet Union take immediate and effective countermeasures. The sea approaches to all other countries will entail navigation in enclosed waters directly menaced by Russian air fleets ... not only of the sea lanes of approach, but also the ports of disembarkation.
>
> If the British Commonwealth and the United States of America are to be in a position to defend their vital interests

in the Middle East, then the best and most stable area from which to conduct this defence is from Pakistan territory. Pakistan is the keystone of the strategic arch of the wide and vulnerable waters of the Indian Ocean.[46]

The NWFP comprised of 95 per cent Muslim population, essentially the Pathans who were either settled in districts or lived in the tribal areas. The former included cities such as Peshawar from which the Pathans had been brought into British administration. The latter area lay along the mountainous border along Afghanistan and was inhabited by nomadic Pathan tribes who were kept in administrative control by the distribution of large annual subsidies. The Pathans always allied with those who tried to unseat the British from India, which is why, in the provincial elections of 1937, they gave their support to the Congress. Since the area comprised of 95 per cent Muslim population, communal division on the lines of 'Islam in danger' could not be exploited, which was a disadvantage for Jinnah's strategy. The Pathan tribes of the day were led by Khan Abdul Ghaffar Khan, also known as 'Frontier Gandhi', who had come under the Gandhian influence after the latter had extended support to the Khilafat movement around 1920. After the Congress government in the NWFP resigned in 1939, there emerged a power vacuum in the region. Exploiting this vacuum, Jinnah announced his scheme to create a separate independent Islamic state in the subcontinent.[47] However, so strongly were the Pathans against the divisive messages of the League that even in the 1945 elections, the Congress party won 30 seats against the League's 17, and, consequently, a Congress provincial government headed by Dr Khan Sahib returned to power.

---

[46]The Strategic and Political Importance of Pakistan in the Event of War with the USSR (unsigned memorandum), 19 May 1948, Mountbatten Papers, British Archives, Hartley Library, University of Southampton.
[47]Secunder, Kermani, 'How Jinnah's Ideology Shapes Pakistan's Identity', BBC, 18 August 2017, https://tinyurl.com/4s2d52dk. Accessed on 10 November 2023.

ATLANTIC CHARTER: AMERICAN PRESSURE ON THE BRITISH FOR INDIAN INDEPENDENCE

At this juncture, it is also important to understand how the British interests played out vis-à-vis the freedom struggle in India and other external geopolitical factors at the time. In 1941, then American President Franklin Roosevelt and then British PM Winston Churchill signed an agreement—the Atlantic Charter. The Charter they drafted included eight 'common principles' that the US and Great Britain would be committed to supporting in the post-War world. Most importantly, both the US and Great Britain were pledged to support the restoration of self-governments for all countries that had been occupied during the War and allowing all peoples to choose their own forms of government. While the British got the Americans to support their War effort, what it also did with respect to India was to allow for American intervention in the British handling of the Indian independence. As soon as the Charter was signed, the British knew that they'd have to grant India independence sooner rather than later. In order to do so, they needed to keep their military and strategic interests in the region safe. Keeping the NWFP under British control was top priority. However, until they figured out how exactly they'd safeguard this all-important frontier, they'd have to keep throwing crumbs to the Congress leaders in order to appear to the Americans as though they were making genuine efforts to advance towards Indian independence. It is at this crucial point in the sensitive geopolitics of the time that Nehru and Gandhi seemed to have fully missed—the strength of retaining control over the NWFP.

THE VIOLENT QUIT INDIA MOVEMENT

With increasing American pressure to put India on the path of self-governance, Churchill sent Sir Stafford Cripps, a great strategist and planner, in March 1942 with an offer that can be summarized as follows.

It was decided that immediately after the War, India would have full independence inside and outside the Commonwealth on the basis of a constitution framed by Indian leaders. In the interim period, leaders of Indian political parties would be asked to enter the Viceroy's Executive Council and enjoy considerable autonomy except for the conduct of the War that would remain in British hands. However, they would have to accept the right of any British Indian province or princely state to stay out of the proposed Indian union post Independence if they so chose. In addition, the Cripps proposal was to be 'accepted as a whole' or 'rejected as a whole', which meant that the Indian parties' agreement to assume office in the Government of India would commit them to accept the seed of the partition of India whenever the British withdrew.

Nehru's individual peaceful disobedience of resigning from provincial governments in 1939 to protest against the British War efforts, on the lines of Gandhian principles of ahimsa and satyagraha, hadn't really worked as envisioned. Over 2 lakh recruits offered themselves to the British Armed Forces every month, when they had the capacity to only absorb about 50,000. Even powerful businessmen who were financiers to the Congress were producing goods for the British Indian Army. The Congress's call for peaceful disobedience had no effect on ground. In fact, the only impact it had was the arrest of powerful party leaders when they gave instigating speeches. About 1,500 leaders were jailed, after which Gandhi retreated to his ashram. So much of a failure was it that the British intelligence is said to have quoted Nehru in a report saying that, 'No one expects Gandhiji's movement to bring success, but its moral value is what counts.'[48] In absolute numbers, it was such a colossal failure that the strength of the British Indian Armed Forces rose from 1.9 lakh at the beginning of the war to over 20 lakh towards the end.[49]

---

[48]Commentary, Director, Intelligence Bureau, 21 May 1940, Oriental and Indian Collection, British Library, London.
[49]Sarila, Narendra Singh, *The Shadow of the Great Game: The Untold Story of India's Partition*, HarperCollins India, Noida, 2009.

However, the Cripps offer revitalized the Congress leadership to adopt yet another resolution—the Quit India movement on 8 August 1942. However, with the prompt arrests of Gandhi and other senior members of the Congress, Gandhi's non-violent struggle was never carried out. Instead, the movement fell into the hands of the revolutionaries—the group within the Congress that had little faith in Gandhi's non-violent methods. The violence was targeted particularly to cut off communications and transport. Nearly 250 railway stations and an equal number of post offices and police stations were destroyed by the freedom fighters. Large railway lines as well as telephone and telegraph wires were also targeted. The uprising was so severe that the Viceroy stated that 'it was the most serious revolt against the British rule since the Great Mutiny of 1957'.[50] The violence of the revolutionaries within the party was so widespread that in 1943, Gandhi had to fast for 21 days in the prison to quell his own movement.

Global opinion, which was, by then, anti-colonization and pro-Indian independence, shook as people saw the Congress's hyper-nationalism at a crucial time of the World War. The Quit India movement was, in fact, perceived to be silent support for the Axis powers against the Allies. In fact, the movement, as Nehru–Gandhi had envisioned, was ineffective and ill-timed. It is also around this time that Gandhi's advice to other world leaders was simply distanced from the violent actions that followed his call-for-action and, frankly, also seemed preposterous. For instance, in a meeting in 1940 with then Viceroy Linlithgrow, Gandhi suggested, 'Let Germany take possession of your beautiful Island. If Hitler chooses to occupy your homes, vacate them. If he does not give you free passage out, allow yourself man, woman and child to be slaughtered.'[51] His letters to Hitler and Mussolini urged them to follow his path of satyagraha and also requested the Jews to pray for Hitler,[52] but failure to fully understand the plight of the victims

---

[50]Ibid. 135

[51]Ibid. 34.

[52]Ibid.

in the gas chambers made the world perceive his suggestions as irrational. While his acts of social mobilization and service to society are commendable and he remains an inspirational figure, the fact was that around 1940, in the middle of a World War, no leader of a country could afford to 'turn the other cheek' to an invading army which would annihilate millions. Satyagraha used as a tool to encourage moral awakening against social and civil equalities against oppressing groups is perhaps genius, but the same tool simply cannot be deployed against aggressive armies attacking free nations or even communities with contrary ethical values like jihadis or separatists.

Having said that, the words 'Quit India' had caught on among the general public in India and across the world. American people's sympathy for Indian independence was growing, and there was a serious prospect of a general movement of agitation against Great Britain in favour of independence of India.[53] When the American Secretary of State raised similar concerns in diplomatic talks with the British, he was told that they would resume the course of conversation with the Indian leadership as soon as 'this movement of violence' terminated.[54] The Americans also stopped war supplies to India under the Lend-Lease Act with the British in the middle of War, with a real threat of Japanese invasion into India. Once the Japanese threat receded and the War ended, Churchill devised that the only way to hold off the American pressure for Indian independence would be to have them disenchanted with the Congress leadership and believe in Jinnah's usefulness.

---

[53]Foreign Relations of the United States, US FR 1942, Vol. I, Hull's conversation with Halifax, 24 August 1942, Office of the Historian, United States Government, pp. 726–7.
[54]Ibid.

FEAR OF REVOLT WITHIN THE BRITISH ARMED FORCES

After the British had quelled the violence of the Quit India movement on ground and Gandhi, Nehru and other senior leaders of the Congress were in prison, another larger movement was gathering steam, this time far from the homeland. This movement would eventually be one of the primary reasons to demotivate the British from staying in India for a prolonged period. Subhas Chandra Bose, who had been confined by the British in 1941 to his home in Calcutta (now Kolkata), had disappeared. As we have seen earlier, after his resignation from the Congress in 1939, he denounced Gandhi's pacifism and formed the Forward Bloc,[55] harbouring his belief that 'Britain's difficulty is India's Opportunity'.[56] During his preceding imprisonment, he gained great popularity especially among the urban youth of all communities, including Muslims. This is evidenced by the Muslim students in Calcutta threatening to launch an agitation for his release. Their threats found support in the then chief minister (CM) of Bengal, Fazal-ul-Haq, as well as his opponent Nizam-ud-din.[57] Fearing a large-scale revolt, the British kept him under intense police surveillance. And then, one day in 1941, he disappeared from his home despite the heavy police scrutiny. It is believed that he escaped to Peshawar and crossed into Afghanistan. When he showed up at the Italian Embassy, they treated him like a hot potato and passed him on to the Germans. Once he reached Germany, he set up the Free India Centre, from where he spread anti-British propaganda over the German radio. It is here that he created and broadcast the slogan

---

[55]Bose, Subhas Chandra, 'Why Forward Bloc', *The Alternative Leadership: Speeches, Articles, Statements and Letters June 1939–1941*, edited by Sisir Kumar Bose and Sugata Bose, Netaji Research Bureau, Kolkata, pp. 1–4.

[56]Sareen, T.R., Subhas Chandra Bose, Japan and British Imperialism', *European Journal of East Asian Studies*, Volume III, Issue 1, 2004, pp. 69–97.

[57]MSS/EURF 125/9, Vol. V, Viceroy to Secretary of State, 21 July 1942, India Office, Oriental and Indian Collection, British Library, London.

'Jai Hind'.[58] Soon, he was shipped out of Germany to Southeast Asia, where he really blossomed. The revolutionaries' Quit India movement, led by the Bose faction, was so powerful that then Viceroy Lord Wavell had expressed in a letter to the King after the war:

> I can never entirely rid my mind of the recollections that in 1942 at almost the most critical period of the war in India, when I was endeavouring as Commander-in-Chief to secure India with very inadequate resources against Japanese invasion, the supporters of the Congress made a deliberate effort to paralyse my communications to the eastern front by widespread sabotage and rioting ... The loyalty of the police and the Indian Army in face of a really serious challenge to British rule is problematic.[59]

After the fall of Singapore in 1942, many Indian officers who had sworn allegiance to the King, and thousands of Indian soldiers of the British Army very easily switched sides to join the Japanese, which was orchestrated by Bose. Mesmerized by his courage, charisma and leadership, over 60,000 Indian prisoners of war in Japanese hands pledged him support, and Indians in the region helped with the finances, thus enabling him to form the Indian National Army (INA).[60] Such was the ground support for Bose's INA that it led Churchill to remark, 'There is no point in having an army "that might shoot us in the back".'[61] This perception was reinforced by the mutinies that took place in several branches of the armed forces in the following years.

While the tension between the officers and soldiers in the

[58]Sarila, Narendra Singh, *The Shadow of the Great Game: The Untold Story of India's Partition*, HarperCollins India, Noida, 2009, p. 124.

[59]Wavell, Archibald Percival, *Wavell: The Viceroy's Journal*, edited by Penderel Moon, Oxford University Press, London, 1977, p. 499.

[60]Mansergh, Nicholas, *Transfer of Power*, Vol. VI, S. No. 286, Her Majesty's Stationery Office, London, 1970.

[61]Moon, Penderel, *The British Conquest and Dominion of India*, Vol. II, India Research Press, Delhi, 1999, p. 1129.

British Indian Army was growing, the British were realizing that they could no longer depend on India as a reliable source of acquiring human resource capital to fight their wars loyally.

GLOBAL PRESSURE AGAINST THE RAJ

By 1945, World War II had ended in favour of the Allies and a new post-War world was beginning to take shape. There was growing global dissent of colonizers and the act of colonization, which resulted in public pressure to enforce the right to freedom and grant independence to countries that wanted it. The British troops were clamouring after years of fighting to go home. Despite British victory, its power and prestige had been diminished by the War. They had lost Singapore, Burma and one of their finest ships to the Japanese. They'd never be able to demonstrate the background of strength and influence in Asia again—that credibility had crumbled. The machtpolitik, which had for so long enabled Britain to rule a million people with one man on the top, was no longer going to work against the aggressive on-ground campaigns in South Asia. To deal with this situation, Viceroy Wavell held consultations in London with the members of the India committee of the war cabinet headed by Clement Attlee (who would succeed Churchill as the PM) on a proposal of holding a conference of Indian leaders to discuss the formation of a politically representative Viceroy's Executive Council. He shared PM Churchill's view, which has also been detailed in a report titled *The Security of India and the Indian Ocean* on the latter's orders:

> [T]he USSR is the only major power which would be capable of seriously threatening our interests in India and the Indian Ocean area by 1955–1960. It is of paramount importance that India should not secede from the Empire or remain neutral in war ... We must ensure that whatever constitutional changes occur, we retain the right to station military strategic reserves in India ... There might be political objections to stationing the strategic reserve in India proper after she has been

grated Dominion Status … Central Headquarters India have suggested Baluchistan as an alternative to India proper, on the ground that it may be relatively easy to exclude this territory from the Dominion of India.[62]

Wavell's diary entry stated the following about his meeting with Churchill in March 1945: 'The PM then launched into a long jeremiad about India which lasted for forty minutes. He seems to favour partition of India into Pakistan, Hindustan and Princestan.'[63] Initially, Churchill was even reluctant to let such a conference take place, but after pressure from the Americans to make constitutional advances in India and assurance from his people that the conference was set up to fail, he agreed. Thus, the Simla Conference called by the Viceroy on 25 June 1945 was essentially a smokescreen to mislead the Americans and prop up Jinnah as the sole representative of all Muslims in India. Jinnah used the conference to make his case for Pakistan. It was later revealed that he was continuously receiving council from the British leadership to stick to his demands and that as long as he did that, he would be granted Pakistan.[64] Obviously, the conference failed. Jinnah had wrecked it by being completely non-cooperative and refusing to let any mutually agreeable resolutions emerge from it. He benefitted greatly from his act of sabotaging the conference, though. His political stock came to be at an all-time high and that ended up being a serious blow to his Muslim opponents, many of whom began to switch sides from the Congress in order to join the League. Nehru did not qualify to attend the conference and Gandhi chose not to attend it, even though he was in Shimla.

Two global events took shape after the Simla Conference that

---

[62]The Security of India and the Indian Ocean, Post-Hostilities Planning Staff Report, 19 May 1945, PHP (45) 15 (O), Oriental and Indian Collection, British Library, London.

[63]Wavell, Archibald Percival, *Wavell: The Viceroy's Journal,* edited by Penderel Moon, Oxford University Press, London, 1977, p. 120.

[64]Menon, V.P., *The Transfer of Power in India,* Longmans, Green and Co., London, 1957, p. 241.

put Constitutional advances towards Indian independence on a fast track: Churchill lost the general elections to Clement Attlee (the election of a Labour Party PM was much of a signifier of the ground sentiment against War and the Empire that Churchill had nursed)—a reality that simply could not be ignored anymore; and America dropped bombs on Hiroshima and Nagasaki, which led to Japan's unconditional surrender. This coaxed the Americans to press down on the British even more heavily on the need to apply the Atlantic Charter to the colonies in Asia and grant them independence sooner rather than later. There was so much pressure from across the Atlantic that Attlee admitted in his autobiography, 'Britain could not continue to hold on to India because of "American pressure against the Empire".'[65] Though Attlee's government made a case for a united India in its public pronouncement, behind closed doors, it was simply trying to arrive at the least controversial way to partition the country, and there's enough documentation to demonstrate this. In addition, a great famine had hit Bengal due to British mismanagement of food supplies at the time of War, which severely impacted the Empire's credibility. Added to that was the stress of severe financial crunch back home.

Also, in 1945, Bose was believed to have been killed in an air crash over Formosa.[66] This excited folks all over the country towards his brand of fighting for freedom once again. The winter of 1945 was rough for the British—the disciplinary trial of Bose's INA officers had backfired and increased public dissent against the Raj in India.

NEHRU'S SUGGESTION FOR BALKANIZATION OF INDIA

Simultaneously, Nehru was itching to lead India. It was at this time that it was announced that elections to the central and

[65]Hodson, H.V., *The Great Divide: Britain–India–Pakistan*, Oxford University Press, New Delhi, 1997, p. 127.

[66]Rajpal, Roktim, 'Did Netaji Subas Chandra Bose Really Die on This Day 77 Years Ago? New Book Has a Chapter on Tragedy| Review', *India Today*, 18 August 2022, https://tinyurl.com/ymc3nasj. Accessed on 10 November 2023.

provincial legislatures would be held in the winter of 1945. In the meantime, an executive council having the support of the main Indian parties would be formed to help run the government. In November, when Attlee's point man for India, Sir Stafford Cripps, reached out to Nehru, the latter warmly responded, 'Many things have been done during the past few years which have hurt me ... but at no time did I doubt that you had the cause of India at heart. We shall do our utmost to avoid conflict and restrain the hotheads.'[67] When Cripps received this warm correspondence from Nehru, he was delighted. It was quite contrary to his and Attlee's expectation of a full-blooded revolt launched by the revolutionaries due to growing sentiment. At that point, the British had very few means of disposal to quell such a movement, and it would certainly have led to loss of control over that situation, bringing disgrace to Britain in the eyes of the world, particularly the US for the fact that Britain was simply no longer strong enough to control its colonies.

Now that he had Nehru's ear, Cripps urged him, 'I am so glad that you are as convinced as I am, that we must do our utmost to restrain the use of force on either side.'[68] He then sneaked in the all-important question, 'If you were in the Viceroy's place, what line of action would you lay down to be followed after the elections? Let me have an off-the-record answer to that!'[69] This question seemed to have tickled Nehru's ego, and he wrote a 3,600-word reply to it on 27 January 1946. It is important to note here that the content of this letter clearly contains Nehru's consent for India's partition and, indirectly, the violent communal acts that followed in the years leading up to, during and after Partition. Nehru's demand for the British to immediately accept the independence of India, with the Constitution being determined by the people of India without British interference, included the following points:

---

[67]CAB/127/143, 75800, Nehru to Cripps, Public Records Office, The National Archives, London.
[68]Ibid.
[69]Ibid.

1. The matter of the division of India should be left to the people of India themselves and the British should not encourage it. The idea was to have a loose Indian federation with safeguards to protect the minority interests and in which powers of defence, external affairs, communications and currency would be with the federating unit.

2. In a case where the inhabitants of any territorial unit wished to opt out, it could be done only after a plebiscite, and the inhabitants could not carry with them those who didn't wish to opt out.

3. In the event of separation, defence should still remain common.

4. Since the NWFP was unlikely to vote for separation from the Union of India, Pakistan would be an impossibility.

5. Some princely state may be encouraged not to join the Indian union if there is a Pakistan. However, only the larger states, perhaps a dozen, could really survive as independent federal units. All others must be absorbed into provinces or amalgamate to form big enough federal units with the same democratic liberties and forms of administration as in the provinces.

He ended his letter with a threat of impending violence should the British ignore his suggestions, stating, 'An increasing number of young men and women are convinced that only a big struggle can produce something worthwhile.'[70]

Very quickly, the news of Nehru's and, thus, the Congress party's flexible attitude on separatism reached the British leadership in London. In a following conversation that Nehru had with a Labour Party MP Woodrow Wyatt, he conceded that 'the British might have to declare for Pakistan but there must be a plebiscite in border districts ... so that solid blocks of Hindu territory are not included in Pakistan'.[71] Armed with this information and acceptance, Attlee

---

[70]Ibid.

[71]Mansergh, Nicholas, *Transfer of Power*, Vol. VI, Her Majesty's Stationery Office, London, 1970, p. 532.

dispatched a cabinet mission led by Sir Stafford Cripps to India to break the deadlock between HMG and Indians and also between the Congress and the Muslim League.

GANDHI'S OFFER TO JINNAH

The strangeness of the Gandhi–Jinnah relationship between 1942 and 1944 is also noteworthy here. While in prison in this time period, Gandhi made repeated attempts to contact Jinnah to no avail. As soon as he was released, he visited the latter at his Malabar Hill home in Bombay to make an offer. The offer he made was that he could possibly convince the Congress party leaders to allow district-wise referendums in the provinces claimed by Jinnah for Pakistan. Describing the episode, Jinnah's biographer noted: 'One day when Mahatma Gandhi went to see Quaid-i-Azam [the great leader] they ended their arguments and talked, simply of their daily lives ... Jinnah mentioned that, among his ills, one of his feet was troubled with a nervous rash. The Mahatma sank to the floor and insisted on removing Jinnah's socks and shoes.'[72] Gandhi's offer clearly demonstrated that by then, he had most certainly accepted the idea of Pakistan and was only now negotiating the extent of its territory. His action of camaraderie with Jinnah made Jinnah's stature grow in the eyes of the Muslims inside and outside the League. Jinnah, of course, armed with the confidence in his relationship with the British, rejected Gandhi's offer outright.

It is important to note here that in the provincial elections of 1946, the Muslim League emerged as the largest Muslim grouping. They won considerably in the Muslim-minority areas. The all-important NWFP formed a Congress government. In Punjab, a large proportion of Muslims continued to side with the unionists who formed a coalition government with the Hindus and the Sikhs. The Congress formed a majority government in Assam too. Bascically, the Muslim League came to power in only two of the five provinces claimed by Jinnah for Pakistan—Sind and Bengal.

---

[72]Bolitho, Hector, *Jinnah: Creator of Pakistan*, John Murray, London, 1954, p. 25.

They did make heavy electoral gains as their vote share increased from 5 to 15 per cent in Muslim-minority provinces.[73] These results clearly indicate that the provinces where the Muslims didn't feel threatened by a Hindu-majority government did not sway with the communal narrative created by the League. It was only in the Muslim-minority provinces where the 'Islam in danger' narrative seemed to have really worked.

THE CABINET MISSION PLAN OF 1946

The Cabinet Mission, which had now made its way to India, was armed with strong advice from the beginning. The assistant secretary of the India office in London advised Cripps and the Secretary of State:

> Mr. Gandhi has frowned upon a truncated Pakistan ... If the Cabinet Mission can avoid a discussion with Mr. Gandhi in the opening stages there may be an advantage ... If there is any hope of compromise, it is likely to be best worked out with Maulana Azad and Nehru ... If Mr. Gandhi has not committed himself [at the beginning] he may be affected by the views of his supporters if they are sufficiently unanimous.[74]

On landing in Delhi, the Mission had lengthy discussions with the Indian politicians for several days and, on 16 May 1946, produced a plan for British withdrawal from India. Meanwhile, they proposed to set up an interim government with the leaders of Indian political parties replacing the nominated members of the Viceroy's Executive Council. Elections were proposed to be held for the Constituent Assembly, which would draft the constitution of the country, and there would be an all-India union government comprising a legislature consisting of the representatives of

---

[73]Sarila, Narendra Singh, *The Shadow of the Great Game: The Untold Story of India's Partition*, HarperCollins India, Noida, 2009.
[74]CHF 127/128, Francis Turnbull, Public Records Office, The National Archives, London.

the provinces that would deal with foreign affairs, defence and communications. The rest of the powers would vest in autonomous provinces. As per their plan, the proposed Constituent Assembly would represent one of the three following groups:

A. The six provinces with non-Muslim majorities excluding Assam: Bombay, Orissa (now Odisha), the Central Provinces, Bihar and the United Provinces
B. The Muslim-majority areas in the northwest: the Punjab, the NWFP, Sind and Baluchistan
C. Bengal and Assam

The legislators belonging to Groups B and C (which included all the provinces demanded by Jinnah for Pakistan) were to draw up constituents of their respective groups. The provinces would have no choice but to join the groups in which they had been placed. After 10 years, the constituents of Groups B and C would have the option of opting out of the union. Woodrow Wyatt, the same MP in whom Nehru had confided the acceptance of the idea of Pakistan, now convinced Jinnah to accept the Cabinet Mission Plan, as it gave him a definite timeframe for Pakistan's creation. Jinnah was reluctant to accept the plan at first since it didn't grant an immediate Pakistan. He, however, was so desperate that, on many occasions, he had iterated that even if he was given a matchbox-sized Pakistan, he'd accept it.[75] But, with the Cabinet Mission Plan, he would get the entire Pakistan as he envisioned without any cut-outs albeit after 10 years.

The Congress party's interpretation of the plan was different. They thought that since they held majority over the NWFP in Group B and Assam in Group C, these groups were unlikely to

---

[75]Ahmed, Akbar S., *Jinnah, Pakistan and Islamic Identity: The Search for Saladin*, Routledge, New York, 1997. This was recounted by Sahibzada Yaqub Khan, adjutant of the Viceroy's bodyguard and later commandant of the Governor General's bodyguard in Pakistan, during a conversation in a private dinner in 1947 with Lord Ismay, Mountbatten's then Chief of Staff who had returned from a meeting with Jinnah. Ismay told the guests that his impression was that if Jinnah was offered even a matchbox with the work Pakistan on it, he would take it.

break out of the Indian union as a whole. The short-term benefits of an interim government also attracted the Congress leadership to accept the plan. By achieving a majority in the Constituent Assembly, they assumed that they could achieve a united India. They reserved their position on the long-term arrangements and accepted the short-term provisions of the plan. Meanwhile Cripps arranged a visit for Nehru to the Mountbattens in Singapore, where he was courted to such an extent that he became enamoured by them. The Mountbattens would play a significant role in the years to come, which we shall see later. It was also during this visit that he is said to have first met Mrs Edwina Mountbatten while rescuing her from tripping and falling to the ground as she was being pushed by a sea of people. This relationship would go on to have numerous serious consequences for India.[76]

Moving on, both the Muslim League as well as the Congress accepted the Cabinet Mission Plan. Gandhi described the Cabinet Mission proposal as 'the seed to convert this land of sorrow into one without sorrow or suffering'. He added, 'After four days of searching examination of the State paper issued by the Cabinet Mission and the Viceroy on behalf of the British government, my conviction abides that it is the best document that the British Government could have produced in the circumstance.'[77] At the Congress party annual meeting, held on 10 July 1946, Maulana Azad gave a moving speech in favour of the Cabinet Mission Plan, after which it was accepted.[78] In the same annual meet, Azad pushed for Nehru's presidency, sidelining Patel, whom the right-wing factions of the party were gunning for. Jinnah called the Cabinet Mission Plan '[a] plan where Muslims would get nearest to Pakistan than they could have ever hoped to get.'[79] This was a crucial time in the story of Indian independence. Somehow, the

---

[76]Sarila, Narendra Singh, *The Shadow of the Great Gam: The Untold Story of India's Partition e,* HarperCollins India, Noida, 2009, p. 273.
[77]Mosley, Leonard, *The Last Days of the British Raj,* Harcourt, Brace & World, Inc., New York, 1961, p. 24.
[78]Ibid.
[79]Ibid.

two warring groups were finally on the same page. It was a time to sit tight—there was much to gain from silence. However, Nehru made an unforgivable, monumental blunder, which reversed all the gains in the days to come.

2

PARTITION: PART II

NEHRU'S MONUMENTAL MISTAKE OF 1946

In what is considered a monumental mistake, Nehru called a press conference a few days after taking over the Congress presidency once again in 1946 to brief the media on the Congress's policies. Circumspection should have been the order of the day, especially since the fortunes of India were in balance. The Congress leadership had a way forward to constitutionally push all that they wished for a united India, provided that they handled the situation with maturity and silence. But Nehru launched into what his biographer Michael Brecher calls 'one of the most fiery and provocative statements in his forty years of public life ... a serious tactical error'.[1] When asked by the press if the Congress's approval of the Cabinet Mission Plan meant that they accepted it fully, in his next words, which he should have chosen very, very carefully, he doubled down and said that as the president of the Congress, he had every intention of modifying the plan. He said:

> The big probability is, from any approach to the question, there will be no grouping. Obviously, Group A [the Hindu-majority provinces] will decide against grouping. Speaking in betting language, there is a four to one chance of the NWFP deciding against grouping. That means that Group B collapses. It is highly likely that Bengal and Assam will decide against grouping ... Thus you will see this grouping business approached from any point of view does not get us on at all.[2]

[1]Brecher, Michael, *Nehru: A Political Biography*, Oxford University Press, India, 1959.
[2]Mosley, Leonard, *The Last Days of the British Raj*, Harcourt, Brace & World, Inc.,

He essentially said that once in power, the Congress will use all its might at the centre to alter the Cabinet Mission Plan as per its fancies. While this was a genius political strategy, the fact that he laid out a secret strategic manoeuvre on a platter for public consumption was a gargantuan mistake. The fact was that the Muslim League and the Congress had deep distrust for each other, but both had accepted the Cabinet Mission Plan. In these circumstances, Nehru's words were a direct act of sabotage, not only towards the British government's proposal but also towards his own party's goals that were meant to be discreet. Even now, several folks wonder if he made these remarks underestimating the ability of Jinnah and the Muslim League to react or if they were just haphazard remarks made by a politician who did not understand the importance of maintaining diplomatic silence at crucial junctures. Several times in the following years, when asked by the media, Nehru maintained radio silence on this subject.[3] One of his closest colleagues, outgoing Congress President Maulana Azad, described this incident in his autobiography with these words:

> Jawaharlal is one of my dearest friends and his contribution to India's national life is second to none. He has worked and suffered for Indian freedom and since the attainment of independence he has become the symbol of our national unity and progress. I have nevertheless to say with regret that he is at times apt to be carried away by his feelings. Not only so, but sometimes he is so impressed by theoretical considerations that he is apt to underestimate the realities of a situation. The mistake of 1946 proved … costly.[4]

And indeed it did. Jinnah, who was already suspicious of the Congress party, reacted like a man on fire. Not only did he pull out

---

New York, 1961, pp. 27–8.

[3]Ibid.

[4]Azad, Abul Kalam, *India Wins Freedom: An Autobiographical Narrative*, Orient Longmans, Kolkata, 1959.

his support for the Cabinet Mission Plan, but he also convinced his supporters to renounce all titles they held from the British government and set aside 16 August 1946 as Direct Action Day—a day when the Muslims of India would violently demonstrate their determination to achieve their holy land, Pakistan. For the foreseeable future, any possibility of a unified, independent India was crushed, and only one man was to blame—Nehru.

The British archives contain a copy of the Muslim League's proclamation for Direct Action Day, and it reads:

> It was in Ramzan that the Quran was revealed. It was in Ramzan that the permission for Jehad was granted by Allah. It was in Ramzan that the Battle of Badr, the first open conflict between Islam and Heathenism was fought and won by 313 Muslims (against 900 in AD 634) and again it was in Ramzan that 10,000 Muslims under the Holy Prophet conquered Mecca (in AD 630) and established the kingdom of Heaven and commonwealth of Islam in Arabia. The Muslim League is fortunate that it is starting its action in this holy month.[5]

Now, Bengal was the only province that had a Muslim League CM. What followed on 16 August seemed to be an outcome of a cosy, conspicuous, mutually convenient arrangement between the British leadership and Muslim League CM, Shaheed Suhrarwardy. British Governor Sir Frederick Burrows willingly overlooked the violence that killed thousands of Hindus, so that the Muslim League could prove the point that it needed to in order to convince the world that Hindus and Muslims could not coexist and, hence, creation of Pakistan was inevitable.[6] Muslim mobs were provoked by fiery speeches by the Muslim League leaders while the British gave orders to the police to stand down and let the events unfold.[7] One

---

[5]Mansergh, Nicholas, *Transfer of Power*, Vol. VIII, S. No. 197, Her Majesty's Stationery Office, London, 1970, para 6.
[6]Ibid. Paras 7–9, 14 (2).
[7]Akbar, M.J., *Nehru: The Making of India*, Viking, London, 1981, p. 382.

must recollect here that only about three years ago, in 1943, over three million people had died of starvation in Bengal during the Great Famine, which was fully attributable to the mismanagement of supplies and resources by the British Indian government. Once again, Bengal's destiny called for bloody murders of over 5,000 people, with millions rendered injured.[8] Thousands of Hindu women were raped and murdered. Children were brutally killed. For over 72 hours, this bloodbath was allowed to prevail before any action was taken.[9]

On 16 August, when Bengal was to burn, Nehru made a half-hearted visit to Jinnah in the morning to convince him to abort the impending violence. Unable to do so, he went on with his day, just like he would have on any other regular day. The British had promised to include representatives of political parties in the Viceroy's Executive Council (to be called the Cabinet) as part of the interim government. Nehru, completely insensitive to the massacre taking place in the eastern part of the country, preoccupied himself with holding first meetings to pick his cabinet ministers. Bengal was one of the richest provinces in the world when the British first discovered it; it had been a thriving port and a rich business centre—a splendid provider of wealth for the British. The Bengalis were among the most intelligent, creative, poetic and affluent individuals in South Asia. Sadly, though, after centuries of exploitation, it had been turned into a black hole, with life sucked out of it. And now it was left in the hands of the Muslim League to conduct its dastardly acts with full support from the British. The warning signs of the looming massacre were all there—the call to violence from Jinnah, followed by the silence from the British government. However, it is not fair to absolve the Congress and its leadership of all blame either. They ignored all

---

[8]Bhaskar, C. Uday, 'Direct Action Day the Core of Pak Malignancy', *The Economic Times*, 16 August 2011, https://tinyurl.com/zp2bsxsj. Accessed on 10 November 2023.

[9]*Recurrent Exodus of Minorities from East Pakistan and Disturbances in India: Report to the Indian Commission of Jurists by Its Committee of Enquiry*, The Indian Commission of Jurists, New Delhi, 1965.

blaring alarms and went about their business. Making a last-minute call to Jinnah on the morning of the D-Day simply wasn't enough when thousands of human lives were at stake. What was even more surprising was Gandhi's silence and absence in the attempt to avert the tragedy. He did enter the scene, however, when the violence had spread to Bihar and other parts of the country, where angry Hindus were attacking Muslims as retribution for the Bengal killings and urged them to stop violence.

Wavell, the then British viceroy, made an attempt to get both the Muslim League and the Congress back on the table to accept the Cabinet Mission Plan, possibly to soothe any pushback arising from the global perception that the British sat pretty and allowed the Bengal massacre. British PM Attlee feared that a wave of civil disobedience would sweep the country, further affecting his government's perception back home. Here is where he got his judgement wrong. The Nehru–Gandhi faction of the Congress was not ready for another movement. In a later conversation with the media, Nehru admitted, 'We were tired men. We were not prepared to go to jail again.'[10] When Viceroy Wavell failed to convince Gandhi and Nehru to come back to the table and accept the Cabinet Mission Plan as the British had intended it, he was sacked by HMG, to be replaced by the infamous Admiral Louis Mountbatten. He was, however, ordered to bring the interim government into being. And so, on 2 September 1946, the interim government was sworn in.

LARGE-SCALE MUTINIES IN THE ARMED FORCES

This was the time when all the main men of the moment had trust issues with each other: Gandhi and Nehru didn't trust Jinnah; Jinnah didn't trust the Congress; Wavell didn't trust Nehru–Gandhi; and PM Attlee didn't trust Wavell since he had failed to gather consensus on the Cabinet Mission Plan. Added to this

---

[10]Mosley, Leonard, *The Last Days of the British Raj*, Harcourt, Brace & World, Inc., New York, 1961.

potboiler of players—all distrustful of each other—was the feeling of revolution that Bose's rumoured death in 1945 had created among his lakhs or possibly crores of supporters. With Nehru's sabotage, the communal violence unleashed in parts of the country and the inability and disinterest of Congress leadership to quell the violence, several elements in the country felt deeply resentful of the way the Congress was handling the situation. To them, there seemed no way in the foreseeable future for the British to grant India her freedom while keeping her undivided. Added to the tension were the heightened public feelings for Bose's idea of how freedom should be won due to the disciplinary trials of INA officers by the British. So overwhelming was the public emotion and uproar against the Raj that Nehru, too, decided to harness this and win some sympathy when he legally chose to represent these officers on trial. However, the hand-in-glove tactic of talking to the British and making settlements behind the scenes was simply not going down well with the people of India. Factions within the Congress, with soldiers of Bose's INA, launched large-scale mutinies in the Royal Indian Navy, Royal Air Force, the Royal Corps of Signals and the engineers. There was growing uncertainty about the loyalty of the Indian Army. Soon, rebellion in the Indian Army had erupted as well and several people began to believe that the moment to 'do or die' was now when the British were exhausted after the war and demoralized in India instead of the less opportune year of 1942, when Gandhi had launched the Quit India movement. So frustrating was this for Viceroy Wavell that, in a top-secret memorandum in the winter of 1945–46, he wrote to the Secretary of State,

> We are now faced in India with a situation of great difficultly and danger ... the Congress leaders (revolutionaries) intend to provoke or pave the way for mass disorder ... counting on the INA as a spearhead of the revolt. They would suborn the Indian Army, if they could, and hope that their threats will impair the loyalty and efficacy of the Police ... There is no doubt about the growth of Hindu enthusiasm for the Congress.

The British members of the ICS (Indian Civil Service) and IP (Indian Police) are dispirited and discontented.[11]

The Intelligence Bureau's opinion was that communal disorders were the antidote to the agitation which was heavily building up against the Raj. They feared that an even more aggressive, full-blown nationwide revolution may prove to be an antidote to Jinnah's 'direct action threats'.[12] Very aware of losing ground in India and deeply concerned about Britain's strategic interests in the NWFP and growing public pressure, in February 1947, PM Attlee announced in the House of Commons that the British will withdraw from India no later than June 1948, when power would be transferred into the hands of a responsible Indian government.[13] For this, he deputed Louis Mountbatten, a man who would lead the process of catalysing and authorizing the bloody partition of the country with the help of his wife, Edwina Mountbatten.

∽

A few months before this, Nehru and Patel had already been saddled with responsibilities as part of the Viceroy's Executive Council. Nehru was made its vice-president just a few months earlier in September. The Council came to be known as the Cabinet and Nehru as its vice-president was termed as the PM of the interim government. Nehru also took the foreign affairs portfolio, whereas Patel got home affairs. Seeing their fellow members in the Cabinet and their top leader being called 'prime minister' incited a feeling of victorious thrill among the Congress nationalists. Jinnah, who chose to stay out of the Viceroy's Executive Council, remarked sharply, 'You cannot turn a donkey

---

[11]Mansergh, Nicholas, *Transfer of Power*, Vol. VI, S. No. 194, Her Majesty's Stationery Office, London, 1970.

[12]Sarila, Narendra Singh, *The Shadow of the Great Game: The Untold Story of India's Partition*, HarperCollins India, Noida, 2009, p. 193.

[13]Mansergh, Nicholas, *Transfer of Power*, Vol. IX, Her Majesty's Stationery Office, London, 1970, p. 438.

into an elephant by calling it an elephant.'[14] Now that the British had saddled Nehru and Patel with responsibilities of governance, their belief that 'Pakistan is likely to come from Congresstan' was beginning to look more and more achievable.[15] Just like in 1942, while the Congress leaders were in prison for three years and Jinnah was given a free hand to grow the Muslim League's base, this time around, too, with the Congress looking the other way, riding high on power, perhaps a settlement with Jinnah could be sneaked in by helping him grow his party and further cut the Congress to size.

NEHRU–MOUNTBATTEN AXIS

For a couple like Louis and Edwina Mountbatten, their role in India was nothing short of a coronation, much in line with their lineage. Louis Mountbatten was a cousin of King George VI, and Edwina was one of the richest heiresses in England and considered one of the most sought-after eligible single women in London due to her 'fierce brilliance and elegance'.[16] Married in July 1922, this was an alliance that had royal blood balanced with great fortune. However, neither his royal connections nor his wife's wealth distracted Mountbatten from his utter devotion to rise up the ranks in the Royal Navy. Many of his colleagues called him 'an undersexed workoholic' and believed that he was not averse to taking shortcuts to further his career.[17] To many, it wasn't his skill that enabled him to move upwards in his career so swiftly but the close relationship with the royal family. With this kind of pedigree,

---

[14]Sarila, Narendra Singh, *The Shadow of the Great Game: The Untold Story of India's Partition*, HarperCollins India, Noida, 2009, p. 228.

[15]Mansergh, Nicholas, *Transfer of Power*, Vol. Vol. IX, Her Majesty's Stationery Office, London, 1970, p. 304 enclosure.

[16]Ziegler, Philip, *Mountbatten: The Official Biography*, Collins, London 1985, p. 156.

[17]French, Patrick, *Liberty or Death: India's Journey to Independence and Division*, HarperCollins, London, 1995, p. 284; Sarila, Narendra Singh, *The Shadow of the Great Game: The Untold Story of India's Partition*, HarperCollins India, Noida, 2009, p. 271.

it would only be fitting for him to deliver to HMG their core interests in India, retaining the crucial NWFP while staying behind the smokescreen, absolving the British of all blame for Partition. If he could keep both India and Pakistan as dominions in the British Commonwealth, he'd truly be hailed as a hero back home. In addition, Louis Mountbatten truly believed that for Britain 'to continue to play a major role in the post-War world, the old Empire should be transformed into a multiracial and worldwide association of free nations remaining linked to Britain through membership in the Commonwealth.'[18]

So, when the Mountbattens were deputed to India, they came with a clear plan. Seeming nothing short of royalty, they brought a staff of over 7,500 as well as some of their closest officers who had worked in India for a long time. They also retained some of outgoing Viceroy Wavell's officers, one of which was V.P. Menon—the reforms commissioner.[19] Lord Mountbatten was charming, handsome and flamboyant. He made sure that there was no high-handedness in dealing with his Indian interlocutors. He showed no hesitation to stoop low in order to conquer.[20] These qualities made him a wily negotiator for Nehru and Patel to deal with. Now, Nehru was already acquainted with the Mountbattens as he had visited them in Singapore a few years ago, returning to India absolutely smitten by them. And why wouldn't he have been? Nehru and the Mountbattens were natural partners—they were aristocrats working for popular interests. For Nehru, who was 'a man consumed by self-doubt and self-accusation even in triumphant moments', Mountbatten's serene self-confidence, totally devoid of doubt, drew Nehru to him like a bee to nectar.[21] It is believed that Nehru found it so easy to talk to the Mountbattens that he often spoke to them without reservation.

---

[18]Mountbatten to Narendra Singh Sarila, 1958, and Sarila, Narendra Singh, *The Shadow of the Great Game: The Untold Story of India's Partition*, HarperCollins India, Noida, 2005, p. 297.

[19]Mosley, Leonard, *The Last Days of the British Raj*, Harcourt, Brace & World, Inc., New York, 1961, p. 93.

[20]Ibid.

[21]Ibid. 94.

As soon as they settled in the Viceregal House, Lord Mountbatten got going, working 12 hours a day. He began to hold early morning informal strategy meets with his close associates to plan the tactics for the day. He had written to Gandhi and Jinnah to come and see him even before he was sworn in, but it was Nehru who was his first official visitor. The men had a three-hour talk, at the end of which Mountbatten realized that Nehru, on being prodded, became gossipy and malicious about his friends and colleagues.[22] The information that he'd extract from Nehru in later conversations was put to use very strategically in negotiating with the other men of the moment. While Nehru was floored by Mountbatten's charm, the latter had measured Nehru in and out in just one conversation. His biggest takeaway was that Nehru could be flattered and persuaded.[23] That was all that mattered to Louis Mountbatten. Armed with this, he asked Nehru his opinion of Jinnah, to receive a reply that 'Jinnah was a mediocre lawyer with an obsession for Pakistan',[24] which was, of course, a watered-down assessment of Jinnah. If this was truly what Nehru assumed of the man, he was meant to be doomed. Jinnah was very intelligent, dangerously crafty and could give most men in the Congress a run for their money.

Just in that one conversation, Mountbatten had won Nehru over. But his attachment to the Mountbatten ménage subsequently deepened with increasing contact with Edwina. He was in awe of her, and as he met her more frequently, the close contact with her stirred in him emotions which were soon much stronger than mere admiration.[25] So much was Nehru under their spell that when Lord Mountbatten made it clear to him that Gandhi was an unrealistic man, thus difficult to negotiate and deal with, Nehru found it rather easy to sideline Gandhi, the man who had declared him his political heir of sorts. Gandhi, on the other hand, was not

---

[22]Ibid.

[23]Ibid.

[24]Ibid.

[25]itvindia, 'CNN IBN Pamela Mountbatten 22 7 2007', *YouTube*, https://tinyurl.com/mweeabxj. Accessed on 15 November 2023.

impressed with the Mountbattens. On returning from Bihar, where he had been on a tour to quell the violence that was a response to the Direct Action Day massacre in Bengal, Gandhi met Lord Mountbatten twice on consecutive days. On the first day, Gandhi went on a three-hour monologue about his early life and struggles, but on the second, he proposed that Louis Mountbatten invite Jinnah to set up a government immediately, fully leaving it on him to decide whether his government would contain all Muslims or both Muslims and Hindis to break the Congress–Muslim League deadlock.[26] Gandhi added that such a government, headed by Jinnah, should be given an absolutely free hand, with the exception of a Viceregal veto, to rule India.[27] Rebuffed by the Congress on discovering his proposal, Gandhi promised to the party that he would take no further part in the discussions with the Viceroy and play nothing more than a minor advisory role in the Congress.[28] It is believed that Team Mountbatten worked closely with its friends within the Congress to leak and sabotage Gandhi's unworkable proposal[29] so as to achieve this exact goal—to sideline Gandhi from crucial decision making in the days to come.

V.P. Menon observed that within only four days of his arrival in India and his conversations with Nehru, Jinnah and Gandhi, Mountbatten had made up his mind about which way he wanted to lead the negotiations.[30] He knew that an agreeable solution in accordance with the Cabinet Mission Plan was not possible, and an alternative plan for the transfer of power needed to be found and implemented without loss of time. The Congress, even before his arrival, had begun to increasingly make decisions without Gandhi. And one such major decision was the resolution passed by the Working Committee on 8 March 1947, essentially accepting 'a

---

[26]Mountbatten, L.M., *Mountbatten's Report on the Last Viceroyalty: 22 March–15 August 1947*, edited by Lionel Carter, Manohar, 2003, Para A, Sub-Para 11.

[27]Mosley, Leonard, *The Last Days of the British Raj*, Harcourt, Brace & World, Inc., New York, 1961, p. 95.

[28]Ibid. 96.

[29]Ibid. 95.

[30]Ibid. 98.

division of Punjab into two provinces so that the predominantly Muslim part may be separated from the predominantly non-Muslim part'. In a note sent by Nehru to the Viceroy attaching the resolution, he had also added, '[T]his principle (of communal division in the Punjab) would, of course, apply to Bengal also.'[31]

Within the Congress, V.P. Menon had managed to convince Patel that Jinnah would be willing to accept a truncated Pakistan. He also insisted that instead of having interference from the Muslim League at the centre, which could hold up legislation and instigate waves of communal riots across undivided India, they'd be better off giving Jinnah amputated limbs from Punjab and Bengal. When the party passed this resolution, the idea was that the British would never agree to divide Punjab and Bengal as a pre-condition for Independence. But as the days grew nearer, the inevitability of such a scenario dawned on everyone. Patel was the first to hold talks with Mountbatten in this respect. The former was too intelligent to allow himself to be played and persuaded by Mountbatten for something he didn't want. An idea of a strong centre, the safety of Congress financiers from the influence of the League, the possibility of the Congress solely ruling India and being able to make strong decisions without interruptions from the League were extremely attractive to him. So, he played along and allowed himself to open up to the idea of Partition in his conversation with Mountbatten.

Once Mountbatten had Patel in his corner, his next project was to turn Nehru. An extensive web was spun around the Mountbatten–Nehru axis, with one of Mountbatten's closest officers, Campbell-Johnson, becoming a frequent at the Nehru breakfast table. He developed a firm friendship with Indira, who had considerable sway over her father and became a primary lubricant of this axis.[32] Meanwhile, Nehru frequented the Viceregal House, getting very close to Edwina. The two women eventually influenced him to accept the idea of partitioning the country,

---

[31]Ibid. 100–1.
[32]Ibid. 102.

the first of many decisions that were taken under this Nehru–Mountbatten web. In fact, so overpowering and crucial was Edwina's role in influencing Nehru's thoughts from this point forward that her daughter Pamela Hicks, in her personal accounts, revealed the 'deep love' that Edwina and Nehru had for each other. She confessed that her mother had several lovers in the past and that did upset her father terribly, but her father became quite friendly with Nehru.[33] Pamela went on to say that with her father so busy, her mother was often lonely, and so was Nehru, who had been a widower for over a decade by now. The famous fable has it that every night at 2.00 a.m., Nehru would write an incredibly romantic letter to Edwina, revealing his deepest feelings and insecurities coupled with the tender language of a lover. It is understood that a stack of these letters were found by Edwina's bedside when she died.[34] As Pamela put it, often with regard to policies, her father would state his opinion in conversation with Nehru, but it would be Edwina who would drive the point home by playing to his emotions and deeply influencing his being. Pamela reiterated that the relationship between Edwina and Nehru was very useful to her pragmatist father. Often, when it was particularly tricky to get Nehru's consent, Lord Mountbatten would say to Edwina, 'Do try to get Jawaharlal to see that this is terribly important....'[35]

The other problem was also how involved Indira, who would go on to hold the Congress's reigns and become India's future PM, was with Campbell-Johnson, who was, of course, forging a relationship with her to use her as a tool to get into her father's mind.[36] Despite being used, the Nehru family, which later became the Gandhi family as a result of Indira's marriage to Feroze Jehangir Gandhi (previously Ghandy), maintained a close friendship with the

---

[33]itvindia, 'CNN IBN Pamela Mountbatten 22 7 2007', *YouTube*, https://tinyurl.com/mweeabxj. Accessed on 15 November 2023.

[34]Ibid.

[35]Mountbatten, Pamela, *India Remembered: A Personal Account of the Mountbattens during the Transfer of Power*, Pavilion Books, London, 2007, p. 18.

[36]Mosley, Leonard, *The Last Days of the British Raj*, Harcourt, Brace & World, Inc., New York, 1961, p. 102.

Mountbattens. Close colleagues of Nehru like Azad continued to wonder how a vociferous opponent of Partition was persuaded to accept it within a month of the arrival of the Mountbattens. However, at the time, little did they know that Nehru had already shown signs of acceptance of the idea of Pakistan in his letter to Cripps before the Cabinet Mission Plan arrived in India and, subsequently, to MP Woodrow Wyatt in a personal conversation.[37] In his private thoughts, he certainly knew that the country was going to be partitioned but allowed the overwhelming sentiment of infatuation for Edwina; his fondness for Mountbatten in addition to Indira's opinions seemed to cause him to finally come to terms with it in public.

EYES ON THE PRIZE: THE NORTH-WEST FRONTIER PROVINCE

It is pertinent to note that at this crucial time of the Mountbattens' arrival in India, when they'd be open to opinions based on their on-ground experiences, Nehru stayed pre-occupied with the Asia Relations Conference that he had planned since taking over as 'prime minister'.[38] Nehru thought that he had ushered in the beginning of a new era in Asian history by encouraging overwhelming participation so as to bring in several shades of opinion at the conference. However, nothing really came out of it in the long run—no participating country acted on the resolution to set up national units of this organizations. In fact, it was such a failure that even a second session of the Asia Relations Conference did not take place.[39] Meanwhile, to achieve this global glory that he had dreamt of, Nehru fully ignored internal affairs and the deteriorating law and order situation in several parts of the country.

Mountbatten very much had his eye on the prize—the NWFP. But for him to keep the prize under Britain's control, he needed

---

[37]CAB/127/143, Nehru to Cripps, 27 January, 1946, Public Records Office, The National Archives, London.
[38]Sarila, Narendra Singh, *The Shadow of the Great Game: The Untold Story of India's Partition*, HarperCollins India, Noida, 2009, p. 276.
[39]Ibid.

to ensure that it slipped away from the hands of the Congress government, which was the ruling party in the frontier. As soon as he arrived in India, he received information from the governor of the NWFP, Sir Olaf Caroe, perhaps one of the most knowledgeable minds on Pathan and tribal affairs, that there was considerable on-ground tension between the current Congress government led by Dr Khan Sahib, brother of Khan Abdul Ghaffar Khan, and the Muslim League supporters. He recommended that the British dissolve the Congress government and impose governor's rule in the province to maintain peace, after which he advised holding fresh elections.[40] When Lord Mountbatten consulted a preoccupied Nehru, the latter strongly opposed fresh elections and called for dismissal of the governor but was also soft on the idea of a referendum, conceding that 'it would be desirable to obtain the views of the people before the final turnover of power was effected'.[41] He also stated, in continued conversations that 'it would not be right to impose any form of constitutional conditions to a community which is a majority in a specific area'.[42] To Mountbatten, these words were music. Clearly Nehru implied that he was agreeable to not only non-Muslim parts of Punjab and Bengal to be given a free choice but also to all of the British provinces, including those that were already with the Congress party, such as the NWFP, and showed any form of resistance to constitutional conditions. To Mountbatten, this was pure ammunition; he'd hold on to this information and use it to bargain if it came down to it, in the battle for control of the NWFP.[43]

As soon as these words were spoken, Mountbatten and his staff began a draw up a plan of withdrawal from India that would entail that all elected representatives to the assembly from each and every British province, including those under the Congress's control and

---

[40]Ibid. 281.

[41]Mountbatten, L.M., *Mountbatten's Report on the Last Viceroyalty: 22 March–15 August 1947*, edited by Lionel Carter, Manohar, 2003, Part B, Para 46.

[42]Ibid.

[43]Sarila, Narendra Singh, *The Shadow of the Great Game: The Untold Story of India's Partition*, HarperCollins India, Noida, 2009.

the Indian princes, be given a free choice to choose an affiliation for their territories in any matter they wished to. Now, the NWFP, a wholly Muslim province, could not be detached from India as long as its representatives to the all-India Constituent Assembly supported its affiliation to India. The way to bypass this would be to hold fresh elections or some form of referendum to wrest power from Congress. Mountbatten launched 'Operation Frontier' on 18 April 1947 and turned down Governor Caroe's request to dismiss a duly elected government. Instead, he worked Nehru and the other Congress leaders to accept a referendum in exchange of leaving Dr Khan Sahib's government in place. He also offered to sack Governor Caroe, who had been causing much grievance to the Congress leadership. To take this a step further, Mountbatten visited Peshawar in the NWFP on 28 and 29 April. Upon his arrival, a crowd of over 50,000 people, mostly the League supporters, had gathered and were sloganeering 'Pakistan Zindabad'. This provided a great excuse for him to stick to his position of argument that 'it would certainly be necessary to know whether the Congress party still had a mandate from the people before a decision would be taken as to who was to inherit the Province at the transfer of power'. Nehru accepted the proposal with the condition to control the organization running the referendum.[44]

And so, to India's great misfortune, the Congress agreed to make an exception in the case of the NWFP and departed from its policy for all other provinces for ascertaining their affiliation to India or Pakistan and instead agreed to a referendum. Had it not done so, elected representatives of the Congress sitting in the Constituent Assembly could have easily chosen to affiliate with India.[45] It remains questionable as to why Nehru agreed to a referendum in the first place.

---

[44]Mountbatten, *L.M., Mountbatten's Report on the Last Viceroyalty: 22 March–15 August 1947*, edited by Lionel Carter, Manohar, 2003, Part B, Para 62.

[45]Sarila, Narendra Singh, *The Shadow of the Great Game: The Untold Story of India's Partition*, HarperCollins India, Noida, 2009, pp. 282–3.

THE SHIMLA RETREAT AND NEHRU'S APPROVAL OF PARTITION

The broad points of the withdrawal plan drafted by Mountbatten and his team were shown to Nehru and Jinnah in the last week of April 1947. The points were so vague that they were simply not enough to get a clear picture.[46] Ismay, one of Mountbatten's closest officers, had left for London to get the plan approved by the British government. Within four days, he had wired back that he had received approval to proceed with the draft plan. So, Mountbatten invited Nehru and his close friend and colleague Krishna Menon (member of British Labour Party and sole interlocutor of Nehru with British socialist leaders) to his Shimla retreat to discuss the plan in detail. The Viceroy wanted to jostle with the Indian leaders for a settlement before either the Congress or the Muslim League had too much time to think about it and any effective opposition to the partition of the country could develop. Now, the draft plan, which came to be called the Dickie Bird Plan, was essentially an adaptation of the Cabinet Mission Plan. On looking at it, V.P. Menon found it absolutely unworkable and told the Viceroy that he had been working on a transfer or power plan of his own as Reforms Commissioner. Of course, he had been secretly collaborating with Patel to come up with workable terms. Menon's plan was simple—power would be immediately transferred to India and Pakistan on the basis of dominion status. By consenting to accept dominion status, the Congress would be ensuring a peaceful transfer of power and a warm continuing relationship with Britain. Also, the civil services in India and the Indian Army, Air Force and Navy, which were manned by British officers at senior levels, would be encouraged to stay and help in the interim period. And finally, the princely states that were so fond of their connection with the Crown would be reassured and willing to federate. Menon assured the Viceroy that he had Patel's commitment that his plan would get accepted by the Congress.[47]

---

[46]Ibid. 286.

[47]Mosley, Leonard, *The Last Days of the British Raj*, Harcourt, Brace & World, Inc.,

On 17 May, a vital press conference was to be held to announce the plan to the press. At this point, the Viceroy still intended for his original Dickie Bird Plan to be announced to the Indian leaders.

However, in Shimla, one night after the three of them had dinner, Mountbatten invited Nehru for whisky and soda in his office at the Viceregal Lodge. They had already spent several days together at Campbell-Johnson's tucked away home, 'The Retreat', also in Shimla, in high spirits. It is believed that after one too many drinks, Mountbatten took out the Plan from his locker in his study and produced it to Nehru. After 30 minutes of reading carefully, Nehru was sweaty, nervous and appalled. His face grew red with anger and green with distress, after which he burst out, 'It won't do. I will never accept a plan like this. Congress will never accept it and India will never accept it either.'[48] The next morning, Nehru submitted written objections to the Dickie Bird Plan and sounded off Menon for not alerting him about it ahead of time over coffee. Mountbatten sent for V.P. Menon and proposed that Nehru be presented with the latter's plan immediately. Menon typed away his plan within four hours, after which it was snatched away by Sir Eric Mieville, another one of Mountbatten's trusted staffers, and taken to Nehru. 'He accepted it, V.P.,' Edwina had whispered in Menon's ear when she walked up to Menon and gave him a kiss.[49] That was that—a document produced in four hours was about to change the course of the Indian continent and perhaps the world. There remains considerable debate as to if Nehru was shown the Dickie Bird Plan only to warm him up to Menon's plan.

THE NORTH-WEST FRONTIER PROVINCE GIFTED TO PAKISTAN ON A PLATTER BY CONGRESS

After Nehru's acceptance, all other Indian leaders in the mix accepted Menon's plan one by one and announced their support

---

[48]Ibid.
[49]Ibid. 126.

for it on 3 June 1947. In fact, on 2 June, Gandhi had a meeting with Mountbatten. If Gandhi had sufficiently resisted the plan, that was going to be the end of it. The Congress's acceptance would be off the table. Even though Gandhi had been pushed to the periphery by the prevailing Congress leadership, his opposition to something would likely be taken most seriously. On 2 June, at the Mountbatten residence, when Gandhi showed up, Lord Mountbatten expected him to be livid, but instead, much to his relief, Gandhi entered his room with his fingers on his lips indicating that it was his *mounvrat* (day of silence). But he did scribble on a piece of paper, 'I am sorry I can't speak. I know you too don't want me to break my silence, do you?' In a follow-up sentence, Gandhi wrote, 'Abdul Ghaffar Khan has asked me to convey to you to dismiss the governor of the NWFP. I do not know whether he is right or wrong. He is truthful. If it can be done decorously, you should do it.'[50] And so, on 3 June 1947, the plan to partition India was announced.

The draft Bill of the plan was drawn up by the British parliamentary machinery and sent to Mountbatten for his comments. He urged them to add 15 August 1947 as the exact date for the transfer of power, for in his opinion, 'any later date will psychologically have adverse effect on present delicate position'.[51] He, of course, was referring to the great communal disharmony and violence that had been breaking out in various parts of the country. To quell this violence, more troops would be required, which would mean calling back some of the troops that had already been sent back home. It also meant that more money would have to be spent on those troops. Considering that the tax revenues coming from India had reduced significantly due to the pressure from the US to make serious constitutional advances and end the Empire rule in India; that Britain's finances were in a total flux; and that the US had tightened their purse strings, PM Attlee

---

[50]Mountbatten, L.M., *Mountbatten's Report on the Last Viceroyalty : 22 March–15 August 1947*, edited by Lionel Carter, Manohar, 2003, Part C, Paras 78–9.

[51]Sarila, Narendra Singh, *The Shadow of the Great Game: The Untold Story of India's Partition*, HarperCollins India, Noida, 2009.

had no choice but to approve 15 August in the draft Bill. With support even from the Opposition, the plan was accepted. Now it was time to implement it. Here was a task that would have taken years to accomplish peacefully and successfully but was rushed into completion in just 72 days. Mountbatten had two crucial things that needed to be done to safeguard British interests within this period of time: the NWFP had to be given to Pakistan with consent of the Congress leadership and the boundary between India and Pakistan needed to be drawn.

In the following week, British Foreign Secretary Ernest Bevin stated in the British Labour Party's Annual Conference that 'the division of India would help to consolidate Britain in the Middle East'.[52] Krishna Menon, who was witness to Nehru's approval to the partition plan during the Shimla retreat, was aghast and wrote in a letter to Lord Mountbatten on 14 June 1947:

> Is this frontier still the hinterland of the Imperial strategy? Does Britain still think in terms of being able to use this territory and all that follows from it? There is considerable amount of talking in this way; and if Kashmir, for one reason or another chooses to be in Pakistan, that is a further development in this direction. I do not know of British policy in this matter. But if this is the British intent, this is tragic...[53]

While all of this was going on, Dr Khan Sahib in the NWFP had begun to advocate for a separate, independent state called 'Pakhtoonistan' because he thought that he and his supporters will be unable to fight the Muslim League propaganda against delivering the province in the hands of the Hindus, that is, the Congress. The Congress, on Dr Khan's advice, made a request to Mountbatten to allow the NWFP referendum to include a third choice—for independence. When Mountbatten met Nehru

---

[52]Sarila, Narendra Singh, *The Shadow of the Great Game: The Untold Story of India's Partition*, HarperCollins India, Noida, 2009, p. 309.
[53]MB1/E 104, Krishna Menon to Mountbatten, 14 June 1947, Mountbatten Papers, British Archives, Hartley Library, University of Southampton.

subsequently, he explained how, to avoid Balkanizations, the option for independence in the case of Bengal and other provinces had been removed. He also reminded Nehru of a conversation in which the latter had agreed that the NWFP could not sustain itself. In lieu of rejecting the Congress's demand, Mountbatten dangled a carrot he had hidden in his heart—he offered to dismiss the governor and assist with the integration of the Indian princely states into the dominions of choice.

Nehru accepted Mountbatten's counter and then convinced his colleagues that they would have to bow down and withdraw their demand for the independence option in the referendum. Dr Khan Sahib was devastated. He felt betrayed by his own people. However, time and again, the NWFP Pathans had voted for his government, unimpressed by the League propaganda. He decided to put up a fight but was once again blocked by his brother Gaffar Khan, who had decided that their party would not contest in this referendum. Gaffar Khan believed that unlike in an election, there was no provision to weed out votes cast by fraudulent means in a referendum. More importantly, he feared massive violence breaking out between the two Pathan groups, and in his nephew Yunus Khan's words, 'Gandhi's pacifism had entered his soul.'[54] In a letter to Mountbatten written on 29 June 1947, Gandhi assured him, 'The referendum would go forward without any interference by the followers of Khan Abdul Gaffar Khan.'[55] That was that—Gandhi and the Congress party handed over the NWFP to Pakistan without much of a fight. Had they not done so, perhaps the British would have never gone ahead with the partition. With their strategic interest still located in the NWFP, they would have possibly convinced Nehru to cooperate in exchange of dismissing the partition plan. They'd have most certainly thrown Jinnah under the bus in the absence of the NWFP. But the Congress failed to capitalize on this asset to prevent the biggest massacre in human history.

---

[54]Mountbatten, L.M., *Mountbatten's Report on the Last Viceroyalty: 22 March–15 August 1947*, edited by Lionel Carter, Manohar, 2003, Part D, Para 71.
[55]Ibid.

Gandhi made his consent for Partition clear by persuading the Congress to accept Menon's plan in the All-India Congress Committee on 14 June. As Menon wrote, 'The Congress was opposed to Pakistan ... Yet, he had come before the All-India Congress Committee to urge the acceptance of the Resolution on India's division.'[56]

INDIA IS PARTITIONED

On the matter of drawing up the borders and ensuring peace prevailed, Maulana Azad was having none of Gandhi, Nehru and Patel's opinion. He warned Mountbatten that even without Partition, there had been riots in Calcutta, Noakhali, Bihar, Bombay and Punjab. If the country was divided in such an atmosphere, there would be rivers of blood flowing in different parts of the country, and the British would be responsible for the carnage.[57] But Mountbatten assured him:

> I shall give you complete assurance and see to it that there is no bloodshed and riot. I am a soldier, not a civilian. Once partition is accepted in principle, I shall issue orders to see that there are no communal disturbances in the country. If there should be the slightest agitation, I shall adopt the sternest measures to nip the trouble in the bud. I shall nor use even the armed police. I will order the Army and Air Force to act and I will use tanks and aeroplanes to suppress anybody who wants to create trouble.[58]

The high-ranking officers who had foreseen the inevitability of the partition as early as 1945 had warned and advised steps to avoid a violent massacre to the British authorities in several letters.

---

[56]Menon, V.P., *The Transfer of Power in India*, Longmans, Green and Co., London, 1957, p. 386.
[57]Azad, Abul Kalam, *India Wins Freedom: An Autobiographical Narrative*, Orient Longmans, Kolkata, 1959.
[58]Mosley, Leonard, *The Last Days of the British Raj*, Harcourt, Brace & World, Inc., New York, 1961, pp. 129–30.

Measures like setting up a central, impartial force to step in to stop the violence that would blow up in the Sikh–Hindu–Muslim areas were proposed. They had recommended for this force to be within a Commonwealth Defence region and advised against the British hurrying to Indianize the impartial forces. Instead they pushed for building the impartial forces so much so that it became the nucleus of an army that would in the future reunite the subcontinent. It is understood now that when the suggestion to retain a single force in the subcontinent was made by Mountbatten, Nehru and Jinnah immediately rejected it stating that independence would not have been obtained until they possessed their own troops. Eventually, Jinnah agreed but Nehru rejected the proposal vehemently: 'I would sooner have every village in India put to the flames than keep the British Army here after August 15.'[59] Hence, the decision to split up the Indian Army was made. After repeated pleas from the Commander-in-Chief to retain some troops, even if only to protect the British officers, Mountbatten wrote to the Secretary of State for India in which he explicitly revealed that only by granting complete autonomy (which meant both India and Pakistan having their own armies), with no reservations, could they stand the best chance of India retaining a dominion status indefinitely. This was Mountbatten's true ambition—he had enticed Nehru and his friends to stay in the Commonwealth by dangling the carrot of immediate autonomous independence.

Jinnah, on the other hand, was ecstatic. His joy was becoming hard to conceal even for a man as cold as him. At this point, he believed that he was going to be given the Pakistan of his dreams with an undivided Punjab, undivided Bengal, Sind, the NWFP and even parts of Delhi for that matter. He demanded a corridor traversing through India to connect East and West Pakistan. At this point, little did he know that he was going to be given this sorry moth-eaten state that would include a divided Punjab, a divided Bengal, Sind and the NWFP. However, for this boundary to be decided, the British brought in Sir Cyril Radcliffe, a British Civil

---

[59]Ibid. 129.

Service officer who had never set foot in India before and couldn't really even tell a Hindu apart from a Muslim, to carry out the task in five weeks.[60] Although he was promised help from two separate boards of four judges—two for Pakistan and two for India—they quickly withdrew from taking any responsibility. Radcliffe found himself as the sole decision-maker. In Bengal, he drew a clean line separating the poor, jute-growing eastern region from the wealthy Calcutta and western Bengal. In Punjab, he realized that the task he had on hand was destined to fail. Whatever the shape of the line he drew took, both communities had a lot to lose. He'd essentially be dividing the irrigation system built by Sikh money. The canals had turned a desert into the granary of India capable of feeding the whole subcontinent. The rivers that supplied the water lay in the east and would inevitably come under India whereas the lands that they supplied were all in the west, which would go to Pakistan. Sir Radcliffe quickly drew a line on the map and got out of India as fast as he could, which happened to be on 15 August.

The governor of Punjab, Sir Evan Jenkins, who had preserved peace in Punjab with a heavy hand even on Direct Action Day, repeatedly warned Mountbatten of the dangerous mood that the Sikhs were in and that they'd resort to violent means if the Boundary Commission's report was not in their favour. Their shrine at Nanak Sahib, at least one canal system and arrangements to bring at least three-quarters of the Sikh population from West to East Punjab were among the expectations that the Sikhs had laid out to the British. The tension in Punjab rose so swiftly that on 13 July, Jenkins once again warned Mountbatten, 'The communal feeling is now unbelievably bad. The Sikhs believe they will [be] expropriated and massacred in West Punjab and smothered by the Hindus and Congress generally in East Punjab. They threaten a violent rising immediately.'[61] He urged the Viceroy to immediately announce the results of Radcliffe's report to stop the panic and urgent madness of large chunks of population moving from India

---

[60]Ibid. 194.
[61]Ibid. 207.

to Pakistan and vice versa. He also recommended that a force be moved into the area along the likely line of partition to preserve peace. Thus, on consultation with Sir Claude Auchinleck, the supreme commander of the emerging Indian and Pakistani armies and outgoing Commander-in-Chief, ordered to set up the Punjab Boundary Force consisting over 50,000 officers, a high-proportion of them being British. To Mountbatten, setting up the Punjab Boundary Force meant that he had kept the promise made to Azad that he'd maintain peace.

The air in the rest of the country was jubilant in anticipation of Independence. Worried that the announcement of the awarding of Partition may kill the moment of celebratory joy that he had worked so hard for, the Viceroy reserved it until after Independence. Gandhi, still convinced that Patel and Nehru had made a grave error in accepting a hurried division, was persuaded by the governor of Bengal to station himself in Bengal so that violence could be averted. And that's exactly what Gandhi did. Taking CM Shaheed Suhrawardy along, the two men visited places where violence was likely to erupt, held prayer meetings and toured extensively. Gandhi ended up being the one-man boundary force for Bengal. Punjab, on the other hand, lay ravaged, with the blood of Sikhs, Hindus and Muslims flowing endlessly as the rest of India and Pakistan celebrated Independence. The 50,000-men-strong Punjab Boundary Force was instructed by the British to stick to their barracks and only protect British officers.

The partition of India and Pakistan remains one of the bloodiest events of the twentieth century. What could have been done differently? What the British had desired was access to Gilgit in northern Kashmir where they had set up seismic monitoring stations and strategic access to the Middle East. The Congress leadership, with Nehru helming all foreign affairs matters, was so clueless about geopolitical realities that they simply couldn't cut deals with the British using pressure from the Americans, the way Jinnah did. Had they negotiated with the British to let the latter keep Gilgit as a long-lease property (akin to Hong Kong) and allow limited strategic operations, perhaps Pakistan's territory would have been much more limited. It is not unrealistic to say that Baluchistan may have been part of India, and so would all of Kashmir, the Katarpur corridor and perhaps even parts of Sind. Had it been better thought through, perhaps our leadership could have negotiated a greater land mass around the Siliguri corridor so as to enable easier access to the Northeast (Indira Gandhi had the opportunity to renegotiate this on the creation of Bangladesh in 1971 with the help of Indian Armed Forces but passed it despite India being in a position of strength). At the very least, the bloodshed of Partition could have been avoided as Jinnah's wings would have been significantly clipped.

In fact, neither the Indian leadership, who are political heirs of the decisions related to Partition, nor the British take any square responsibility for the death of millions. The partition of India was perhaps the first time in history that Islam was weaponized to drive a wedge in a subcontinent. It is from this appeasement to Jinnah and his extremist demands that the Pakistan was born. It is the violence that Jinnah, supported by the British, perpetrated during Direct Action Day that still seems to dictate Pakistan's unsaid policies of harbouring violent, terrorist elements in the name of religion. This causes great loss of lives all around the world even today. It is about time the world wakes up to these events in history and begins to have a clearer look, pinning accountability on those who were part of the nexus that enabled such a state to be created to satisfy their own interests.

SECTION II
TERRITORIAL INTEGRATION

3

INTEGRATION OF THE PRINCELY STATES

Alongside the final days of Partition, the question of integrating over 600 princely states into one of the dominions, India and Pakistan, came into prime focus. However, out of all of them, Kashmir and Hyderabad were the only two that had the power and size to sustain themselves, if they chose independence. They were so intertwined with India geographically and historically that choosing independence or aligning with Pakistan would have been disastrous for India's security and strategic interests.

From the third decade of the century, the princely states' relationship with the British Crown had been made official via an arrangement known as the 'doctrine of paramountcy'.[1] Paramountcy meant that the princely states had a direct relationship with the King instead of one with the British government administered by the King. Under this instrument of paramountcy, the states were given several privileges that included freedom to govern without interruptions in exchange for allowing the British Indian government to station armed forces, run communication lines and so on. Come Independence, this doctrine of paramountcy would lapse and would certainly leave the states helpless and vulnerable, without the protection of the British Crown. In order to facilitate accession, the States Department was formed, and Patel was chosen to lead it, who, in turn, convinced V.P. Menon to assist him as the

---

[1]Mosley, Leonard, *The Last Days of the British Raj*, Harcourt, Brace & World, Inc., New York, 1961, p. 161.

secretary of the department.[2]

Once again, the British played a contrasting role to create confusion among the states acceding to either dominion. On one hand, Sir Conrad Corfield, the British political advisor to the Chamber of Princes (a representative organization of the heads of the princely statesman), along with Secretary of State for India, Lord Listowel, made it a point to destroy all evidence that they had on the rulers of the princely states that could potentially come in handy for the future Indian government to pressurize them to accede to India.[3] Additionally, they lobbied the big states to start thinking about independence as a third option instead of acceding to either dominion. While on the other hand, Mountbatten appeared vaguely supportive of convincing the states to accede to the dominion of their choice as per the task entrusted to him by the King just before he left for India to become the last viceroy.[4] Just a few days prior to his departure from London, he was summoned by the King in the capacity of a cousin, and the King confessed how worried he was on the issue of the princely states. He asked Mountbatten to consider it an important task to solve their problem, especially since they shared a direct relationship with the Crown under the instrument of paramountcy.[5] The task at hand was tricky: while Mountbatten didn't care about which way most states went, he certainly had a strong opinion on the ones that were critical to Britain's continued strategic interests in the Indian subcontinent. He, however, tried to remain aloof up until the time the Patel–Menon duo requested his help to convince the states to accede to India. The duo believed that due to his royal blood and the title of the viceroy, the rulers of the princely states were likely to be influenced by him. Mountbatten accepted Patel–Menon's offer but refused to influence the states to accede to

---

[2]Menon, V.P., *Integration of the Indian States*, Orient BlackSwan, Hyderabad, 2014, pp. 85–6.
[3]Mosley, Leonard, *The Last Days of the British Raj*, Harcourt, Brace & World, Inc., New York, 1961, pp. 162–3.
[4]Ibid. 158.
[5]Ibid.

India. He said he'd try to convince them to accede to the dominion of their own choice.[6]

Meanwhile, as per Nehru's letter to Cripps in 1945, he was of the opinion that big princely states (like Kashmir, Hyderabad, Travancore) or a united group of small princely states like the Rajput states could certainly chose independence if they decided so. As mentioned earlier, Nehru was absolutely okay with the Balkanization of India. So, Patel really was a one-man army when it came to ensuring the integration of states with India.[7]

The first meeting between the Chamber of Princes and Mountbatten took place on 25 July 1947, just days before Independence.[8] Decorated with medals, Lord Mountbatten came in a jovial mood in his full uniform. One by one, most states acceded and only a few remained hesitant—Travancore, Kashmir, Hyderabad, Jodhpur and Junagadh being some of them. Travancore was a wealthy state in the south of India and intended to become independent after the lapse of paramountcy. The state had an active, strong communist movement. The Patel–Menon duo and Mountbatten tried to get the ruler to see how the dream of independence would be shattered if the communists took to the streets on the lapse of paramountcy of the Crown and the British Indian Army was unavailable to come to their rescue. Several days later, Patel orchestrated strong demonstrations all over the princely state, some of them violent, with help from the Congress workers, which shook the core of the ruler, and he quickly signed the Instrument of Accession with India.[9]

This demonstrated to the other states the reality of their vulnerability to the Indian defence and political forces when paramountcy lapsed. For several months, the Nizam of Hyderabad had been colluding with Sir Conrad to see if the large number of

---

[6]Ibid. 170.

[7]CAB/127/143, 75800, Nehru to Cripps, Public Records Office, The National Archives, London.

[8]Mosley, Leonard, *The Last Days of the British Raj*, Harcourt, Brace & World, Inc., New York, 1961, p. 172.

[9]Ibid. 176.

troops of the British Indian Army stationed within his state could be recalled before paramountcy lapsed. Hyderabad was surrounded on all sides by Indian territory. Remaining independent would be a strategic and security nightmare—another Poland, as Mountbatten put it. He didn't withdraw the troops in advance, and as soon as the British left on 15 August, more Indian forces moved in, forcing accession to India.[10]

Junagadh was a state that was mostly Hindu but the ruler was a Muslim. It had the Gir forest, a Hindu temple of significance and also an important Jain temple in Girnar. Geographically, in the middle of its kingdom, there were other smaller princely states (Mangrol states) that had already acceded to the Indian dominion. Also, much of Junagadh's enclaves were in other Kathiawar states like Bhavnagar, Baroda and Gondal. While Junagadh's ruler sweet-talked Patel–Menon, giving them repeated assurances, he simultaneously opened a channel of communication with Jinnah and the Muslim League leadership too. Eventually, when Jinnah offered him a blank cheque, he decided to accede to Pakistan without thinking of what would happen to his kingdom, which would be surrounded on all land sides by India.

He was odd, with a fetish for pet dogs and hunting. It is believed that he had four wives, over 150 dogs and luxurious arrangements for all the dogs. Every time his dogs mated, he announced a holiday in the state. So peculiar was his love for his pet dogs that it is believed that the night he fled from the kingdom for Pakistan, with his choice of pet dogs and his four wives, one of the wives got off the plane to fetch a child she had left behind in the palace. Without waiting for the wife and the child to return, he cramped in two more of his dogs on the plane instead and took off.[11] While Jinnah had no strategic gains from a largely Hindu state that was separated from Pakistan by sea, he still wanted to see the Congress's reaction to Junagadh's accession. Was India prepared to give away a Hindu-majority state to Pakistan just because of its ruler's decision?

---

[10]Ibid. 191.
[11]Ibid.

After all, while Junagadh was only a test case, the real meat for Jinnah was Kashmir, which was a reversed situation—a Hindu ruler with a largely Muslim population. Patel was too politically wily to not have seen through this, so he activated the Congress ecosystem in the smaller states, which were interspersed in the middle of Junagadh's territory and had acceded to India, to create unrest and disturbance. Then, on the pretext of maintaining law and order (and since Jinnah took no action), armed forces were sent in. Junagadh was always expendable to Jinnah. He was unwilling to deploy any more forces fighting internal unrest and also wanted to set an example that would come in handy while negotiating for Kashmir.[12]

So, when the day of independence rolled around, all states had signed Instruments of Accession except three—Junagadh, Hyderabad and Kashmir. Junagadh's and Hyderabad's accession to India soon came through, but Kashmir's fate remained hanging.

---

[12]Ibid. 181–6.

4

KASHMIR

ashmir, which we popularly consider the crown of India, met its unfortunate fate of forceful partition a few months after Independence. The crux of the problem was that British strategic interests remained a vital element in the northern and western parts of the former state of Jammu and Kashmir, and the outgoing British leadership colluded with Pakistani leadership to invade the princely state. They didn't stop there—in order to face the least amount of resistance from the Indian Armed Forces, Nehru and the Congress leaders, who failed to see the geopolitical powers at play, were misled into actions that compromised the territorial integrity of the region that was and continues to be an integral part of India.

In order to fully understand the above statement, it is essential first to list out why certain areas of Jammu and Kashmir remained of extraordinary importance to the British (marked as 'Pakistan Occuped' in Map 1), even after Independence.

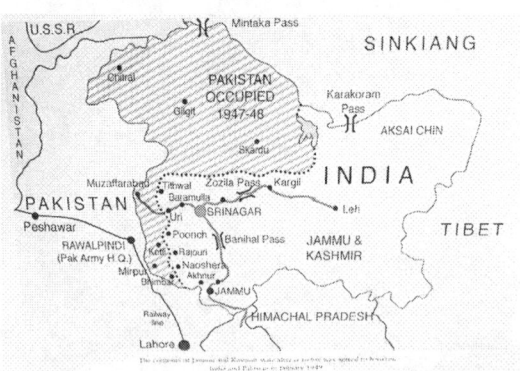

Map 1: Contours of Jammu and Kashmir after the 1948 ceasefire
Source: Sarila, Narendra Singh, *The Shadow of the Great Game: The Untold Story of India's Partition*, HarperCollins India, Noida, 2009.

Let us look at the contours of the state to further understand the developments. The state extended from the subcontinental plains to the Pamirs. Some massive mountain ranges divide it in such a way that it allowed for people of various religions and cultures to coexist. The Karakoram mountain range separates it from Central Asia while the Himalayan range runs through its middle. The Pir Panjal range, part of the Himalayan range, separates these highlands from the southern foothills, where Jammu is situated. The Kashmir Valley is situated in the western reaches of these mountains, and Srinagar is built on the Dal Lake. Even though the Valley occupied less than 10 per cent of the state's total geographic area, it contained well over half of the region's population of about 4 million in 1947. The only all-weather road from this Valley isolated by the mountain ranges runs along the Jhelum in the western part of the state. The second largest fair-weather road runs between Jammu and Srinagar through the Banihal Pass, but closes down in the winter. The northern part of the state was inhabited by the Shia Muslims, eastern Ladakh along Tibet by Buddhists, the province of Jammu by the Dogras and other Hindus, and its western strip, along Pakistan, by the Sunni Muslims of the same make as the Punjabi Muslims.[1] Even though about 80 per cent of the Valley had Sunni Muslims and the other 20 per cent Sikhs and Hindus (Kashmiri Pandits), they were tied together by a unique Kashmiri identity, popularly known as Kashmiriyat, that unified them.[2] It is this Kashmiriyat that made them very distinct from the Punjabi Muslims who went to Pakistan.

Until the fourteenth century, the Kashmir Valley and some of the surrounding areas were ruled by a series of Hindu and Buddhist dynasties.[3] However, they were then taken over by the Mughal rulers. In the late-sixteenth century, it is believed that

---

[1]Razdan, P.N., *Gems of Kashmiri Literature and Kashmiriyat: The Trio of Saint Poets – I*, Samkaleen Prakashan, Pune, 1999.

[2]Ibid.

[3]Kaw, M.K., *Kashmir and Its People: Studies in the Evolution of Kashmiri Society*, A.P.H Publishing, New Delhi, 2004.

Emperor Ashoka spent his summers in Srinagar. By the eighteenth century, the area was taken over by the Afghans, who were defeated by Sikh King Ranjit Singh in 1819.[4] It is from Ranjit Singh that the British wrested the Kashmir Valley during the Anglo-Sikh War and awarded it to Gulab Singh for his loyalty to the British Empire. Gulab Singh's descendants then ruled the then princely state of Jammu and Kashmir up until a few months after Indian independence.[5]

☞

It is heartbreaking to see distorted maps of Kashmir today, with various limbs cut off and territories being attributed to Pakistan and China. When references by responsible diplomats of several countries and international organizations are made to 'Azad' Kashmir, it ignites rage in the hearts of Indians across the world. But very few fully understand how 'Azad' Kashmir came to be created and what the role of each party involved in this creation was. Many questions still cloud the minds of people. Why did India let Pakistan occupy Kashmir? Why didn't Nehru act aggressively to take back India's lost territory? Was it India's territory to 'take back' in the first place? If it was, why did Nehru agree to divide the state in his correspondence with the British? What were Britain's strategic interests and compulsions because of which they wanted certain areas of the state to be handed over to Pakistan? And if they did play such a role, why don't they own up to it in international forums and media?

MAHARAJA HARI SINGH'S INHERITANCE AND FAMILY DYNAMICS

The Kashmir problem is a very complex one with multiple players, each shifting the blame onto the other to get out of being held

---

[4]Malhotra, Iqbal Chand and Maroof Raza, *Kashmir's Untold Story: Declassified*, Bloomsbury India, New Delhi, 2019, p. 22.
[5]Ibid. 26.

accountable. But my endeavour in this section will be to pin each of these players' actions to them by trying to explain their role and relationships at the time. Before Independence, Jammu and Kashmir was a princely state ruled by Maharaja Hari Singh. Maharaja Hari Singh's grandfather Gulab Singh had already signed the Treaty of Chushul on 17 September 1842, along with the Qing Emperor of China and then Dalai Lama of Tibet. This treaty restored the boundaries of the Sikh Empire to Aksai Chin, which lay at the south of Sinkiang and also gave to the Dalai Lama a *jagir* (ownership) of three villages near Mansarovar.[6] This somewhat ambiguous treaty drafted in those days became the basis of both Indian and Chinese claims to Aksai Chin from 1949.[7] In addition to these inherited territories, the British had sold the entire territory, which included the Kashmir Valley and all territories east of River Indus and west of River Ravi, to Gulab Singh for a meagre sum of 75 lakh *nanakshahi* currency, which would be used to compensate Gulab Singh for helping them during the Anglo-Sikh War.[8] The northern part of the princely state, which included the Gilgit region that had remained of particular interest to the British after Independence, was included as part of Gulab Singh's acquired territory. All of this was recorded in the Treaty of Amritsar signed between the British and Gulab Singh in 1846.

Gulab Singh relinquished his throne in 1856 to make way for his youngest son Ranbir Singh with approval from the British. Ranbir Singh, like his father, maintained close ties with the British and expanded his empire to share common borders with Russia, Sinkiang and Tibet. Between 1855 and 1865, the British carried out the Great Trigonometric Survey of India, as part of which they surveyed all areas of the state and officially recorded the entire territory. In this survey, the British officer on duty recorded that

---

[6]*Frontier and Overseas Expeditions from India: Vol. VI,* Low Price Publications, New Delhi, 1907–1911.

[7]Lamb, A., *The China India Corder: The Origins of the Disputed Boundaries,* Oxford University Press, London, 1964.

[8]Malhotra, Iqbal Chand and Maroof Raza, *Kashmir's Untold Story: Declassified,* Bloomsbury India, New Delhi, 2019, p. 27.

the northeastern border of the state extended 100 miles north of Karakoram Pass towards Sinkiang as he crossed over to Khotan in Sinkiang from Leh. Until that point, it was believed that the northeastern boundary extended only about 50 miles from Karakoram Pass. This new data was officially included in Indian cartographic records by the British.[9]

Ranbir Singh left the throne to his son Pratap Singh, who was rather ambitious and took part in pro-Russian activities, angering the British. In turn, the British stripped him of his authority and took over the state administration in 1889, violating the Treaty of Amritsar and the Queen's proclamation of 1858 in the name of treason.[10] Pratap Singh's powers were partly reinstated in 1905, but he came under a heavy shadow of his younger brother Raja Amar Singh, whom the British worked closely with. In exchange for his loyalty to the British against his brother, Amar Singh was given the commitment that his son Hari Singh will succeed Pratap Singh as the next Maharaja (Hari Singh was also the only male descendent of Gulab Singh after Pratap Singh).[11] Pratap Singh, who was childless, was bitter about this development in light of the role that his brother Amar Singh had played against him, and he decided to adopt a son who could succeed him, leaving out the British-backed Hari Singh. He adopted Jagat Dev Singh (descendant of the younger brother of Gulab Singh) of Poonch, despite the British making it clear that an adopted son would not be made the Maharaja.[12]

However, in 1925, when time came for succession, the viceroy at the time was delayed in naming Maharaja Hari Singh as the successor for three weeks, creating the initial seeds of contempt against the British in Maharaja Hari Singh's mind. Other petty issues like a certain British officer addressing him as 'Raja' instead

---

[9]Ibid. 28.
[10]Ibid. 30–1.
[11]Ibid. 34.
[12]Ibid. 35.

of 'Maharaja' added fuel to the fire.[13] Meanwhile, the family drama continued. Raja Jagat Dev Singh's grandfather Dhyan Singh, who was Gulab Singh's younger brother, had been made the Raja of Poonch, whereas Gulab Singh had been made Raja of Jammu by their father Ranjit Singh. But on Dhyan Singh's untimely death, widely believed to be orchestrated by Gulab Singh, the latter had consolidated his power over Poonch, only to grant it back to Dhyan Singh's descendants later with the reduced status of a jagir. Very bitter about the loss of his inheritance and reduced rights over Poonch, Raja Jagat Dev Singh decided to militarize and mobilize the tribal Muslims of the region against the British and Maharaja Hari Singh in the fourth decade of the century.[14] We shall come back to why this is important to note.

THE IMPORTANCE OF GILGIT AGENCY

On 26 March 1935, Maharaja Hari Singh leased Gilgit and its vassal states, namely, Chitral, Hunza, Nagar Haveli, Puniyal, Chilas Yasin, Yashkoman and Koh-e-Khizr, to the British for a period of 60 years for a nominal amount of ₹75,000. The newly leased region came to be known as Gilgit Agency and was administered by the Political Department from Delhi (the contours of which are depicted in Map 2),[15] similar to some agencies in the NWFP like Khyber and Malakand, with political officers stationed there reporting to the Viceroy through Peshawar. Gilgit lay in the northern areas of the state, sharing a border with the NWFP in the east, Afghanistan in the northwest and Sinkiang in the northeast. In the time period around 1935, Sinkiang was a potboiler of political tension due to the crumbling authority of the Kuomintang government and the rise of Mao Zedong's Red Army, which was closely allied with Russia. Meanwhile, in Khotan, there was threat from the Muslim warlord Ma Hushan spreading to Ladakh. With northern borders under

---

[13]Ibid. 38–9.
[14]Ibid. 51–2.
[15]Ibid. 54.

threat, the British simply could not trust Hari Singh to protect the British Indian Empire and, as a solution, prevailed on the Maharaja to lease out Gilgit and its vassal states to them. Simultaneously, they introduced a constitution in the state of Jammu and Kashmir under the pretext of calming down political unrest simmering against the Maharaja's rule.[16] While the constitution of 1934 only lasted five years, another amended one was brought in 1939. The intent of the British to bring in the constitution was to keep the Maharaja preoccupied with political upheaval in the Valley and divert his attention from the northern borders.[17]

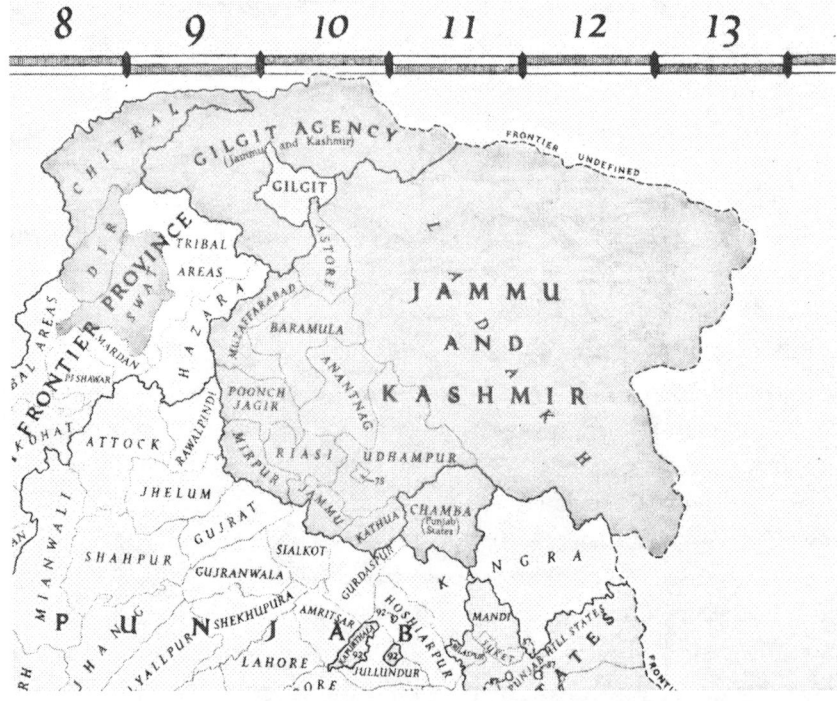

Map 2: Gilgit Agency on the map of Jammu and Kashmir before Independence
Source: https://tinyurl.com/mv74565a. Accessed on 22 November 2023.

---

[16]Ibid. 42.
[17]Ibid.

The first political agent to take charge in Gilgit Agency was Major Kirkbridge, and he did so on 1 October 1935. In 1942, during World War II, the Soviets suffered defeat at the hands of the Nazis. This led the war-lord Sheng Shicai in Sinkiang to shift loyalty from the communists to the Kuomintang. He carried out massive infrastructure projects that linked Sinkiang to mainland China, alongside wiping out Soviet spies and the Chinese Communist Party cadres who were deeply involved with the Soviets. As Sinkiang became mainstream China, these developments certainly didn't go unnoticed in New Delhi. There was an overwhelming understand that the Soviets were not going to take this integration quietly and that there would be a response.

Around the late 1930s and early 1940s, another important development that was taking place was one of new war weaponry, specifically nuclear weaponry. The Americans, British, Russians as well as Germans were in a cut-throat competition to master the power of the atom in order to make the atom bomb.[18] The US, United Kingdom (UK), Canada and France had, from the 1930s, collaborated on the Manhattan Project, a consortium of the aforementioned nations to collaborate and build a weapon using nuclear fission, i.e., an atom bomb. On the other side, the Soviet scientific community had been making proposals to develop a 'superweapon' all through the 1930s, culminating in a formal proposal in 1940. The discovery of the Soviets mining uranium in Sinkiang threw New Delhi into panic. The British government in India felt an urgent need to develop a network of spies that would collect samples of uranium, beryllium and other ores being mined by the Soviets in Sinkiang. This network of spies was supposed to be supplemented by a network of couriers that would secretly carry these samples across the border to Gilgit, from where they'd be further shipped to the US to continuously evaluate the progress made by the Russians on the readiness of the nuclear weapon.[19]

---

[18]Ibid. 54.
[19]Ibid.

To further pursue this systematically, two things were done in 1942–43: the British posted a Pashto-speaking Indian Army officer Capt. William Brown to the Gilgit Agency and the US government opened a consulate in Tihwa, the capital of Sinkiang headed by Consul Edmund Cubb.[20] There is solid circumstantial evidence that Clubb would hand over ore samples to a network of couriers controlled by Capt. Brown, which would then be carried to Gilgit from Kashgar.[21] With Shicai's loyalty shifting to Kuomintang, trade routes between Gilgit and Sinkiang had opened up, and, in fact, a protocol was signed by the governments of India and Sinkiang to permit trade via pack animals. Of course, Capt. Brown's role was to ensure that the ores were carried undercover, under the pretext of trading other commodities.[22]

The US developed the atomic bomb and deployed it over the Japanese cities of Hiroshima and Nagasaki, which brought an end to World War II. A year later, despite the top secret 1944 Hyde Park Aide-Mémoire signed between President Roosevelt and PM Churchill that allowed for continued collaboration between the two nations on development of nuclear weapons (the papers of which disappeared with Roosevelt's demise),[23] the US government passed the Atomic Energy Act 1946 (McMahon Act) that would restrict sharing of nuclear information with other countries. Britain was left out of the loop, and it had to ramp up its own efforts to get back in the race.

In 1944, with the defeat of the German Army on the eastern front of Sinkiang, Soviet penetration increased once again, and it became necessary to keep a strong vigil on their mining activities in the area. Additionally, the US was trying very hard to maintain a global monopoly on the supply of uranium. If the British were to use their own skills and resources to make the atom bomb, they needed to upgrade the existing informal Brown network of

[20]Ibid. 55.
[21]Ibid.
[22]Ibid.
[23]'Hyde Park Aide-Mémoire', *The National Museum of Nuclear Science and History*, https://tinyurl.com/y7x6ns9y. Accessed on 16 November 2023.

informants to a full-scale espionage network of spies that would be capable of reading the intelligence generated by the locals. Britain needed to continuously spy on the progress made at the Semipalatinsk Test Site (where the Soviets were testing the bomb). They also needed to keep an eye on the relationship between the Soviets and the mines in the Koktogai Valley, in addition to building their own relationship with their mines, so that they could secure the ores necessary for their nuclear progress. To give more context about just how frequent these activities were, between 1945 and 1965, the Soviets conducted over 110 above-ground nuclear tests at the Semipalatinsk Test Site, which was an 18,500-km patch of land.[24]

In order to do this, the British brought in Col Roger Bacon as the political agent in Gilgit (Capt. William Brown was transferred to Waziristan in the NWFP) with an undercover mandate to construct and commission a seismic monitoring station to detect the nuclear tests being conducted. This station was established in the Gilgit Agency within the Hindu Kush mountain range and went by the code name 'Stowage'.[25] The proximity to Semipalatinsk enabled the station to receive strong signals as soon as the tests were conducted. The daily output from Stowage was reported to both the British and US governments, the papers of which are possibly still undisclosed as of today. To complement this seismic monitoring station, Col Bacon established two additional acoustic stations in the Gilgit Agency, which were code named 'Beaver' and 'Tagday'.[26] In addition, the Royal Air Force ran debris collection flights from Peshawar, coinciding with the nuclear tests. So, the British had established a deep-seated nuclear monitoring empire in the Gilgit Agency, whose role was absolutely crucial for the British quest of making the atom bomb and continuing to achieve its own nuclear milestones.

---

[24]Malhotra, Iqbal Chand and Maroof Raza, *Kashmir's Untold Story: Declassified*, Bloomsbury India, New Delhi, 2019, p. 58.
[25]Ibid.
[26]Ibid. 59.

The British intended for the Gilgit Agency to go to Pakistan or remain as Pax Britannica[27] on the lines of the Hong Kong model, where they would continue to administer it as their leasehold property after Independence, so that they could keep complete control over these strategic activities. But when Maharaja Hari Singh decided to accede to India, the British activated a complex web that would ensure that Gilgit Agency fell into Pakistan's hands. Nehru and the Congress failed to see how vital of a cog it was for British interests. Not only did they not fight hard enough to retain it with India, but they also failed to use it as a bargaining chip to further Indian interests. So uninterested or uninformed was Nehru of the importance of the Gilgit Agency that in his brief to Mountbatten on 17 June 1947 on Kashmir, he left out the Gilgit Agency completely while describing the contours of the state.[28] Obviously, the omission of Gilgit from Nehru's note didn't go unnoticed and gave off the sentiment that Gilgit was dispensable to him. Additionally, four months after the invasion of Kashmir by Pakistani *kabalis* (tribal invaders), on 20 February 1948, Nehru wrote to Krishna Menon, then Indian high commissioner in the UK:

> Even Mountbatten has hinted at partition of Kashmir—Jammu for India and the rest including the lovely Vale of Kashmir to Pakistan. This is totally unacceptable to us ... Although if the worst comes to the worst I am prepared to accept Poonch and Gilgit being partitioned off.[29]

THE RISE OF SHEIKH ABDULLAH

The Kashmir Valley before the 1930s was mostly intellectually disconnected from India and the world. There were little

---

[27]Ibid. 69.
[28]Sarila, Narendra Singh, *The Shadow of the Great Game: The Untold Story of India's Partition*, HarperCollins India, Noida, 2009, p. 337.
[29]Wolpert, Stanley, *Nehru: A Tryst with Destiny*, Oxford University Press, New York, 1996, p. 435.

opportunities for higher education within the state, and the Muslim residents seldom got a chance to serve in the Maharaja's government. Born in 1905 just outside Srinagar to a shawl salesman, Abdullah's family was plunged into poverty after the untimely death of his father.[30] A bright kid, he pursued his higher education at Aligarh Muslim University but was miffed that the state refused to fund his education. He eventually got a teaching job but soon abandoned it for active political involvement.

Around that time, the Muslim residents were protesting the Maharaja's unfair and discriminatory treatment towards them. In response to their demonstrations, he used the police to arrest several activists. In 1931, his police force even shot down nine of them, which led to Muslim unrest spreading beyond the Kashmir Valley to Jammu, where several hundred British troops were brought in to help the Maharaja restore order. This was the first time that affairs in Jammu and Kashmir got international attention. Two things transpired during these protests—a British personnel who was made in charge of the commission investigating the situation, Sir Bertrand Glancy, recommended to the Maharaja to create a constitution that would politically allow a platform for political dissenters,[31] and Abdullah and another Muslim leader Mirwaiz Mohammad Yusuf Shah emerged as popular leaders of the dissenting Muslims. They were jailed by the Maharaja, which only increased their popularity. In 1932, the duo formed a political party called the Muslim Conference, which brought together all political forces that opposed his rule. Hari Singh's Dogra community and the Valley's Sikh population, which had lived there from the time of Maharaja Ranjit Singh's conquest, along with the Kashmiri Pandits, stood at the receiving end of the ever-growing strength of the Maharaja's Muslim subjects. The political mobilization of the large Muslim population had established a communal divide.

---

[30]Krishnan, Revathi, 'Lion of Kashmir, Sheikh Abdullah's Nationalism Clashed with Nehru's Indian Nationalism', *The Print*, 8 September 2019, https://tinyurl.com/wt79xeej. Accessed on 17 November 2023.

[31]Hasan, Mohibbul, 'British Policy towards Kashmir and the Glancy Commission' *Social Scientist*, Volume 48, Issue 7/8, 2020, pp. 3–16.

While at Aligarh University, Abdullah gained a very cosmopolitan, secular outlook, which only strengthened as time passed. After he was released from jail in 1933, he even made peace with Hari Singh and married the half-Kashmiri daughter of a wealthy Croatian businessman who owned a chain of hotels in the state.[32] His progressive outlook got even stronger when he met Jawaharlal Nehru in 1938. Both men were enamoured by socialism and the Soviet way of life. Abdullah even began to operate the Muslim Conference as an extension of the Congress,[33] which triggered the ultra-conservative Mirwaiz. Eventually, the differences between Mirwaiz and Abdullah reached a breaking point, due to which they dissolved the Muslim Conference in 1939.[34] In its stead, Abdullah founded the National Conference. After the Pakistan Resolution (the Lahore Resolution, presented by A.K. Fazlul Huq at the three-day general session of the Muslim League in Lahore on 22–24 March 1941, is popularly known as the Pakistan Resolution because it called for independent states based on religion) was passed by the Muslim League in Lahore in 1941, several Muslims urged Mirwaiz to resurrect the Muslim Conference. He obliged.[35] This resurrected Muslim Conference became the trump card for Jinnah and the Muslim League to begin sowing communal seeds within the Kashmiri people.

Maharaja Hari Singh remained more or less occupied in playing the balancing act of managing opposition voices until he eventually acceded to India. In 1944, the PM of the state, Ram Chandra Kak, arranged for Jinnah's visit to Srinagar to have him mediate between the two warring parties. Kak had his own agenda, which was mostly to remain independent or accede to Pakistan.[36] The

---

[32]Malhotra, Iqbal Chand and Maroof Raza, *Kashmir's Untold Story: Declassified*, Bloomsbury India, New Delhi, 2019, p. 43.

[33]Ibid. 45.

[34]Abdullah, S.M., *The Blazing Chinar: An Autobiography*, Gulshan Books, Srinagar, 2016.

[35]Malhotra, Iqbal Chand and Maroof Raza, *Kashmir's Untold Story: Declassified*, Bloomsbury India, New Delhi, 2019, p. 45.

[36]Ibid. 64.

National Conference's cosiness with the Congress wasn't helping to mount pressure on Hari Singh to accede to India as Hari Singh was growing suspicious of Nehru's role in fuelling discontent. However, Jinnah was unsuccessful, and he ended up endorsing the Muslim Conference as the only real representative of Muslim issues in the state. Due to this, Kak was able to introduce the idea of Pakistan to Hari Singh.

In May 1946, Abdullah launched the Quit Kashmir movement against the Maharaja, during which Abdullah condemned the 1846 sale of the Valley by the British to Gulab Singh in incendiary speeches.[37] He emphatically declared that this was an invalid act, and, therefore, the Maharaja, as the descendant of the Dogra dynasty, was also an invalid ruler. He insisted that the Maharaja leave Kashmir immediately and hand over power to the people of the state. It had taken 15 years of British Machiavellian intrigue to unleash the forces that had shaken the seemingly unshakeable rule of Gulab Singh's descendants. Around the same time, Kak began to exploit the differences that arose between Sheikh Abdullah's National Conference and Mirwaiz Mohammad Yusuf Shah's Muslim Conference. Kak's deft political intrigue isolated the Muslim Conference from the Quit Kashmir movement to a large extent. While Kak placed the state under martial law and arrested almost the entire top leadership of the National Conference and hundreds of its workers, he spared the Muslim Conference his wrath.[38] Sheikh Abdullah, following an arrest and a three-year imprisonment sentence for sedition, left the National Conference leaderless and in disarray. The Quit Kashmir movement found immense support from folks in the Kashmir Valley but fizzled out in other parts of the state.

However, failing to see the bigger picture, all that Nehru's wisdom allowed him to conclude was that Abdullah was the most

---

[37]Hiro, D., *The Longest August: The Unflinching Rivalry Between India and Pakistan*, Bold Type Books, 2015.

[38]Malhotra, Iqbal Chand and Maroof Raza, *Kashmir's Untold Story: Declassified*, Bloomsbury India, New Delhi, 2019, p. 62.

popular leader in Kashmir. The latter was eventually arrested and put behind bars. As a close friend, Nehru decided to put his weight behind Abdullah and began to convince Kak to release him, but Kak stood his ground. Nehru decided to visit Kak in person in an additional attempt. However, as he was crossing from Punjab into Kashmir, he was detained at the Uri Dak Bungalow on Kak's orders. For the thin-skinned Nehru, this was a personal blow, one he'd avenge by bringing the Maharaja down. As per a close aide's report recorded in a note on Nehru's reaction on being detained, 'He violently trampled his foot on the floor and told them that one day the Maharaja of Kashmir would have to repent and apologise to him for the discourtesy shown to the president-elect of the Indian National Congress [Nehru].'[39] A month later, due to the intervention of then Viceroy Wavell, Nehru went to Srinagar to visit Abdullah in prison. He also attended one of his trials. However, during his visit, Hari Singh, who had a low opinion of him for colluding with the British, did not attempt to meet him.[40] The differences between Hari Singh and Nehru kept growing in the times to come. After joining the Congress and enjoying the perks of power, Karan Singh, son and heir-in-waiting to Hari Singh, wrote in 1982, '[I]nstead of welcoming Nehru and seeking his cooperation, we had arrested him. I have no doubt that his arrest was the turning point in the history of the State.'[41]

There is an obvious disconnect here: Nehru seemed to have put all his trust in his friend Abdullah, whose popularity among the Muslims in the Valley wasn't impressive or dominant. The Muslim Conference had enchanted the Muslims of Kashmir with the option to join Pakistan—this option found PM Kak's support—whereas

[39]Lamb, A., *Kashmir: A Disputed Legacy, 1864–90*, Roxford Books, London, 1991; Rijiju, Kiren, 'Opinion | Union Law Minister Kiren Rijiju Writes: Nehru's 5 Blunders on Kashmir – The Real Story', *News18*, 14 November 2022, https://tinyurl.com/486fkncn. Accessed on 17 November 2023.

[40]Malhotra, Iqbal Chand and Maroof Raza, *Kashmir's Untold Story: Declassified*, Bloomsbury India, New Delhi, 2019, p. 62.

[41]Singh, Karan, *An Examined Life: Essays and Reflections by Karan Singh*, HarperCollins, Noida, 2019.

Abdullah and the National Conference had really lost ground with the supporters as the Kashmiri cause was abandoned for Nehru's views—the National Conference was only partially able to revive its base when it launched the Quit Kashmir campaign against the Maharaja. Outside the Valley, Abdullah's popularity fell flat. Hari Singh was still the decision-maker and ruler of the princely state as well as the only legal authority to decide its future. However, Nehru hedged his bets on his protégé and friend Abdullah because he found it hard to get along with Hari Singh ever since the Maharaja had arrested him. This potboiler of multi-pronged politics exploded in 1947, catalysed by some other players in the mix, as we shall see later.

DISBANDMENT OF INDIAN ARMY UNITS ON THE NORTHERN FRONTIERS

Ever since 1944, the British were meticulously planning potential actions to ensure that strategically important parts of Jammu and Kashmir would remain under their control after Independence. After the dismissal of Sir Olad Caroe as the governor of the NWFP on Gandhi's request,[42] Sir George Cunningham, who was the governor of the NWFP before Caroe, was brought back. Only this time, he was returning from Britain after spending a considerable amount of time with former PM Winston Churchill and Lord Hastings Ismay, who was not only Churchill's military advisor during World War II but also on Mountbatten's core team when the latter came to India as its last viceroy. They are believed to have had detailed discussions on Britain's withdrawal plans from India, and, in many circles, it is strongly understood that it is during these conversations that the lines between India and Pakistan were drawn.[43] The Boundary Commission headed by Sir Radcliffe remained merely an eye-fog.

---

[42]Mountbatten, L.M., *Mountbatten's Report on the Last Viceroyalty: 22 March–15 August 1947*, edited by Lionel Carter, Manohar, 2003, Part C, Paras 78–9.

[43]Malhotra, Iqbal Chand and Maroof Raza, *Kashmir's Untold Story: Declassified*, Bloomsbury India, New Delhi, 2019, p. 69.

Cunningham, since 1944, had begun to put in place a series of measures, by which Hindu and Sikh Indian Army soldiers on the northern frontiers were methodically replaced by the Muslim-staffed Frontier Scouts and Frontier Constabulary. He had recommended that the Indian northern frontiers must be defended by Muslim staffed scouts and *khassadar*s (tribal levies).[44] Furthering this plan of action, in 1946, the Indian Army's Commander-in-Chief announced the replacement of regular troops with scouts and khassadars in all frontier areas. It was to be a gradual withdrawal in five phases and completed over a course of two years. What this did was to make vulnerable all areas that could be overpowered with the Muslim tribesmen, should Kashmir accede to India.

THE POONCH PROBLEM

As discussed earlier, Raja Jagat Dev Singh was frustrated with the diminution of his status and wanted to mobilize his Muslim subjects against Maharaja Hari Singh. Over 90 per cent of Poonch's population consisted of Punjabi Muslims, who were very different from the Muslims of the Valley. Over 60,000 of them had served in the Indian Army during World War II, and it was this group that would eventually form the nucleus of the tribal revolt against the Maharaja in October 1947. Being a Dogra, he was well aware that he needed to appoint someone to lead them. He found his carpenter's son Ibrahim Khan as the right man for the job and financed his law degree in London. In 1940, Raja Jagat Dev Singh died under mysterious circumstances, and his son was prevented from taking over Poonch. Jagat Dev's wife immediately took her son and fled to Nepal, and the jagir fell under the control of Hari Singh. This triggered Ibrahim Khan, who decided to avenge the injustice to Jagat Dev's family by Hari Singh.[45] After coming under control of Hari Singh, the Poonch jagir lost its autonomy and became a part of the Jammu province. As a result, heavy taxes

---

[44]Ibid. 93.
[45]Ibid. 52.

were levied on its people. Ibrahim Khan led the people of Poonch to protest against the Maharaja's autocracy. He also contested the 1947 state elections on a Muslim League ticket and won. His transformation as agent provocateur of the Punjabi Muslims in Poonch was now complete.

MOUNTBATTEN VISITS HARI SINGH: HINTS AT ACCESSION TO PAKISTAN

One of the first actions that Mountbatten took on taking charge as the viceroy was recommending Lord Listowell, Secretary of State for India, to return the Gilgit lease back to Hari Singh on 29 April 1947.[46] For his first action on Kashmir to be related to the Gilgit Agency, anyone who studied the events keenly would recognize just how much of a priority it was for the British to retain hold over it. During the multitude of events taking place across India around this time, the Gilgit Agency really was the hidden joker in the deck for the British. No Congress leader had any idea about this, even when Mountbatten clearly prioritized it in one of his foremost actions on Kashmir. When Mountbatten recommended that the lease be rescinded to Hari Singh, Britain was fairly confident that the entire princely state of Jammu and Kashmir would accede to Pakistan due to the Muslim-majority population.[47] Britain had to take control of Gilgit out of Hari Singh's hand in order to operate the seismic monitoring stations—this is why the lease was executed in the first place. The British government's orders, which overrode the ones issued by Mountbatten, were to secure the 'cast-iron' safety and continued existence of the three British nuclear monitoring stations in Gilgit, notwithstanding the transfer of power, as per the decision of the Gen 163 Cabinet Committee. Since the balance was tilted in favour of Maharaja Hari Singh's likelihood of opting for Kashmir's

---

[46]Menon, V.P., *Integration of the Indian States,* Orient BlackSwan, Hyderabad, 2014, p. 415.
[47]Dasgupta, C., *War and Diplomacy in Kashmir: 1947-48,* SAGE, New Delhi, 2002, pp. 54–5.

accession to Pakistan, it became imperative to ensure that the entire kingdom, including the Gilgit Agency, was peacefully passed off to Pakistan.[48] That perhaps drew him to make this decision of rescinding the Gilgit lease back to the Maharaja, which seemed rather appropriate up until a few months down the line when he realized that Hari Singh had other intentions, and that Plan B had to be immediately activated.

Over the next couple of months, Mountbatten learnt that Jammu and Kashmir and Hyderabad were keen on remaining independent and continuing the existing arrangement with regard to trade, defence and communications with the Indian union. He requested the British political agents to convince the respective rulers not to announce this decision until he had a chance to personally visit them.[49] Just before his scheduled visit on 17 June, Nehru had readied a note for him on Kashmir that clearly said, 'The normal and obvious course appears to be for Kashmir to join the Constituent Assembly of India. This will satisfy both, the popular demand and the Maharaja's wishes.'[50] Nehru intended for the contents in this note to unfold but under his conditions.

On 17 June, Edwina and Louis Mountbatten visited Srinagar. The latter and Hari Singh were old friends—they had served together as aides-de-camp to the Prince of Wales (who later became King Edward VIII) during his pretty long visit to India in 1921. Mountbatten broached the topic of accession with Hari Singh during a car ride in the latter's Bentley when he was at the wheel.[51] Mountbatten later recounted the episode, 'I explained to HH [His Highness] that his choice was between acceding to India or Pakistan and made it clear that I had assurances from Indian leaders that if he acceded to Pakistan they would not take

[48]Malhotra, Iqbal Chand and Maroof Raza, *Kashmir's Untold Story: Declassified*, Bloomsbury India, New Delhi, 2019, p. 79.
[49]Ibid.
[50]Sarila, Narendra Singh, *The Shadow of the Great Game: The Untold Story of India's Partition*, HarperCollins India, Noida, 2009.
[51]Ibid. 343.

it amiss.'[52] For Hari Singh, this was a fairly clear indication that his old pal preferred Kashmir's accession to Pakistan. After all, he had gone through great lengths to seek assurances from Indian leaders for such a situation. A source that had had access to the Mountbatten papers, which remain unavailable to the others even today, additionally noted with reference to this incident that the Viceroy had told Hari Singh to not take a decision till the Pakistan Constituent Assembly had been convened.[53] Mountbatten had to be at his diplomatic best to retain the garb of neutrality with regard to accession of the princely states. Britain wanted Kashmir to accede to Pakistan but with India's consent, and Mountbatten had to run with that stand in all his dealings with regard to the subject. After Hari Singh read Mountbatten's preference, he retreated into a shell. He was absolutely unwilling to join Pakistan and needed to weed out any members within his government who were making moves that would force this eventuality onto him. On the other hand, he also didn't have the best relationship with Nehru and Abdullah. He was intimately aware of and uncomfortable with the closeness of their relationship. And so, he retreated. Karan Singh, in his observations of Mountbatten's visit, noted,

> I suspect that in his heart of hearts my father still did not believe that British would actually leave ... Independence could perhaps have been an attractive proposition but to carry that off would have required careful preparation and prolonged negotiations and diplomatic ability ... Instead of taking advantage of Mountbatten's visit to discuss the whole situation meaningfully and trying to arrive at a rational decision, he [Hari Singh] first sent the Viceroy out on a prolonged fishing trip to Thricker [where Mountbatten shocked our staff by sunbathing in the nude] and then— having fixed a meeting just before his departure—got out of it on the plea that he had suddenly developed a severe attack of

---

[52]Ibid.

[53]Hodson, H.V., *The Great Divide: Britain–India–Pakistan*, Oxford University Press, New Delhi, 1997, p. 442.

colic ... Thus the real chance of working out a viable political settlement was lost.[54]

Despite the horn touted by Karan Singh and other Congress leaders, the fact remains that ever since 1931, Hari Singh's loyalty to India had not been in question. Even at the 1930 Roundtable Conference in London, he had said, 'I am an Indian first and then a Maharaja,'[55] clearly indicating that his priorities were for his nation first and self later. The second instance of his intent to accede to India even before Mountbatten's visit was during the visit by Acharya Kripalani, the Congress president of the time, to Kashmir in May 1947. *The Tribune* published a piece on 20 May 1947, where Kripalani was noted to have clearly said, 'Hari Singh was keen to accede to India and that it was not correct on the part of the National Conference to raise the demand of "Quit Kashmir" against Hari Singh. He is not an outsider. He appealed to the National Conference in particular to give up the call of "Quit Kashmir".'[56] He was so clear that even Nehru's note to Mountbatten preceding his visit to Srinagar clearly indicated Hari Singh's wish to join the Indian union. He wrote, 'The normal and obvious course appears to be for Kashmir to join the Constituent Assembly of India. This will satisfy both the popular demand and the Maharaja's wishes.'[57]

However, during Mountbatten's visit, Hari Singh chose to stay mum on the subject after having read Mountbatten's view on Kashmir's accession. Mountbatten, however, realized that something was amiss and that Hari Singh was not going to easily

---

[54]Singh, Karan, *Heir Apparent: An Autobiography*, Oxford University Press, Delhi, 1982, pp. 47–8.

[55]'Remember Maharaja Hari Singh', *Daily Excelsior*, 23 September 2017, https://tinyurl.com/35ermj2x. Accessed on 20 November 2023.

[56]Rijiju, Kiren, 'Jawaharlal Nehru and the Real Story of His Five Blunders on Kashmir, Writes Kiren Rijiju', *Firstpost*, 14 November 2022, https://tinyurl.com/25tmc6yz. Accessed on 28 November 2023.

[57]Rijiju, Kiren, 'Opinion | Union Law Minister Kiren Rijiju Writes: Nehru's 5 Blunders on Kashmir – The Real Story', *News18*, 14 November 2022, https://tinyurl.com/486fkncn. Accessed on 17 November 2023.

accede to Pakistan. Interestingly, Ismay had accompanied them during the visit and he met with Col Bacon, the political agent in Gilgit, to discuss future strategy. He is also believed to have met PM Kak and possibly learn of Hari Singh's intent. With this information, immediately on Mountbatten's return to New Delhi, Britain activated Plan B—a sequence of events that had to be orchestrated to protect British interests should Hari Singh accede to India. And this is evidenced by what followed next.

BRITAIN'S PLAN B: OPERATION DATTA KHEL

In the first week of July 1947, Col Bacon summoned Major William Brown, having been promoted from his previous rank of captain, and his trusted deputy Capt. Jock Mathieson to inform them that they should be prepared to take positions as the commandment and deputy commandment of the Gilgit Scouts in a few weeks and that he had spoken to the Maharaja and Chief of Staff of Kashmir State Forces Gen. Scott to do so. Since the Gilgit Scouts were under the Kashmir state administration, when the Gilgit lease would be rescinded to the Maharaja, the officers would have to resign from British service in order to join the Kashmir state services. This would also keep any actions carried out by these officers at an arm's length from the British government, which holds accountable the actions of all its service officers. Since the endeavour they were embarking on was top secret and likely to taint Britain's image if their activities were discovered, they had to do it outside the British service. The fact that their actions had Britain's stamp of approval was proven when Major Brown was given the honour of 'Most Exalted Officer'. A report in the 1948 *London Gazette* read, 'The King has been graciously pleased on the occasion of the celebration of His Majesty's Birthday to give orders for the following appointments to the Most Exalted Order of the British Empire: "Brown, Major (Acting) William Alexander, Special List (ex-Indian Army)."'[58]

---

[58]Sarila, Narendra Singh, *The Shadow of the Great Game: The Untold Story of India's Partition*, HarperCollins India, Noida, 2009, p. 334.

The newsletter that cited the above award also added, 'No further details are available from official sources for what might have been recorded as a somewhat equivocal award.'[59] In no way would a British officer who was responsible for carrying out a coup against Britain's wishes, albeit after leaving British services, be entitled to receive such an honour.

On 30 July, within an awfully crunched period of time, Major Brown took charge. The next day, he, along with Col Bacon, met the rulers of certain vassal states—namely, the Raja of Puniyal, the governor of Koh-e-Khizr, Ishkoman from the Khuswat family of Chitral and Raja Mehboob of Yasin—and made them aware of the plan to execute Operation Datta Khel. Datta Khel really was the coup d'état that would put Gilgit Agency in Pakistan's control.[60] Between Gen. Scott, Col Bacon and Major Brown, along with officers posted in the Pakistani army, this coup was to be carried out.

In parallel, Governor Cunningham was building his clout within the tribesmen in the NWFP. This is the region where an army for the coup would be built. Around the time of Independence and just before, several tribesmen had come to him, literally begging him to allow them to go and kill the Sikhs. His hold over the tribesmen had been so strong that, according to his records, 'I would only have to hold up my little finger to get a lashkar [army] of 40,000 or 50,000.'[61] He had encouraged and involved himself in the local tribal politics with tactful political manoeuvring in order to really determine the best men who could be sent to Kashmir. He had deployed two strong recruiting agents—the CM designate of the NWFP Khan Abdul Qayyum Khan and Muslim League supporter Pir of Manki Sharif—to lobby the Pashtuns for the Kashmir invasion.[62] This effort to raise the disparate tribal army

---

[59]Ibid.

[60]Bulletin of Military Historical Society of Great Britain, Volume 46, Issue 182, 1995, Oriental and Indian Collection, British Library, London.

[61]Hajari, N., *Midnight's Furies: The Deadly Legacy of India's Partition*, Houghton Miffin Harcourt, USA, 2015.

[62]Schofield, V., *Kashmir in Conflict: India, Pakistan and the Unending War*, I.B. Tauris, London, 2003.

really was the centre point of the decades-long conflict that was about to mar Kashmir.

THE DELAY IN ACCESSION

With the lack of any progress in talks after Kripalani's intervention, in July 1947,[63] Hari Singh once again reached out to Indian leaders with a request to accede to India.[64] This is when Nehru began to show his true designs with regard to Kashmir. He rebuffed the Maharaja and enlisted his conditions for considering Jammu and Kashmir's accession to India, which included releasing Sheikh Abdullah from prison and bringing and an immediate change in the internal administration of the state.[65] At this point in time, Nehru was against accepting the request from Hari Singh until his conditions were met. This resulted in Hari Singh being the only ruler not invited for the meeting between the Chamber of Princes and Mountbatten, where the latter played a crucial role in urging the states to accede to the dominions before the lapse of paramountcy.[66] Sardar Patel was livid over Nehru's conditions to Hari Singh for accepting Kasmir's accession to India. He had attacked Nehru by saying, 'I regret our leader [Nehru] has followed his lofty ideas into the skies and has no contact left with earth or reality.'[67]

Meanwhile, in the first week of August 1947, Gandhi visited Hari Singh and warned him of a coup taking place in the highlands. He is also believed to have urged the Maharaja to release Sheikh Abdullah from prison, so that the accession talks

---

[63]Rijiju, Kiren, 'Opinion | Union Law Minister Kiren Rijiju Writes: Nehru's 5 Blunders on Kashmir – The Real Story', *News18*, 14 November 2022, https://tinyurl.com/486fkncn. Accessed on 17 November 2023.

[64]Ibid.

[65]Ibid.

[66]Sarila, Narendra Singh, *The Shadow of the Great Game: The Untold Story of India's Partition*, HarperCollins India, Noida, 2009, p. 345

[67]Ibid.

could go forward. Additionally, he recommended PM Kak's arrest.[68] On Gandhi's departure and after some investigation, Hari Singh found that Kak was involved with the Muslim League leaders and immediately arrested him as he was trying to flee the country from Srinagar with the help of some British officers.[69] Another major development that took place a few days before Independence was that the Punjab Boundary Commission released a provisional map of the partition line, under which three tehsils of Gurdaspur in eastern Punjab were shown to be awarded to India, despite a Muslim-majority population, on the grounds of accessibility to good irrigation.[70] Before this, the Maharaja, even though was clear that he wanted to join the Indian union, was worried about being completely cut off from Indian mainland should the connecting land links in eastern Punjab be awarded to Pakistan. For Hari Singh, the state would become very difficult to administer and security would certainly become a challenge if it acceded to India, while remaining vulnerable to an attack due to having an entire western frontier in common with Pakistan. The fact that the three major roads connecting mainland India to Jammu and Kashmir would go to Pakistan made it all the more worrisome for him. The three tehsils provided a strong land link between Kashmir and India, despite no usable concrete road, especially in the winters. This was a huge development and certainly catalysed the Maharaja's efforts to plead for adhesion to India more forcefully.

After Kak was arrested, he was replaced by Major Gen. Janak Singh, who immediately sent out standstill agreements to India and Pakistan in order to allow continuing trade, communications and service arrangements, which the state had enjoyed with British India. To clarify, the standstill agreement with Pakistan became operative on 15 August 1947 and was only with regard to communications,

---

[68]Sharma, O.P., 'Gandhi's Only Kashmir Visit', *Kashmir Life*, 2 October 2017, https://tinyurl.com/s7m5w6zd. Accessed on 21 November 2023.
[69]Bell, C. and B. Ellemen (eds), *Naval Mutinies of the Twentieth Century: An International Perspective*, Routledge, London, 2013.
[70]Hasan, Z., *The Times and Trial of the Rawalpindi Conspiracy, 1951: The First Coup Attempt in Pakistan*, Oxford University Press, Karachi, 1998.

supplies and postal and telegraphic arrangements.[71] However, the standstill agreement sent to India proposed that 'Jammu and Kashmir Government would welcome standstill agreements with the Union of India on all matters on which these exist at the present moment with the outgoing British Indian Government.'[72] It is to be noted that the existing arrangements comprised of the use of Indian Forces if there was an internal rebellion in one of the states, in addition to all other matters of defence and national security. India delayed signing the dotted line[73] on the standstill agreement—something that Pakistan did in a matter of days.

With no headway, Hari Singh's PM M.C. Mahajan, who succeeded Major Gen. Janak Singh, once again reached out to Nehru regarding further development on accession to the Indian union in September. Regarding this meeting, Mahajan later wrote in his autobiography,

> I also met Pandit Jawaharlal Nehru, the Prime Minister of India. The Maharaja was willing to accede to India and also to introduce necessary reforms in the administration of the state. He, however, wanted the question of the administrative to be taken up later on. Panditji wanted an immediate change in the internal administration of the state.[74]

Nehru, for inexplicable reasons, was fully enamoured by Abdullah and was willing to put Abdullah's interests over prioritizing accepting Hari Singh's proposal for Kashmir's accession to the Indian union without any delay. He believed that Abdullah represented 75 per cent Muslims of the state and that he deserved to lead them, even before accession was announced. Abdullah,

---

[71]Lamb, A., *Kashmir: A Disputed Legacy, 1864–90*, Roxford Books, London, 1991.

[72]'Appendix 1: Standstill Agreement with India and Pakistan, August 12 1947', *Strategic Analysis: A Monthly Journal of the IDSA*, Volume 25, Issue 7, 2001, https://tinyurl.com/mpj6664m. Accessed on 28 November 2023.

[73]Malhotra, Iqbal Chand and Maroof Raza, *Kashmir's Untold Story: Declassified*, Bloomsbury India, New Delhi, 2019, p. 91.

[74]Mahajan, Mehr Chand, *Looking Back: The Autobiography of Mehr Chand Mahajan, the Former Chief Justice of India*, Har-Anand Publications, India, 2018.

on the other hand, was keeping his cards close to his chest. He appeared to have convinced Nehru that only he could persuade the Kashmiri Muslims to accept accession to India, provided that he was made the head of the new government. Meanwhile, he had a channel of conversation open with the Pakistani leadership[75] and also with Ibrahim Khan of Poonch, encouraging them to think about a model for an independent Kashmir where Ibrahim Khan and Ghulam Abbas (the new president of the Muslim Conference) would be the heads of government and Abdullah would hold some post in the proposed government. He was certainly working behind the scenes, behind Nehru's back—a fact that Nehru couldn't see, as he was blinded by what was shown to him by Abdullah and his ecosystem.

Hari Singh, compelled by his desire to join the Indian union in addition to the prodding by his wife, her brother and the mobilization of state forces by the Hindu Mahasabha, reached out to Nehru once again in October, this time after releasing Abdullah from prison on 29 September 1947, which seemed to be Nehru's pre-condition. But Nehru rejected the Maharaja's request, posing the condition that he would accept Kashmir's accession only when Abdullah was given the full honour of heading the state. It may be important to note here that the invasions into Kashmir from Pakistan had already begun, a fact that Nehru was well aware of. A letter dated 27 September 1947 from Nehru to Sardar Patel, who was keeping in touch with the Maharaja, is quite telling of the former's wishes with regard to the question of Kashmir's accession. It says:

> I understand that the Pakistan strategy is to infiltrate into Kashmir now and to take some big action as soon as Kashmir is more or less isolated because of the coming winter. It becomes important therefore that the Maharaja should make friends with the National Conference so that there may be this popular support against Pakistan. There is no other recourse

---

[75]Ibid. 109.

open to the Maharaja but this: to release Sheikh Abdullah and the National Conference leaders, to make a friendly approach to them, seek their cooperation and make them feel that this is really meant and then to declare adhesion to the Indian Union.[76]

This was precious time lost. While Nehru was playing hardball with the Maharaja, prioritizing Abdullah's interests, the tribal invasion of Kashmir had officially begun. Sympathizing with the Maharaja, and fully aware of how unreasonable Nehru was being in this dire time, Patel wrote to Hari Singh on 2 October, after Abdullah's release, 'I need hardly say how pleased we all are at the general amnesty which Your Highness has proclaimed [with respect to Abdullah's release]. I have no doubt that this would rally round you the men [that is, Nehru] who might otherwise have been a thorn in your side. I can assure Your Highness of abiding sympathy with you in your difficulties.'[77]

OPERATION GULMARG: A MULTI-PRONGED ATTACK ON KASHMIR'S SOVEREIGNTY

Abdullah had now been released from prison and was contemplating his next move. Ibrahim Khan was sitting in Murree with an army of Punjabi Muslims who were in the mood to avenge the injustice done to them and recapture Poonch from the Maharaja's rule. Cunningham had also prepared a tribal army that was ready to invade Kashmir at the drop of his finger. Additionally, Major Brown in Gilgit, heading the Gilgit Scouts, was well prepared to orchestrate a coup against the new governor, Ghansara Singh, in the Gilgit Agency, which was called Operation Datta Khel. The infiltration by the tribal army through the western frontier of the state led by Pakistani and strategically positioned British officers were really the essence of Operation Gulmarg.

---

[76]Shankar, V. (ed.), *Sardar Patel: Selected Correspondence—1945–1950*, Vol. I, Navjeevan Publishing House, Ahmedabad, March 1977, p. 230.
[77]Ibid. 232.

However, a letter written by a British officer (Lt Gen. Frank Messervy, general commanding officer of the Northern Command, which included 14 battalions along the frontier), with an appendix titled 'Operation Gulmarg—The Plan for Invasion and Capture of Kashmir', fell into the hands of a Sikh officer, Major Onkar Kalkat.[78] According to the letter, the commencement date of the operation was 20 October, 1947. Major Kalkat escaped to India and is said to have taken the contents of the letter to then Defence Minister Baldev Singh on 19 October 1947.[79] He asked the British-staffed Intelligence Directorate to verify Kalkat's claims, but they didn't seem to pay heed and, thus, no action was taken. Baldev Singh didn't really follow up either, not taking the claims seriously and choosing to brush them under the carpet.[80] However, the news did flag the British officers of the fact that the Indian leadership had gotten wind of the British involvement in Operation Gulmarg, and, thus, it was decided that the British mercenaries would stand down and the invading army would be fully composed of non-British men.[81]

Gen. Scott, the Commander-in-Chief of the Jammu and Kashmir State Forces had first reported the situation on border encroachments on 31 August 1947.[82] He followed this report up with another one on 4 September, noting the increased infiltration of armed Muslims into the state from Rawalpindi.[83] Soon after, he was sacked by Hari Singh for colluding with Kak. The fact that Hari Singh's information on Gen. Scott was absolutely correct is corroborated with the fact that on leaving the Jammu and Kashmir

---

[78]Malhotra, Iqbal Chand and Maroof Raza, *Kashmir's Untold Story: Declassified*, Bloomsbury India, New Delhi, 2019, p. 95.
[79]Prasad, S.N. and P. Dharm, *Operations in Jammu and Kashmir 1947–48*, Thomas Press, New Delhi, 1987.
[80]Malhotra, Iqbal Chand and Maroof Raza, *Kashmir's Untold Story: Declassified*, Bloomsbury India, New Delhi, 2019, p. 98.
[81]Ibid. 101.
[82]'762nd Meeting: 23 January 1857', *Security Council Official Records, United Nations*, https://tinyurl.com/2b5xx8ep. Accessed on 28 November 2023.
[83]Ibid.

service, he immediately joined as an advisor to the Pakistani military. On 17 September 1947, about 400 armed men drew away herds of cattle belonging to the locals in Ranbir Singh Pura.[84] And on the very next day, 18 September 1947, Pakistan suspended railway lines between Sialkot and Jammu, violating the standstill agreement they had signed with Jammu and Kashmir.[85]

Meanwhile, around the same time, Ibrahim Khan managed to set up a base in Murree (a hill station about 33 km from Poonch, on the other side of the border), using it as a command post that he fully controlled. The Poonch uprising had now acquired a formal command structure. Several kinds of weapons began to be collected, including old muzzle-loaders. Ammunition was prepared and its supplies came to be smuggled across the Jhelum into Poonch and Mirpur, where he had already built a quasi-military organization of demobilized men who had served as soldiers in World War II. This force acquired strength as more and more officers, especially the Muslims, began to abandon the state forces to join Ibrahim Khan's instead. By early October, this force had grown so powerful that it had gained control of the entire Poonch district, except for the town of Poonch, which was still under the control of Jammu and Kashmir forces. Enthused by this success, Sardar Muhammad Ibrahim Khan, as he came to be known, proclaimed the formation of a provincial Azad Kashmir government in Pallandari, a township in Sudhanoti district in the third week of October 1947.[86]

On 30 September 1947, hundreds of armed invaders entered Dhirkot within Jammu and Kashmir territory.[87] The Jammu and Kashmir government took this issue up with the Pakistani government, along with the issue of supplies of essential commodities like salt, petrol, cloth and rice being cut off.[88] However, it failed

---

[84]Ibid.

[85]Ibid.

[86]J. Bhagyalakshmi, *Capital Witness: Selected Writings of G.K. Reddy*, Allied Publishers, New Delhi, 1991.

[87]'762nd Meeting: 23 January 1857', *Security Council Official Records*, United Nations, https://tinyurl.com/2b5xx8ep. Accessed on 28 November 2023.

[88]Ibid.

to receive a satisfactory reply. A few days later, on 4 October 1947, a fight broke out between state forces and the armed men in the Chirala area near the Jhelum, ensuring that a state of war had been reached.[89] A few days later, on 10 October, two sections of the Pakistani army, followed by armed men, attacked the village Pansar in Jammu.[90] This was the first organized episode of an act of aggression by Pakistani forces against Jammu and Kashmir's sovereign territory.

There were growing warning signals of a large-scale invasion. On 15 October, PM Mahajan met a group of Hindu and Sikh refugees who had reached Srinagar after crossing the border at Domel. They had reported seeing large concentrations of tribal Pathans (Kabalis) in the area around Abbottabad and Man Shera.[91] A panicked Hari Singh, on having received these concerning reports from PM Mahajan, cabled PM Clement Attlee:

> People all along the border have been licensed and armed with modern weapons under the pretext of general policy which does not appear to have been followed in the case of internal districts of West Punjab … whereas military escorts are made available for several other purposes, none is provided for safe transit of petrol and other essentials of life. Protests merely invites promises which are never implemented. As a result of obvious connivance of the Pakistan Government, the whole of the border from Gurdaspur side up to Gilgit is threatened with invasion which has actually begun in Poonch.[92]

However, his letter couldn't find any assistance or sympathy from the British PM. On 18 October, the British officers and bureaucrats, posted or on holiday in the Valley, were given emergency

---

[89]Ibid.

[90]Ibid.

[91]Malhotra, Iqbal Chand and Maroof Raza, *Kashmir's Untold Story: Declassified*, Bloomsbury India, New Delhi, 2019, p. 98.

[92]'762nd Meeting: 23 January 1857', *Security Council Official Records*, United Nations, https://tinyurl.com/2b5xx8ep. Accessed on 28 November 2023.

evacuation orders,[93] and the next day, they were ferried by 20 Royal Armed Forces buses and trucks away from Srinagar into the 'safety zone' of Rawalpindi via Baramulla, Uri and Muzaffarabad.[94] Hari Singh was offended by this mysterious exodus of the British officials. Now that we have a clearer picture, we understand that Baldev Singh's complacency of ignoring Major Kalkat's warning for Operation Gulmarg cost us. But then, would Nehru have acted any differently than Baldev Singh had this information come to his attention?

The invaders continued their march across the Jhelum Valley. On 22 October, the PM alerted the PM of the NWFP, Abdul Qayyum, and the deputy commissioner of Rawalpindi about continuous infiltration of armed men from Hazara and Rawalpindi districts into the state, asking them to act immediately to put a stop to it.[95] However, his appeal fell on deaf ears, and the raiders continued their progress towards Srinagar. This invasion force of the Kabalis had taken over Muzaffarabad (7 miles from the border), making their way towards Uri. The Kabalis destroyed the electricity sub-station in Mahura on the outskirts of Uri, which supplied power to Srinagar. Here is where their march was temporarily halted due to the destruction of the bridge and armed resistance by 150 men of the Kashmir Army headed by Brig. Rajinder Singh, the first Indian to be awarded the Mahavir Chakra (posthumously) after Independence. It took over two days for a mile-long diversion road to be built—a commendable task requiring considerable engineering skill. Clearly, sophisticated engineering and civil regiments of the Pakistani army had to have been deployed for the same, for it was a task incomprehensible to be accomplished by the Kabalis.[96] Meanwhile, the raiders lost

---

[93]Abdullah, S.M., *The Blazing Chinar: An Autobiography*, Gulshan Books, Srinagar, 2016.

[94]Malhotra, Iqbal Chand and Maroof Raza, *Kashmir's Untold Story: Declassified*, Bloomsbury India, New Delhi, 2019, p. 98.

[95]'762nd Meeting: 23 January 1857', *Security Council Official Records*, United Nations, https://tinyurl.com/2b5xx8ep. Accessed on 28 November 2023.

[96]Ibid.

patience, got side-tracked and plundered the town of Baramulla, raping and pillaging their way through it, even ignoring orders of their commanders.[97] It is these three days in Baramulla where the invaders paused due to their own distractions that gave Hari Singh the time to speak with the Indian government. At the end of three days, it was only when the loot from Baramulla had been dispatched to the NWFP, Poonch and Rawalpindi that the advance to Srinagar resumed. Lack of disciplined leadership was obviously their Achilles' heel. Just imagine, had the letter concerning Operation Gulmarg not fallen into the hands of Major Kalkat, the British wouldn't have been just silent partners. Instead, they would've executed their original plan, by which the invading force would have been led by British mercenaries. What a difference it would've made to have the invaders in uniform and headgear versus in tribal attire![98]

Srinagar, which had already plunged into darkness due to the destruction of its electricity sub-station, became vulnerable to the tribal invaders— the Azad Kashmir *fauj* (army)—in a matter of a few days. The media ecosystem of Azad Kashmir was planned meticulously by the Pakistani government as well. Around the first week of October, Hari Singh suspended the publication of the Kashmir Times. The owner Abdul Rahman Mittha was appointed as the director of public relations of the Azad Kashmir government and its resident editor G.K. Reddy as Azad Kashmir's deputy director of public relations immediately.[99] So cohesive was the relationship between the Pakistani government and Azad Kashmir that on 21 October, Reddy received a call from a public relations officer in the Pakistani Army, and the latter told him that the Ramkot post of the Jammu and Kashmir government was going to be attacked by Kabalis that night. On delivering the news, he demanded that it should be published as coming from the Azad Kashmir headquarters

---

[97]Malhotra, Iqbal Chand and Maroof Raza, *Kashmir's Untold Story: Declassified*, Bloomsbury India, New Delhi, 2019.

[98]Ibid. 101.

[99]Ibid. 110–11.

in Pallandri. He also added that while further news of the invasion would come from the army headquarters in Rawalpindi, Pallandri was the place that it should be sourced to and mentioned in all press releases.[100] In short, while the Pakistani army was doing most of execution of the attack, their actions were to be attributed to Sardar Ibrahim Khan's Azad Kashmir Army in Pallandri.

ACCESSION TO INDIA

On 24 October, as Baramulla was being plundered, Hari Singh wired the Indian government, appealing for help.[101] On 25 October, the Defence Committee met in New Delhi and decided to depute V.P. Menon and Field Marshall Sam Manekshaw (director of military operations) to Kashmir in order to assess the on-ground situation. Rather curiously, in the meeting, Mountbatten suggested that Hari Singh sign the Instrument of Accession to India prior to India dispatching its troops. Recording this in his diary, Campbell-Johnson writes, 'He [Mountbatten] considered it would be the height of folly to send troops into a neutral State where we had no right to send them, since Pakistan could do exactly the same thing, which would only result in a clash of armed forces and war.'[102] Nehru once again raised his demand, which he had been making all along to the Maharaja—that for India to accept his request for acceding to it, Abdullah must be entrusted to form an emergency government under Mahajan.[103] It may be important to note here that from 15 October, Sheikh Abdullah had moved in with Nehru in New Delhi.[104] The Defence Committee was constituted on 30

---

[100]Ibid. 109–10.

[101]'762nd Meeting: 23 January 1857', *Security Council Official Records*, United Nations, https://tinyurl.com/2b5xx8ep. Accessed on 28 November 2023.

[102]Campbell-Johnson, A., *Mission with Mountbatten*, Macmillan Publications, London, 1985.

[103]Rijiju, Kiren, 'Opinion | Union Law Minister Kiren Rijiju Writes: Nehru's 5 Blunders on Kashmir – The Real Story', *News18*, 14 November 2022, https://tinyurl.com/486fkncn. Accessed on 17 November 2023.

[104]Abdullah, S.M., *The Blazing Chinar: An Autobiography*, Gulshan Books, Srinagar, 2016.

September 1947, comprising a mix of Indian and British members. The Indian members were PM Nehru, Deputy PM Patel, Defence Minister Baldev Singh, Finance Minister R.K.S Chetty and a minister without a portfolio, N. Gopalaswami Ayyangar. Ayyangar had been the PM of Kashmir from 1937 to 1943 and enjoyed a close relationship with Sheikh Abdullah. Some say that his presence in the Nehru Cabinet was a consequence of this camaraderie he shared with Abdullah and his contribution to resolve the Kashmir problem. The British members of the committee were Mountbatten (who was offered by Nehru to chair the Defence Committee) and three British Commanders-in-Chief of the armed forces.[105]

Menon and Manekshaw flew to Jammu to the Maharaja, who, in his desperation, agreed to Nehru's terms and signed the Instrument of Accession at midnight, which was carried back to New Delhi by Menon. Recounting the incident, Manekshaw later noted, 'He [Maharaja Hari Singh] kept saying you must send soldiers. And we said, "We can't send soldiers into your state unless you accede to India."'[106] In an attached letter to the Instrument of Accession, the Maharaja clarified:

> I have accordingly decided to do so [accede to India] and I attach the Instrument of Accession for your acceptance by your Government. The other alternative is to leave my State and my people to free-boosters. On this basis no civilised Government can exist or be maintained. This alternative I will never allow to happen as long as I am Ruler of the State and I have life to defend my country.[107]

Additionally, Menon and Manekshaw did two things during their visit: they took stock of the situation via a briefing from PM Mahajan and, on learning that the invaders were already at

---

[105]Sarila, Narendra Singh, *The Shadow of the Great Game: The Untold Story of India's Partition,* HarperCollins India, Noida, 2009, p. 357.

[106]Brut India, 'The MAN In Sam Manekshaw', *YouTube,* 8 July 2020, https://tinyurl.com/3bw4wxzv. Accessed on 21 November 2023.

[107]Anand, Adarsh Sein, 'Kashmir's Accession to India', *Journal of the Indian Law Institute,* Volume 6, Issue 1, 1964, pp. 69–86.

Baramulla, barely 30 miles away from Srinagar, and that the Muslim element in the Maharaja's army had revolted, advised the Maharaja to relocate to Jammu for his safety. The Maharaja and his family immediately left for Jammu and the Menon–Manekshaw duo took PM Mahajan with them to New Delhi.

While the duo was away, in another Defence Committee meeting on 25 October 1947 chaired by Mountbatten, the Commander-in-Chief of the Indian Army read out a telegram from the headquarters of the Pakistani army, stating that about 5,000 tribesmen had captured Muzaffarabad and Domel, and considerable tribal reinforcements could be expected.[108] As soon as Menon, Manekshaw and PM Mahajan landed on 26 October, another Defence Committee meeting was called at PM Nehru's residence. Interestingly, this was attended by his pal and houseguest Sheikh Abdullah in addition to the committee members. Sam Manekshaw informed Mountbatten and the committee members that the invaders were now only about 9 km away from Srinagar, and if they took control of Srinagar, India would lose Jammu and Kashmir since it wouldn't be able to fly troops and other equipment in. In Manekshaw's words:

> So, he [Mountbatten] looked at Nehru and Nehru talked and all, until Sardar Patel lost his temper. He said, 'Jawaharlal, do you want Kashmir or do you want to hand it over?' He [Nehru] said, 'Of course, Kashmir is ours now.' So he [Sardar Patel] said, 'Will you issue orders?' But before he could issue orders, Sardar Patel said, 'You have received your orders.' So, I walked out and we started flying troops into Kashmir.[109]

After a long discussion in the Defence Committee meeting regarding acceptance of accession, Mountbatten, then Governor General of India, accepted the Instrument of Accession of Jammu

[108]'762nd Meeting: 23 January 1857', *Security Council Official Records*, United Nations, https://tinyurl.com/2b5xx8ep. Accessed on 28 November 2023.
[109]Brut India, 'The MAN In Sam Manekshaw', *YouTube*, 8 July 2020, https://tinyurl.com/3bw4wxzv. Accessed on 21 November 2023.

and Kashmir to India. He, however, insisted that accession should be coupled with the will of the people being ascertained. However, his acceptance of the Instrument of Accession resulted in the union of Jammu and Kashmir within the Indian federation. Accession was unconditional, voluntary and absolute, not subject to any exceptions and no different than from those executed with some 500 odd states.[110] After the Instrument of Accession had been accepted by the Governor General of India, he wrote a semi-official letter to the Maharaja and, among other things, he mentioned that 'it is my Government's wish that, as soon as law and order have been restored in Kashmir and its soil cleared of the invader, the question of Kashmir's accession should be settled with reference to the people'.[111] While this statement had provided the basis for the controversy feeding into Pakistan's fetish, the truth remains that Mountbatten's statement in no way changed the legality and irreversibility of accession. Furthering the intent in the Instrument of Accession, Mahajan explained in his autobiography:

> [T]he Indian Independence Act did not envisage conditional accession. It could not envisage such a situation as it would be outside the Parliament's policy. It wanted to keep no Indian State in a state of suspense. It conferred on the Rulers of the Indian States absolute power in their discretion to accede to either of the two Dominions. The Dominion's Governor-General had the power to accept the accession or reject the offer but he had no power to keep the question open or attach conditions.[112]

That the accession of Kashmir stands the legal test is explained best by Mountbatten himself when he said to Ismay, 'The decision to

---

[110]Anand, Adarsh Sein, 'Kashmir's Accession to India', *Journal of the Indian Law Institute,* Volume 6, Issue 1, 1964, pp. 69–86.

[111]*White Paper on Jammu and Kashmir,* Government of India, 1948, p. 47.

[112]Mahajan, Mehr Chand, *Accession of Kashmir to India: The Inside Story*, Sulakhani Devi Mahajan Trust, 1969, pp. 19–20.

hold a plebiscite in no way invalidated the legality of the accession of Kashmir to India.'[113]

As soon as the Maharaja acceded to India, several folks in the high-power corridors were perturbed in Britain, in Pakistan and some in India too. Attempts have been repeatedly made, even today, to paint Hari Singh as the indecisive, power-hungry king who wanted Kashmir to be independent. Several historians since 1947 have twisted the facts of history and cherry-picked information to drive this narrative. Karan Singh has enjoyed multitude privileges from successive Congress governments while continuing to further the narrative that it was indeed his father who was responsible for the delay of Kashmir's accession to India. This seems like it was done to protect Nehru and the Congress government who turned a deaf ear to Hari Singh's repeated appeals for Kashmir's accession to India. Not only were his appeals for accession ignored in order to protect Sheikh Abdullah's interests, but the proposal to sign a standstill agreement was dismissed by the Indian leadership as well until Nehru's conditions were met. Hari Singh did not feel the need to lay out his cards to Mountbatten, whom he thought was advocating Kashmir's accession to Pakistan, or to Jinnah and the Muslim League, who had begun to threaten him via multiple means. For instance, 24 August 1947, *Dawn*, the official mouthpiece of the Muslim League, declared, '[T]he time has come to let the Maharaja of Kashmir know that he must make his choice and choose Pakistan. Should he fail to join Pakistan, the gravest possible trouble will inevitably ensure.'[114]

Thus, simultaneous with the acceptance of accession, 28 Dakota aircraft were immediately flown to Srinagar, loaded with troops and arms. To their pleasant surprise, they found Patiala gunners guarding the Srinagar airfield, which had been under their control since 17 October.[115] Clearly, the lack of a standstill agreement had

---

[113]MB1/G25, Mountbatten to Ismay, 8 November, 1951, Mountbatten Papers, British Archives, University of Southampton.

[114]Anand, Adarsh Sein, 'Kashmir's Accession to India', *Journal of the Indian Law Institute*, Volume 6, Issue 1, 1964, pp. 69–86

[115]Iqbal Chand Malhotra, Maroof Raza, *Kashmir's Untold Story: Declassified*, Bloomsbury India, 2019, p. 104.

not hindered the Maharaja of Patiala to send troops, infantry and artillery to Kashmir, which helped the state in its time of crisis. In fact, it may not be incorrect to say that it was Patiala, the largest Sikh princely state that came to defend Kashmir before anyone else did. On their return journeys, the Indian Air Force planes would bring back wounded soldiers, civilians and refugees. The Indian Armed Forces were now in action. In a matter of days, 35,000 Indian troops were posted to defend the Valley.

On 28 October, in a candid letter to his sister Vijayalakshmi Pandit (who was gifted the important portfolio of India's first ambassador to the Soviet Union [1947–48]), Nehru wrote, 'If we had vacillated by a day, Srinagar might have been a smoking gun,' accepting how time-sensitive the accession was.[116] He added that Sheikh Abdullah had been entrusted with the formation of a government. He further stated, 'For my part, I do not mind if Kashmir becomes more or less independent, but it would have been a cruel blow if it had just become an exploited part of Pakistan.' In order to fulfil Nehru's condition of accession, on 30 October, the Maharaja appointed Abdullah as the chief executive administrator and retained Mahajan as the PM.[117]

Within days, about 4,000 troops surrounded Srinagar and protected the city from the invaders. With Srinagar secure, more troops marched north, securing Baramulla on 8 November, followed by the electricity station in Mahura and finally, a few days later, Uri. On 11 November, as soon as Uri was securely with the Indian government, Nehru, unmoved by the recent events and still bullish on his demand, wrote to Hari Singh to place 'full confidence' in Sheikh Abdullah and formally make him head of the administration, that is, the PM of Jammu and Kashmir.[118]

---

[116]Chaturvedi, Santosh Kumar, 'Indian Politics: 1947–1984', Sardar Patel University of Police Security and Criminal Justice, Jodhpur, p. 27.

[117]Malhotra, Iqbal Chand and Maroof Raza, *Kashmir's Untold Story: Declassified*, Bloomsbury India, New Delhi, 2019, p. 114.

[118]Roy Chowdhary, Adrija, 'What Role Exactly did Nehru Play in the Accession of Kashmir to India?', *The Indian Express*, 13 October 2022.

GILGIT TAKEOVER: EXECUTION OF OPERATION DATTA KHEL

While the Congress leadership was busy defending the Valley, there was a coup brewing in the highlands of Gilgit. With British mercenaries standing down due to Kalkat's intervention, which ultimately resulted in the failure to capture Srinagar, the British deep state began to worry that the Gilgit situation would get similarly messy. Taking proactive action, Major Brown collaborated with the Mehtar of Chitral and the Wali of Swat to mobilize forces in order to offer firm guerrilla resistance to the Indian Army troops should they ascend towards Gilgit. On Col Bacon's instructions, on 30 October, Major Brown offered Governor Ghansara Singh the option to step down and have a safe passage out of Gilgit or hold a referendum in the Gilgit Agency and continue to govern the province until the requisite authority took over. Being a man of honour, unwilling to indulge in an act of treason against the Maharaja, Ghansara Singh rejected both proposals. And, thus, the British began to execute the final closing moves in order to make Operation Datta Khel a success.[119]

On the night of 31 October, Major Brown attacked Ghansara Singh's official residence, outnumbering the latter's staff. As a result of this, the governor was forced to surrender and was then imprisoned.[120] Major Brown, on defeating Ghansara Singh, became the administrator *pro tempore* of Gilgit. He immediately informed Abdul Qayyum Khan and Col Bacon—his 'handlers'—of this crucial development. Now all he had to do was hold on to this power and preserve it until it could be passed on to Pakistan's hands as intended. Three days later, on 4 November, Ghansara Singh officially signed the surrender order drafted by Major Brown.[121] Over the next few days of correspondence, Major Brown and Col

---

[119]Malhotra, Iqbal Chand and Maroof Raza, *Kashmir's Untold Story: Declassified*, Bloomsbury India, New Delhi, 2019, pp. 103–4.

[120]Sarila, Narendra Singh, *The Shadow of the Great Game: The Untold Story of India's Partition*, HarperCollins India, Noida, 2009, p. 357.

[121]Malhotra, Iqbal Chand and Maroof Raza, *Kashmir's Untold Story: Declassified*, Bloomsbury India, New Delhi, 2019, p. 105.

Bacon discussed a lot of defence strategies and concluded that the Burzil Pass situated on the road from Harmosh near Kargil to Gilgit was the weakest link and that it needed to be reinforced with additional scouts and equipment. The commander of the invaders from the Pakistani army, Major Gen. Akbar Khan, who went by the pseudonym Gen. Tariq, was thus instructed to secure the Gurez Valley, which lay between Kargil and Burzil.[122]

A week later, on 11 November, Major Brown was reprised of the arrival of a Pakistani representative by the name of Mohammad Alam who was to arrive on 16 November to take over. Following the handover, Major Brown was to make his way his way to Peshawar for briefings. If any more proof of the British deep state involvement is needed, the same Harvard aircraft flown by Squadron Leader Ahmed, which flew Mohammad Aslam to Gilgit, brought Major Brown to Peshawar on its return journey. On landing in Peshawar, the trio of Major Brown, Col Bacon and Governor Cunningham met for a debriefing. Major Brown prepared a detailed report attached with maps of ground positions should the Indian Army attack. This report was then shared with Charles Duke, the British High Commissioner in Peshawar, who in turn sent it to his bosses in the British government including the Secretary of State.[123] It may be pertinent here to reiterate that it was after pulling off this coup on behalf of the British government that he was perhaps awarded the honour of 'Most Exalted Officer' by the King in July 1948.[124] Technically, Major Brown had aided the Pakistani army in capturing Gilgit, which was an act against Britain's official position—an act of treason. However, the fact that his actions were appreciated and felicitated adds further proof to the fact that Operation Datta Khel, just like Operation Gulmarg, was organized by the British deep state, fully supported by the British government to secure their strategic assets.

---

[122]Ibid.

[123]Brown, W., *Gilgit Rebellion*, Pen & Sword Military, UK, 2014.

[124]Sarila, Narendra Singh, *The Shadow of the Great Game: The Untold Story of India's Partition*, HarperCollins India, Noida, 2009, p. 334.

While how the Indian Army bravely recaptured territory invaded by the Pakistani tribals is outside the subject of this book, a certain factoid stands out particularly. About a year later, in November 1948, an opportunity presented itself to India where we were in a position to recapture Gilgit, but we let it pass. The commander of the 77 Para Brigade, Brig. Kanhaiya Lal 'Bagga', had taken Kargil, and the Para Brigade wanted to go up north on the Astore Road up to recapture Gilgit. He had asked the leadership for permission to do so. However, the permission to march on was denied.[125]

MOUNTBATTEN REVEALS HIS TRUE COLOURS

Until the Indian government had finally accepted Hari Singh's repeated pleas for accession, Mountbatten had managed to more or less keep his wish for Kashmir's accession to Pakistan concealed. Certainly, the Maharaja was on to Mountbatten's schemes, which was evident especially when, during his visit to Kashmir in June 1947, the former didn't bother to grant him an exclusive audience after their brief conversation on arrival when Mountbatten had made a masked reference of accession to Pakistan. But to the Congress leadership, he managed to put up neutral face with regard to Kashmir's accession. By the time it became an issue, he had even garnered Patel's trust due to the way he had assisted in integrating the princely states into the Union, especially Junagadh. So, in addition to offering him the all-important Governor General position, the Indian leadership also made him the head of the Defence Committee after constituting it in September 1947.[126] This gave Mountbatten, and, thus, the British government, unsurmountable power when it came to decisions on India's military actions and strategy.

After Kashmir's Instrument of Accession was accepted, all communications between Mountbatten and his British bosses

---

[125]Singh, R., *Major Defence Operations since 1947*, Prabhat Books, India, 2010.

[126]Sarila, Narendra Singh, *The Shadow of the Great Game: The Untold Story of India's Partition*, HarperCollins India, Noida, 2009, p. 357.

and counterparts show that his metamorphosis had begun.[127] He was going to leave no stone unturned to put into the British lap Kashmir's territory, which was important for protecting Britain's strategic interests and Pakistan's security since Pakistan was the custodian of safeguarding these strategic assets. To fully understand this, we need to first look at why Mountbatten did not sabotage Kashmir's accession in the first place.

To me, there are three reasons. Foremost is that the Maharaja was set on acceding to India. As the ruler, he would be acceding his entire mass of land to the Indian dominion. Second, Mountbatten was desperate to prevent an inter-dominion war, mostly to preserve his own legacy, since such a war would undo all the work that he had done over the past many months. This is evidenced in a letter he sent to the King on 7 November 1947, stating:

> It would still be legally correct to send troops at [Kashmir's] request to a friendly neighbouring country even if it did not accede but the risk of Pakistan also sending troops would be considerable. The accession would fully regularize the position, and reduce the risk of an armed clash with Pakistan forces to a minimum because then they will be entering a foreign country.[128]

Third, he was quite confident that he could convince the Indian leadership to hold a plebiscite or even get them to agree to partition the state. He was certainly not wrong in his thinking; Nehru, as we have seen earlier, was most definitely open to partitioning the state and giving away the western and northern parts, including the Kashmir Valley, to Pakistan. Patel was not particularly opposed to it either, if it meant pushing out the Punjabi Muslims from India. In addition to the aforementioned statement, Mountbatten added in his letter to the King, explaining his reasoning for a plebiscite: 'I still think that a country with so

---

[127]Ibid.
[128]Ibid.

large a Muslim population will finally vote for Pakistan.'[129]

Even though his request for 'accession to be settled by reference to the people' in his letter to the Maharaja remains contested by Pakistan and Pakistan-sympathetic intellectuals, Mountbatten explained the legality of the completed accession procedure to Lord Ismay in a letter written on 8 November 1951, stating, 'The decision to hold a plebiscite in no way invalidated the legality of the accession of Kashmir to India. The position then was that Kashmir was legally part of the Dominion of India.'[130]

However, soon after the last week of October in 1947, after the Indian military entered the state, grave concerns arose in the British government as they grew insecure about their strategic assets under India's rule. Mountbatten was reprimanded in no unclear terms. In a first such instance, merely days after Kashmir's accession, the British High Commissioner brought to Mountbatten's attention the British directive on Jammu and Kashmir, which clearly stated that Kashmir had to go to Pakistan on 'agreed terms'. It added (this time directly blaming Mountbatten for overruling the British government's policy), '[O]n one hand Pakistan had connived at the tribal invasion into Kashmir, "supplied artillery and transport" for the same and on the other India had made "proactive mistakes" in accepting Kashmir's accession since that was not really required for sending military help ... [They] had not consulted Pakistan and used Sikh troops.'[131]

To further prove my point that the British government intended for Kashmir to accede to Pakistan, I'd like to draw attention to two letters from the then British PM Attlee—one to Liaquat Ali Khan and the other to Nehru. To Liaquat Ali Khan, he essentially wrote that if the talks with the Indian leadership (which were scheduled to be held the next day) failed and India used the Instrument of Accession to justify its position in Kashmir, he was to stay put,

---

[129]Ibid.

[130]MB1/G25, Mountbatten to Ismay, 8 November 1951, Mountbatten Papers, British Archives, University of Southampton.

[131]File L/P and S/136/1845-46, British High Commissioner to Mountbatten, Oriental and Indian Collection, British Library, London.

that is, not pull back the tribals.[132] The second letter was the icy cold treatment to Nehru as a response to the latter's explanation for accepting Kashmir's accession to India. In his response, Attlee wrote, 'I do not think it would be helpful if I were to comment on the action your Government has taken.'[133]

Sensing trouble with his bosses, on 1 November 1947, Mountbatten, with Ismay, met Jinnah for four hours in Lahore and assured him:

> It is the sincere desire of the *Government of India* that a plebiscite should be held in Kashmir at the earliest possible date and in the fairest way possible ... They suggest that United Nations Organisation might be asked to provide supervision for this plebiscite and they are prepared to agree that a joint India-Pakistan force should hold the ring while the plebiscite is being held.[134]

INDIA INVOLVES UNITED NATIONS DUE TO BRITISH PUSH

Mountbatten had not taken Indian leaders into confidence before making this commitment to Jinnah. Perhaps he was confident that if Jinnah agreed to take the Kashmir issue to the United Nations (UN), he would be able to convince the Indian leadership. The UN involvement did not arise out of thin air. Sometime in September 1947, even before Kashmir's accession, Gandhi foresaw a violent engagement between India and Pakistan following the bloodbath of Partition and had suggested to Attlee to mediate, ascertain which dominion was overwhelmingly wrong and then withdraw every British officer in the service of that dominion. Attlee had then replied in the negative and essentially said that in a conflict, it is

---

[132]File L/P and S/136/1845-46, Attlee to Liaquat Ali Khan, 29 October 1947, Oriental and Indian Collection, British Library, London.
[133]File L/P and S/136/1845-46, Attlee to Jawaharlal Nehru, Oriental and Indian Collection, British Library, London.
[134]Sarila, Narendra Singh, *The Shadow of the Great Game: The Untold Story of India's Partition*, HarperCollins India, Noida, 2009.

never one side that can be solely blamed.[135] Looking at Gandhi's disappointment, Mountbatten had suggested an alternative solution, which involved the UN. He wrote in his letter dated 29 September 1947 to Gandhi, 'An alternative means is to ask UNO to undertake this enquiry and you would have no difficulty in getting Pakistan to agree to this.'[136] Nothing came out of this proposal until November, when Mountbatten raised it in his meeting with Jinnah.

On returning from Lahore, Mountbatten breached the idea of taking the conflict in Kashmir to the UN with Nehru, Menon and Gandhi. From the get-go, Gandhi and Menon inclined towards it. Nehru, at this time, had taken an indecisive position about involving the UN. A couple of days later, Mountbatten left for London to attend the wedding of Princess Elizabeth with Prince Phillip. On returning, he discovered that Nehru, too, had become open to the proposal. Mountbatten's press attaché, confidant and core team member Alan Campbell-Johnson is believed to have later confessed that Mountbatten did pressurize Nehru to take the Kashmir issue to the UN. In his book, he has also stated, 'Since returning to Delhi [from London] Mountbatten had seen Gandhi and Menon who were both favourably inclined to the invocation of UNO. And today [11 November 1947] he had a further talk with Nehru whose attitude to the idea is now less inactive that it was at Lahore [at the meeting between Nehru and Liaquat Ali Khan a few days earlier].'[137]

Meanwhile, the war in Kashmir was heating up. Mountbatten's mediatory effort between the leadership of the two dominions was not working. In December 1947, Liaquat Ali Khan came to New Delhi to hold talks, following which Mountbatten, Nehru, Baldev Singh and Ayyangar went to Lahore. On 20 December, at the Defence Committee meeting, Indian leaders suggested striking the invaders' camps and lines of communication inside Pakistan. This unsettled Mountbatten, who intervened immediately by suggesting

---

[135]MBI/E/193/2, Mountbatten to Gandhi, 29 September 1947, Mountbatten Papers, British Archives, University of Southampton.
[136]Ibid.
[137]Campbell-Johnson, Alan, *Mission with Mountbatten*, New Age Publishers, New Delhi, 1994.

that the matter should be referred to the UN. To persuade the Indian leaders, he added that 'India had a cast-iron case', referring to a definite win.[138] It is important here to remember that Indian leaders of the time did not have the aptitude or understanding of world politics. While Nehru fancied himself as an expert in foreign affairs, his actions indicated over and over, as also this time, that he simply did not understand how the UN Security Council functioned. He did not know that its members acted in their own national interests and were rather swayed in the wave of interests of the major power blocks. The idealism on which his and his party's preconception was based (that the UNO will function on merit and high ideals which were written in the UN Charter) was rather unwise. What made matters worse was that the Indian PM was not able to separate his personal feelings that he had developed for the Mountbattens from affairs that were in the interest of the Indian State.

Pressurizing Nehru, Mountbatten, in a letter written on Christmas, basically brainwashed the former about how a war with Pakistan was not a good idea. He wrote that it was unlikely that war between India and Pakistan could be confined to only the subcontinent and that it was a fatal illusion to believe that it would be finished off quickly in favour of India. He was clearly threatening Nehru that external forces would intervene, which would have not-so-good implications for India. He added in his letter that embroilment in a war with Pakistan would undermine Nehru's independent foreign policy and progressive social aspirations.[139] Successfully persuaded, in his reply, Nehru agreed to refer the matter to the UN. Even though the caveat under which the Indian leadership accepted approaching the UN was that if the invaders did not vacate Indian territory despite UN involvement, India would march towards the invaders bases to attack, the truth of the matter was that as of 1 January 1948, when the complaint was lodged with the UN, no military preparations were made for carrying out

---

[138]Sarila, Narendra Singh, *The Shadow of the Great Game: The Untold Story of India's Partition*, HarperCollins India, Noida, 2009, p. 371.
[139]File L/WS/1/1139, India Office Records, London.

any such armed operation.[140] In fact, it is evident that Nehru was rather worried about the eventuality of the Mountbattens leaving the country if India was to go to war. To this effect, two days before the complaint being lodged with the UN, he had written to Sardar Patel, 'Among the consequences [of war] to consider are the possible effect on the British Officers in the Army and also the reaction of the Governor General (that he may leave India).'[141]

INDIAN ARMY'S EFFORTS TO RECAPTURE KASHMIR SABOTAGED

A week after Kashmir's accession to India, the general officer-in-command of Kashmir operations, Gen. Kulwant Singh, presented a plan to clear the Pakistanis from the entire captured belt along the border and presented it to the Defence Committee. The acting British Commander-in-Chief of the Indian Army, Gen. Roy Bucher, along with generous help from Mountbatten (chair of the Defence Committee), immediately dismissed the plan, calling it too risky. Despite the Indian leaders in the committee pressing for attack, Singh was instructed 'not to take unnecessary risks'.[142] He was livid with the Indian leadership's placid attitude, and when Mountbatten left for London for Princess Elizabeth's wedding later in the week, Singh laid siege and recaptured the towns of Kohli, Jhangar and Naushera. He had also been able to reinforce the town of Poonch. Unfortunately, when his actions caught the British's eye, he was asked to stop, so he could not recapture Mirpur, Domel and Muzaffarabad.[143] Dismayed by Singh going rogue, the Indian leadership counter-proposed setting up a 'sanitized corridor', that is, a demilitarized zone along the frontier with Pakistan with orders

---

[140]Sarila, Narendra Singh, *The Shadow of the Great Game: The Untold Story of India's Partition*, HarperCollins India, Noida, 2009, p. 371.

[141]Nehru, Jawaharlal, *Selected Works, Vol. IV*, Nehru Memorial Museum and Library, New Delhi, pp. 411–12.

[142]Sarila, Narendra Singh, *The Shadow of the Great Game: The Untold Story of India's Partition*, HarperCollins India, Noida, 2009, p. 358.

[143]Ibid.

that any observed movement within it should be attacked from air after due notice. However, the British were so bent on stalling any such Indian advances that Mountbatten, after referring the proposal to the Joint Planning Staff, disapproved it. The Indian leaders did not have the strength to keep insisting and gave up the idea without argument.[144]

Over the next couple of months, several such attempts from the Indian side were shot down by the British. These attempted included the proposal to destroy the bridges across the Kishan Ganga River, which would have cut off Muzaffarabad from Pakistan, and for the army to push to Domel from Uri.[145] The British also suggested that the Indian Army vacate the town of Poonch, which Gen. Singh had reinforced, but thankfully, the Indian leadership resisted.[146] The war in Kashmir was strange in the way that it was led by the two opposing sides by British Commanders-in-Chief. The British Commanders-in-Chief of the two dominions worked closely in order to eventually achieve what was best for Britain's interest. In their conversations, it emerged that the Indian Commander-in-Chief had no intention to allow the Indian Army into what was considered Azad Kashmir territory, that is, Mirpur and Poonch sectors. I find it extremely curious that no top-rung Indian leader saw through the many manipulations or tried to rectify the situation in India's favour.

In May 1948, while the matter was in the UN for consideration, a last-ditch attempt was made by the brave Indian Army to advance north of Uri to recapture Domel and Muzaffarabad. However, this news was leaked, and the Pakistani army stations, which had official presence along these areas, were reinforced. As a result, although the Indian Army managed to capture Tithwal, a town north of Uri, they were not able to advance beyond 10 km west of Uri on the Jhelum Road. Twelve British officers in the Pakistani army were

---

[144]Foreign Relations of the United States, US FR 1948, Vol. V, Office of the Historian, United States Government, pp. 435–6.
[145]Sarila, Narendra Singh, *The Shadow of the Great Game: The Untold Story of India's Partition*, HarperCollins India, Noida, 2009, p. 360.
[146]Ibid. 361.

posted in the three battalions, which were present in India's Kashmir. As we already know, the Indian Armed Forces were being led by Gen. Bucher, a British officer. The British government thought that if the information that the British were fighting internally leaked into the international community, it would be very embarrassing. There were also rumours that India would ask the British officers in the Pakistani Army to step down, which would significantly strip the Pakistani Army of senior officers.[147] So, Gen. Bucher stepped in, toned down the plans for offensive operations and considerably restricted the use of the Royal Indian Air Force.[148] He was the British Trojan horse—it is believed that Mountbatten encouraged him to stay in touch with Nehru and manipulate him from taking any aggressive action that might put Pakistan at risk.[149] Soon after, the UN Commission for India and Pakistan, which was set up to particularly resolve the Kashmir conflict, arrived, and India had to suspend its military operations.

Clearly, the British deep state had ensured that the Indian Armed Forces were not able to engage and that Pakistan would continue to hold on to the Muzaffarabad–Poonch belt and the Gilgit Agency.[150]

THE UN ROW

India approached the UN on 1 January 1948 for a resolution to the Kashmir conflict under Article 35 of the UN Charter, which provides that any member-state can bring any situation that it

[147]FO 371/69719, 14–16 June 1948, Foreign Office: Political – Far Eastern: India and Pakistan, The National Archives, London.

[148]Subject File 19 – Pt 1 (1947-48), T.W. Elmhirst to Bucher, 23 June 1948, Bucher to Patel, 24 June 1948, Sir Roy Bucher Papers, The National Archives, London.

[149]File No. 19 – Part 1, Bucher to H.M. Patel and T.W. Elmhirst, 24 June 1948, Rau Papers (I Instalment), Nehru Memorial Museum and Library, New Delhi; File No. 7901-87-6-1, Bucher to Elizabeth Bucher, 13 December 1948, Bucher Papers, Nehru Memorial Museum and Library, New Delhi.

[150]File No. 7901-87-6-3, Bucher Papers, January 1951, Nehru Memorial Museum and Library, New Delhi.

considers likely to lead to international conflict to the attention of the Security Council or the General Assembly.[151] India essentially complained of 'a situation existing between India and Pakistan owing to the aid which invaders, consisting of nationals of Pakistan and tribesmen from the territory immediately adjoining India on the north-west, were drawing from Pakistan for operations against Jammu and Kashmir'.[152] India further pointed out in its complaint that Jammu and Kashmir had acceded to India and that the Government of India considered Pakistan's assistance to the raiders an act of aggression against India.[153] Articles 33–38 are placed in the UN Charter under Chapter 6, which is titled 'Pacific Settlement of Disputes'. These six articles essentially lay out that if the parties to a dispute, which has the potential for endangering international peace and security, are not able to resolve the matter through negotiations between them, by any other peaceful means or with the help of a 'regional agency', the Security Council may step in, with or without the invitation of one or another of the involved parties, and recommend 'appropriate procedures or methods of recommendations'.[154]

The matter was first taken up for consideration on 15 January 1948. India was represented by Gopalaswami Ayyangar, who had still not been allocated a portfolio in the Nehru Cabinet. Pakistan was represented by its foreign minister Zafrullah Khan. It denied the charge by India and instead accused India of the same, putting the Kashmir conundrum into the broader context of India–Pakistan and the deteriorating Hindu–Muslim relations. Zafrullah Khan essentially stated that India was seeking to destroy the Pakistani State and was carrying out an extensive campaign of genocide against the Muslims

---

[151]'Kashmir: The True Story', *External Publicity Division*, Ministry of External Affairs, Government of India, 2004.
[152]'Fact Check: Article 35, UN Charter—How India Took Up Pakistan Invasion of J&K', *The Indian Express*, 25 September 2019, https://tinyurl.com/y4ybb676. Accessed on 22 November 2023.
[153]Ibid.
[154]Ibid.

of South Asia.[155] He strengthened their case by adding 'India's actions in Jammu and Kashmir' of involving the army and 'unlawful occupation of Junagadh' as examples. He accused India of obtaining Kashmir's accession by 'fraud and violence' and proceeded to attack it on a variety of issues totally unrelated to India's complaint.[156] Strangely, despite a clear-as-water case of Pakistani aggression on Indian soil, India did not refer the complaint under Article 51 of Chapter 7 of the UN Charter titled 'Action with Respect to Threats to the Peace, Breaches of the Peace, and Acts of Aggression', which would have been a far more apt course of action. Article 51 essentially states that a UN member has the 'inherent right of individual or collective self-defence' if attacked, 'till such time that the Security Council has taken measures necessary to maintain international peace and security'.[157] This would have given India full leverage to continue its military operations and recapture all the territory that was under the control of the Pakistanis. The Article further adds that the exercise of this right must be immediately reported to the Security Council by the member and 'shall not in any way affect the authority and responsibility of the Security Council under the present Charter to take at any time such action as it deems necessary in order to maintain or restore international peace and security'.[158]

Approaching the UN under the wrong article was one of Nehru's greatest mistakes with regard to the sovereignty of Kashmir because it allowed the UN to change the title of the agenda before the Security Council from the 'Jammu and Kashmir question' to the 'India–Pakistan question'. It allowed for powerful countries of the world, which controlled the UN, to interfere in India's internal

[155]Schaffer, Howard B., 'Impasse at the United Nations', *The Limits of Influence: America's Role in Kashmir*, Brookings Institution Press, Washington, D.C., 2009, https://tinyurl.com/36964bmm. Accessed on 27 November 2023.

[156]Sarila, Narendra Singh, *The Shadow of the Great Game: The Untold Story of India's Partition*, HarperCollins India, Noida, 2009, p. 377.

[157]'Fact Check: Article 35, UN Charter—How India took up Pakistan invasion of J&K', *The Indian Express*, 25 September 2019, https://tinyurl.com/y4ybb676. Accessed on 22 November 2023.

[158]Ibid.

matters. It also helped Pakistan make a sympathetic case, play the victim card, lobby for and consolidate support with generous help from the British and, eventually, American forces. Despite hostilities towards Indian land, this major mistake from our side made it possible for the world to paint India as the aggressor and Pakistan as the victim and saviour of law and righteousness.

∽

For about two decades, the UN debated, passed resolutions, appointed new mediators and representatives to solve the Kashmir conundrum. Even today, every now and then, Pakistan and other like-minded member-states raise the issue with the organization. However, the UN's inability to successfully resolve the Kashmir issue and judiciously evacuate captured land by Pakistani tribesmen in Kashmir remains one of its greatest failures to date. Having said that, it may be critical at this point to look at how both India and Pakistani leadership put forth their case and, for the purpose of this book, analyse the Indian argument.

On 15 January 1948, when the matter was first taken up for consideration, the British government began lobbying to sway the narrative in the UK, so that sympathy towards Pakistan's position was created. At the outset, the effort was led by Ismay, who was transferred from New Delhi as a principal advisor to Philip Noel-Baker, the Commonwealth secretary, to primarily counsel him on the Kashmir matter at the UN. Ismay continued to enjoy PM Attlee's confidence as well as ex-PM Churchill's and accompanied Noel-Baker to New York. Britain's position on the Kashmir matter was sensitive. It wanted to protect its strategic assets and also guard its custodian for those assets—Pakistan. In addition, they were aware that all steps needed to be taken to avoid 'the danger of aligning all of Islam' against them. On 10 January, as Ismay prepared to depart for New York, PM Attlee gave his directives in a letter, as follows:

1. Pressurize India through public debate in the Security Council to discourage it from attacking Pakistan
2. Play on Indian respect for legal processes to make India accept the Security Council's recommendations

3. Avoid giving Pakistan the impression that Britain was siding with India against it[159]

As soon as the team from Britain arrived in the US, they began to advocate a joint Anglo-US approach to ensuring that both parties firmly agree to a plebiscite, movement of Pakistani forces to the northern areas, withdrawal of the Indian troops to the southern parts of the state, a joint occupation of the Kashmir Valley and establishing a UN Commission in Srinagar that would serve as an interim government in place of Abdullah's administration.[160] What they ideally wanted was to have the US take a forward position in promoting their solution to the Kashmir conflict in the UN. However, Robert Lovett (the pointsman for the US negotiations at the UN and American Undersecretary of State) was simply cold to the idea for multiple reasons. He primarily believed that American involvement would prompt the Soviets to get involved (which eventually did happen) and take a contradictory stance on the issue. Additionally, the draft resolution of the British, which essentially recommended 'the use of foreign troops from one party to the dispute [Pakistan] in the territory of another party to the dispute [India]',[161] was simply not workable for them. The US took a stand at that point, only to retract it in a few months, stating that 'it was difficult to deny the legal validity of Kashmir's accession to India.'[162] However, despite its initial reluctance, the US did get involved and, in fact, co-sponsored with the UK and others all of the resolutions that the council adopted over the next three months as it tried with little success to resolve the conflict.

Meanwhile, in 1948, the US was warming up to Pakistan. Although the arms deal between the two countries did not take place in the next five years, Liaquat Ali Khan, along with the British,

---

[159]File L/WS/1/1148, Attlee to Noel-Baker, 10 January 1948, Oriental and Indian Collection, British Library, London.

[160]Foreign Relations of the United States, US FR 1948, Vol. V, Office of the Historian, United States Government, pp. 291–2.

[161]Sarila, Narendra Singh, *The Shadow of the Great Game: The Untold Story of India's Partition*, HarperCollins India, Noida, 2009.

[162]Ibid.

was making every effort to sway the US opinion in Pakistan's favour. Khan travelled to the US in October that year and first pitched to the US Secretary of State the possibility of forming a defence alliance against the communist powers. He added that since the US was the strongest and most powerful among free nations, it should strengthen Middle Eastern areas economically and militarily.[163]

In contrast, the Indian leaders were missing from all the behind-the-scenes action, most certainly because they simply did not understand it. Not only that, to make matters worse, they were being played and lapping up instructions and advice being fed to them without any intellectual independence. What this did was make the Indian case extremely weak in its representation to the UN. To illustrate, on 15 August 1948, Mountbatten wrote a lengthy letter to Nehru warning him:

> There was no alternative to the UN approach; if war came, the world would blame India because Pakistan was seen as too weak to seek belligerency; war would mean the Indian leaders abandoning all they have stood for; if the UN declares India an aggressor, even India's best friends would have to conform to the world body's decision; war would result in a communal carnage inside India … and finally India did not have the means to prevail on its own. What have you got? … A few old Dakotas.[164]

At the same time, there is great evidence that the British government was feeding information to Nehru through their 'professional sources' that there were signs that the morale of the Indian Army was beginning to wear thin, that Indian troops had little to no enthusiasm on the Kashmir issue and that leadership was lacking due to inexperience.[165] The intent was to drive home

---

[163]Foreign Relations of the United States, US FR 1948, Vol. V, Office of the Historian, United States Government, pp. 435–6.
[164]MBI/F40, Mountbatten to Nehru, 15 August 1948, Mountbatten Papers, British Archives, Hartley Library, University of Southampton.
[165]File L/WS/1/1144, General Nye to CRO, 22 November 1948, Oriental and Indian Collection, British Library, London.

the point that there was no military solution to the Kashmir problem, and, hence, India must abandon all plans to recapture Pakistan-occupied areas of Kashmir.

The above-mentioned reasons are possibly why Nehru deputed Gopalaswami Ayyangar as the Indian representative. Ayyangar enjoyed good relations with Sheikh Abdullah. A natural choice, however, would have been to depute Sardar Patel in his capacity as the states minister to represent the Indian side. However, due to a deteriorating relationship between Nehru and Sardar, the latter was overlooked. Ayyangar's performance at the Security Council actually swung opinion in Pakistan's favour instead of making a strong, diplomatic case for India. Ayyangar believed that 'high statesmanship' required him not to condemn Pakistan directly for aggression. He went to great lengths to differentiate the actions of the 'Pakistani raiders' from the 'armed forces of Pakistan', focussing on the former.[166] So incorrect was this representation that Pakistan themselves confessed to the presence of their troops in Kashmir to the UN Security Council Commission a few months later. To add to this mess, he made it appear that Kashmir's accession to India was conditional upon the result of the plebiscite.[167] He also did not insist on a time-bound evacuation of Pakistanis from Indian soil and certainly failed to even mention that in case the Security Council was unable to ensure the above, India would do so itself (which India would have had an unquestioned right to do had it filed its initial complaint under Article 51 of the UN Charter). India's image, due to these grave errors, came across as apologetic, while Pakistan's attack on India by calling it perpetrator of Muslim genocide received a great deal of global sympathy. Here, Ayyangar failed to counter-state that millions of Muslims were left behind in India after Partition and were treated as equal citizens with their security and interests protected by the Indian government.[168]

---

[166]Sarila, Narendra Singh, *The Shadow of the Great Game: The Untold Story of India's Partition*, HarperCollins India, Noida, 2009, p. 377.
[167]Ibid.
[168]Ibid.

Adding fuel to the fire was Sheikh Abdullah, driven by his hidden agenda. At this point, Abdullah still hadn't played his cards and was sent as a member of the Indian delegation to the UN.[169] Up till then, he was very much the protector of secularism for the Congress leadership, a friend and a very trusted ally for whom the PM had and was willing to make great, expensive concessions. He began to raise with the Americans a third option for Kashmir—independence.[170] In all future demands, Abdullah stayed inconsistent with his stated preference for the kind of relationship Kashmir should have with India, with the only constant theme being a demand for something less than the full integration of the state into the Indian union. He even proposed to the Americans that there should be a joint India–Pakistan defence arrangement for Kashmir to ensure the state's security against aggression from the Soviets. After he took over the reins of the state, he even pitched to them that if the Americans supported the independence of Kashmir in the UN, he would also be able to get the leaders of Azad Kashmir to cooperate—a clear indication that he was very much hand-in-glove with the Pakistanis.[171]

On 20 January, a formation of the UN Commission on India and Pakistan (UNCIP) was passed in a resolution. In April 1948, five members were appointed to the UNCIP, who made their way to India and Pakistan in an attempt to mediate. While in Pakistan, they were informed of the Pakistan Armed Forces stationed in Kashmir, in India, they observed that there was indecision and disarray. One of the delegates stated, '[Nehru] expressed the thought that we [India] would NOT be opposed to the idea of dividing the state between Indian and Pakistan.'[172] As a result, the UNCIP declared a fresh resolution on 13 August 1948, which called

[169]Schaffer, Howard B., 'Impasse at the United Nations', *The Limits of Influence: America's Role in Kashmir*, Brookings Institution Press, Washington, D.C., 2009, https://tinyurl.com/36964bmm. Accessed on 27 November 2023.
[170]Ibid.
[171]Ibid.
[172]Korbel, Joseph, *Danger in Kashmir*, Oxford University Press, New York and Karachi, 2002, p. 307.

on India and Pakistan to agree to a ceasefire, which was to take effect within four days of the two governments' accepting its terms. Pakistan was to pull back its armed forces from the state and 'use its best endeavours' to secure the withdrawal of tribesmen and other Pakistani nationals from Kashmiri territory. Local authorities under the UNCIP surveillance would administer the areas within the state that Pakistan had held. Once the commission had certified that the invaders had departed and the Pakistani Army was being withdrawn, India would demilitarize and station only the minimal force needed to help local authorities maintain law and order. India and Pakistan were to consult with the UNCIP to decide the 'fair and equitable' conditions for conducting plebiscite to ascertain the wish of the Kashmiri people.[173] India accepted the resolution. Pakistan, on the other hand, put forth so many conditions that their response essentially meant rejection of the resolution.[174] On 1 January 1949, an unconditional ceasefire was accepted by both sides. However, to date, despite multiple attempts, there are some key issues on which solutions have not been found: how the Azad Kashmir armed forces would be disarmed and disbanded; how the bulk of the Indian Army would be withdrawn; which local authorities would govern the 'Azad Kashmir' area in the period before the plebiscite; and who would control the north and north-western parts of Kashmir, An unconditional ceasefire meant that the positions held by India and Pakistan (which included the invaders [who also call themselves Azad forces] and the Pakistani Army) stayed as they were at the time of ceasefire. These positions would be further protected by a small, multinational force—the UN Military Observers Group in India and Pakistan (UNMOGIP)— as it would patrol the 400-mile-long ceasefire line across the state.[175]

It was in 1971 that the third India–Pakistan war took place and the ceasefire line was replaced with a new Line of Control,

---

[173]Ibid. 312.
[174]Schaffer, Howard B., 'Impasse at the United Nations', *The Limits of Influence: America's Role in Kashmir, Brookings Institution Press*, Washington, D.C., 2009, https://tinyurl.com/36964bmm. Accessed on 27 November 2023.
[175]Ibid.

thus ending the mandate of the UNMOGIP.[176] The fact remains that India should have used force and recaptured land from the Pakistani invaders in 1948. The Indian Army was more than capable of doing so as evidenced by even the communique by Gen. Cariappa in November 1948, in which he presented a plan to recapture Mirpur and Muzaffarabad to the Defence Committee. Not only was he denied fresh troops by the Defence Committee for carrying out the assault, but a message had also been sent by the British Indian Commander-in-Chief to the Pakistanis to re-enforce their positions and to equip them with more ammunition. In his explanation, Gen. Bucher had reiterated to Nehru a tale that was being fed to him all along—that the Indian Army was running short of transport, lacked spares and certain types of ammunition—which made the latter conclude that Muzaffarabad and Mirpur were out of reach. During this time, when Liaquat Ali Khan had raised an SOS to Attlee out of fear that the Indian Army would recapture the entire Poonch–Muzaffarabad strip, the latter had replied on 18 November, 'I am taking action to do anything I can to secure the halting of any offensive that may be taking place.'[177]

Contrary to this, several war veterans involved in the war at the time have recounted that the Indian Armed Forces were at an advantageous position and were fully capable of recapturing all the illegally occupied territory in Kashmir. The question that remains unanswerable even today by intellectuals, Congress loyalists and military experts is: why did Nehru not allow the Indian Armed Forces to continue to reclaim invaded territory even when we were at a position of strength and instead abruptly take the matter to the UNSC, even though India was very much within its legal right to reclaim our land by force? The only obvious answer to my mind, after examining multiple accounts written and retold by credible sources, is that he simply didn't care for the land enough (as also evidenced by his correspondence on the subject in the time period

---

[176]Ibid.

[177]Sarila, Narendra Singh, *The Shadow of the Great Game: The Untold Story of India's Partition*, HarperCollins India, Noida, 2009.

clearly stating that he was willing to partition Kashmir and cede these areas to Pakistan). He was especially happy to let it go if he could use the incident to craft his 'global statesman' image in the world affairs at the time. Many years later, in 1971, his daughter and then PM of India, Indira Gandhi, followed the same footsteps. An opportunity had presented itself in 1971 when the Indian Armed Forces were once again in a position to recapture Pakistan-occupied Kashmir (POK), including the northern areas of Gilgit, Skardu and Baltistan. The Soviets had pledged their unconditional support to India to do so.[178] Despite advice given to her by her closest comrades in a meeting attended by Defence Minister Jagjivan Ram, External Affairs Minister Swaran Singh, Finance Minister Y.B. Chavan, Chief of Army Staff Sam Manekshaw and Gopalaswamy Parthasarathi, a foreign policy advisor close to her, that she should give the order to the Indian Armed Forces to recapture POK, she held back. On the way back to her residence, Parthasarathi tried to persuade her to take the 'historic step', to which she had replied, 'When prime ministers and presidents have to take such decisions, they have to take them alone.'[179] Parathasarathi had later opined, 'We lost an irretrievable opportunity to change Asia. In history there are many instances where logic cannot be applied. This was one of them.'[180]

All along, Pakistan has maintained a clear distinction between its army and the invaders (Azad Kashmir force). However, there is resolute evidence to show that the latter was being operated by the highest levels of Pakistani and British leadership. For instance, in November 1947, when Mountbatten met Jinnah to propose taking the matter to the UN, the Pakistani Governor General had made a counter-proposal that both sides should retreat simultaneously. When Mountbatten asked the follow-up question how the tribesmen (who, Pakistan maintained, were acting independently were to be called off, Jinnah replied, 'All he had to do was give them an

[178]Menon, Vandana, 'New Book Claims Indira Gandhi Wanted to Recapture Pak-Occupied Kashmir after 1971 War', *The Print*, 24 March 2018, https://tinyurl.com/yj4yyfef. Accessed on 22 November 2023.
[179]Ibid.
[180]Ibid.

order to come out.'[181] Despite such clear information and facts, the international community has legitimized 'Azad Kashmir'. Very recently, in 2022, the US Ambassador to Pakistan, Donald Blome, visited some areas of POK. His visit was followed by a press release and tweet from the US Embassy of Islamabad, 'I'm honoured to visit during my first trip to AJK [Azad Jammu and Kashmir].'[182] Another example is the 'giving away' of large chunks of land by Pakistan in the Baltistan–Gilgit region to China in order to build the Karakoram Highway as part of the China–Pakistan Border Agreement signed on 2 March 1963. Pakistan had no legal right to 'cede' territory that it had illegally occupied and that legally still belongs to India. However, the Indian leadership was still recovering from the great loss of the Indo-China War of 1962 and did not have the resources or political will to make an effort to counter this. Legitimizing illegally occupied land of a sovereign nation is possibly as criminal as playing a role in doing so. However, western powers, along with politicians like Abdullah and his friends within the Congress party, have, over decades, enabled and used Azad forces as a front to carry out criminal actions that work in their strategic and political interests.

ARTICLE 370

Meanwhile, at the same time, in the Valley, Abdullah was very much asserting his dominance. Concurrent events demonstrated that he was no subservient follower of India, as we have seen glimpses on in his demands during the UN negotiations. He became a political dictator and ran a government that was so arbitrary and extreme that it became difficult for Nehru to defend his actions. The state high court was interrupted repeatedly, thus blocking it from discharging its duties fairly. Almost all opposing voices, which

---

[181]MB1/D86, Personal Reports by Lord Mountbatten: September 1947-October 1947, 7 September 1947, Mountbatten Papers, British Archives, University of Southampton, Para 63.
[182]@usembislamabad, *X* (formerly Twitter), 5 October 2022, 1:25 p.m., https://tinyurl.com/mvry9kdh. Accessed on 28 November 2023.

included a large number of officials who had been part of Hari Singh's old administration, including the governor of Jammu, had been detained.

He opposed following the Mysore-model pattern of integration into the Indian union, that is, that Class-B states (all former princely states, including J&K) would essentially have a constitution that the Constituent Assembly of India would frame.[183] He had a very different vision for Jammu and Kashmir's constitution. There was considerable anxiety in the corridors of power in New Delhi about which way Abdullah would go if he were to be pressed on the matter. He was so unreliable and unpredictable at this point that there was no telling if he would even choose to openly join hands with Pakistan. If he did so, it would be an extremely embarrassing situation for Nehru, who had gone out of his way, making the state vulnerable to attacks, so that Abdullah's wishes could be accommodated. In order to avoid this embarrassment, Nehru continued to give Abdullah an extraordinary amount of latitude in devising machinery for framing the Constitution.

Even in Article 1 of the Indian Constitution, while Jammu and Kashmir was deemed to be an integral part of the Indian union, it was allotted special status under Article 370 (originally 306-A), by which it got 'temporary provisions with respect to the state of Jammu and Kashmir'. This effectively limited the powers of Indian Parliament to the three matters specified in the Instrument of Accession governing the accession of Kashmir to the Dominion of India—defence, external affairs and communication. This was once again confirmed in Article 152 of the 1956 amended version of the Indian Constitution, which, in the section dealing with Indian states, specified that the expression of 'state' does not include the state of Jammu and Kashmir. Everything else apart from the three matters would be decided by whatever form of government the Jammu and Kashmir Constituent Assembly would create. Interestingly, Article 370 was drafted by Gopalaswami Ayyangar in

---

[183]Chand Malhotra, Iqbal and Maroof Raza, *Kashmir's Untold Story: Declassified*, Bloomsbury India, 2019, p. 129.

close consultation with Sheikh Abdullah. The special status enabled the state leadership to exploit the Indian union for huge amount of funds while continuing to run the state like their own fiefdom.[184] It was not until 1953 that Nehru took the bull by the horns and decided to arrest Abdullah for acts of treason against the Indian union. This happened immediately after Abdullah confessed to Karan Singh that he was intending to seek external help to pressurize the Indian government to grant independence to the state of Jammu and Kashmir.[185]

In the 1960s, a master cell set up by fringe elements in the National Conference exploited the ambiguity of the organization's stance on accession to India and began to push the case for separation from India more aggressively. These elements worked closely with Pakistan and were generously funded, supplied with weapons and artillery to perpetrate violence. Abdullah, who was mostly in prison until 1975, was finally released, after which he once again effectively became a one-man government with the support of the Pakistanis and the western deep state. There is enough evidence to show that when he headed the All Jammu and Kashmir Plebicite Front before 1975, the organization regularly received funds from Pakistan to oppose the state's accession to India.[186] Abdullah's second rise had been endorsed by the Muslims in the state who believed that the Hindus in Jammu were trying to break up the state. He finally handed over power to his son Dr Farooq Abdullah, who enjoyed the same autonomy like his father and became the president of the National Conference. Due to their unchallenged power, they enjoyed with the support of the Muslims and, in the hope to continue to do so, they vowed to eliminate the Hindus from the Valley once and for all. With the help of extreme

---

[184]Ibid. 137

[185]Singh, Karan, *Heir Apparent: An Autobiography*, Oxford University Press, London, 1982.

[186]'Enlargement of Cabinet', 'Split in Democratic National Conference', 'Trial of Sheikh Abdullah on Conspiracy Charges', 'Political Developments in "Azad Kashmir"', in *Keesing's Record of World Events*, Vol. 8, edited by Roger East, Longman London, 1961, p. 18290

elements, a dastardly Hindu genocide was systematically carried out as the Rajeev Gandhi government looked the other way.[187] With the Hindus out, the brand of radical Islam grew stronger in the state. These radical elements continued to receive weapons and training from across the border and played an active role in perpetrating acts of repeated terrorism on Indian soil.[188]

However, the Modi government's tough hand on the state administration, by scrapping Article 370 and taking away the state's special status, enabled the Indian government to play a much more decisive role in the affairs of the state.[189] The development of the state, which was halted in exchange for radicalism, was reversed. Just this year, the Emaar Group announced an investment of ₹500 crore to develop malls and infrastructure in the state.[190] This is significant not only because of the sum but also because of the confidence that the Islamic countries have in the future of the state after its integration with the Indian union, presently led by PM Modi. With a zero-tolerance policy on any border transgression as we have seen with Uri and Pulwama, the Modi government continues to wipe the state clean of its radical elements that halted its growth for decades. There finally is a ray of hope that in the time to come, we may be able to return Jammu and Kashmir to its former glory and reclaim the land masses given away to Pakistan and China by former governments.

---

[187]Tikoo, Tej Kumar, 'Kashmiri Pandits offered Three Choices by Radical Islamists', *Indian Defence Review*, 13 March 2022, https://tinyurl.com/yjcmdt4x. Accessed on 28 November 2023; '"How Can We Interfere": Former MP and Senior Journalist MJ Akbar Recalls Rajiv Gandhi's Reply on the Plight of Kashmiri Hindus', *OpIndia*, 16 March 2022, https://tinyurl.com/2hspupcz. Accessed on 28 November 2023.

[188]Bhan, Ashok, 'Pakistan, Kashmiri Terrorists Responsible for Kashmiri Pandit Genocide', *India Legal*, 20 March 2022, https://tinyurl.com/25ufa9r5. Accessed on 22 November 2023.

[189]Mukherjee, Priyanka, 'Article 370 Revoked: When BJP Fulfilled Its Long-Standing Agenda', *The Times of India*, 7 June 2021, https://tinyurl.com/yc28s77z. Accessed on 22 November 2023.

[190]'In J&K's First FDI, Dubai's Emaar to Set Up Rs 500 Crore Mall, IT Towers in Srinagar', *CNBC TV18*, 20 March 2023, https://tinyurl.com/y8uxftze. Accessed on 22 November 2023.

5

CHINA

In the 1950s, while the fate of our beloved Valley was undecided, we had a tense situation with the Chinese on our eastern and northern frontiers. The border dispute between India and China remains unsolved even today. It is the longest border under dispute in the world. The friendship that was solemnized between China and Pakistan during the war time of 1962 has now fully matured into an all-weather partnership, keeping India constantly on its toes. It is in this context that it becomes important to understand how and when the Sino-Indian relationship fouled and its ongoing consequences on India.

China annexed Tibet in 1951 under the pretext that Tibet was an integral part of its mainland and that unification with China was necessary to 'liberate the people'. Tibet was a buffer zone between the Indian and Chinese frontiers, and this move essentially opened a live boundary for us. Tibet appealed to India for help, but we declined and advised it to negotiate a peaceful settlement with China. This was essentially the first time that India was waking up to the possibility of a threat from Chinese expansionism. Our national interest demanded us to engage in dialogue with China, use legal arguments and mobilize world opinion to deter China from making such a move. Tibet was never a full-fledged Chinese province as claimed by the latter: apart from two short periods of Chinese rule in recent history, Tibet had been independent for years with nominal Chinese suzerainty over it. In fact, in 1912, when the Chinese government tried to capture Tibet, it was prevented from doing so by the British Indian government.[1] In

---

[1]Dalvi, Brig. J.P., *Himalayan Blunder: The Curtain-Raiser to the Sino-Indian War of*

1913, when the Tibetans proclaimed their independence and the Dalai Lama was restored to power, a tri-partite conference was held in Shimla, which concluded deliberations in April 1914. According to the agreement, China agreed not to convert Tibet into a Chinese province. Additionally, an agreement was reached on the boundary between Indian and Tibet, all the way from Bhutan to Burma, which came to be known as the McMahon Line.[2] Tibet was proposed to be divided into Inner and Outer Tibet; China was to stay out of the administration of the latter. China did not ratify this agreement since they weren't satisfied with the proposed boundary between Inner and Outer Tibet, but the British Indian government and the Tibetans had signed this agreement. (Even today, the fact that they never signed the agreement forms the basis of the Chinese rejecting the validity of the McMahon Line.)[3] In the west of India, the boundary that divided Kashmir from China was called the Johnson Line.

When China took over Tibet in 1951, they obviously inherited all of Tibet's positions and agreements of the past and were expected to honour the commitments, but they did not. And this is when India should have defended Tibet. Instead, we adopted a policy of appeasement towards China. We even opposed discussion on Tibet's appeal to the UN in November 1950 when the topic came up in the General Assembly.[4] Our actions were typical of a weak nation—we had no allies to muster up global pressure against Chinese aggression due to our PM's non-alignment policy, despite the imminent threat to our national security. We only sent a few diplomatic notes to China, expressing our concern, to which China professed eternal friendship with us, which we believed and accepted at face value.

Recognizing this threat, Patel, barely a year before he died,

1962, Natraj Publishers, Dehradun, 1969, p. 12.

[2]Ibid. 13.

[3]Rowland, John, *A History of Sino-Indian Relations: Hostile Co-existence*, Nostrand, Princeton, 1967, pp. 48–9.

[4]Dalvi, Brig. J.P., *Himalayan Blunder: The Curtain-Raiser to the Sino-Indian War of 1962*, Natraj Publishers, Dehradhun, 1969, p. 15.

wrote a prophetic letter about Chinese ambitions and intentions as well as preparatory measures that India would require to successfully counter an attack.[5] India's Intelligence Bureau Chief B.N. Mullick, who headed the bureau from 1950 until after Nehru died, also warned him that China's move into Tibet was sinister and would threaten India's interests. Mullick also warned Nehru that the Indian ambassador K.M. Pannikkar was 'soft on China'.[6]

While we were dilly-dallying and playing nice with the Chinese, Pakistan recognized the intensity of the Chinese threat to India. In a dinner meeting on 11 July 1961, with American President John F. Kennedy, Ayub Khan threatened to stop an important clandestine operation that the Americans were running over Tibet using East Pakistan as a base, if the latter tilted further towards helping India.[7] He further insisted with the American President that appeasing India at Pakistan's expense would have its cost,[8] to which Kennedy assured him that if China attacked India, he would not sell arms to India without first consulting Pakistan (a promise he didn't keep).[9]

In 1951, China began to patrol Ladakh.[10] At this time, it was already involved in a war in Korea and was vulnerable. Had we addressed the issue with them head-on then, perhaps they would have accepted a compromise on the border. But we did nothing. In fact, PM Nehru did not even bother to inform Parliament of

---

[5]Shankar, V. (ed.), *Sardar Patel: Selected Correspondence—1945–1950*, Vol. I, Navjeevan Publishing House, Ahmedabad, March 1977.

[6] Mullik, B.N., *My Years with Nehru: The Chinese Betrayal*, Allied Publishers, Bombay, 1971, pp. 70–1, 81.

[7]Khan, Mohammad Ayub, *Friends Not Masters: A Political Autobiography*, Mr. Books, Islamabad, 2002, p. 139; Riedel, Bruce, *JFK's Forgotten Crisis: Tibet, The CIA, and The Sino-Indian War*, HarperCollins India, Noida, 2016.

[8]Khan, Mohammad Ayub, *Friends Not Masters: A Political Autobiography*, Mr. Books, Islamabad, 2002, p. 139.

[9]Kux, Dennis, *Disenchanted Allies: The United States and Pakistan, 1947–2000*, Johns Hopkins University Press, 2001, p. 122.

[10]Dalvi, Brig. J.P., *Himalayan Blunder: The Curtain-Raiser to the Sino-Indian War of 1962*, Natraj Publishers, Dehradun, 1969, p. 16.

China's patrolling of Ladakh territory.[11] He clearly failed to realize two important aspects about China—that a strong China would develop an expansionist attitude and that, sooner or later, we would have to prepare to defend ourselves in the northern regions, for which an immediate, long-term plan plus resource allocation would be necessary.

As per its strategy, which we see even today, China began to build strategic infrastructure in Tibet—important roads, airfields and communications to Xinjiang province via Rudok. To build this vital highway that would connect Hotan in Xinjiang to Lhasa in Tibet, they needed to swallow huge chunks of land from the Aksai Chin region of the Indian territory, which they did![12] It was only when a Chinese newspaper announced in September 1957 that the 'Sinkiang-Tibet Highway—the highest one in the world—has been completed'[13] did India learn of it. In fact, after we sent a 20-member team to inspect areas in Aksai Chin that China had taken over, several team members went missing and one was even arrested.[14] The intelligence report of this exercise was kept classified, thus confirming that the contents would have been very telling of the Chinese seizure of Aksai Chin. Moreover, Nehru chose to not notify Parliament of the intelligence-gathering exercise or the arrest of our man. In 1958, Nehru was informed through correspondence by the secretary of foreign affairs that 'there was little doubt that the newly constructed 1,200-kilometre road passes through Aksai Chin'.[15] However, when the Indian press reported the construction of the strategic road, there was an outcry, after which Nehru demanded that China withdraw from India's official territory. China refused, but suggested in a letter instead that it could take Aksai Chin and, in exchange, give up its claim

---

[11] Ibid.

[12] Ibid. 20.

[13] Arpi, Claude, 'When Nehru Lied in Parliament', *Indian Defence Review*, 20 June 2014, https://tinyurl.com/52vwm295. Accessed on 22 November 2023.

[14] Ibid.

[15] Riedel Bruce, *JFK's Forgotten Crisis: Tibet, the CIA and the Sino-Indian War*, HarperCollins India, Noida, 2015, p. 37.

to the Indian territory at the other end of the Chinese–Indian border, in the North-East Frontier Agency (NEFA).[16] Nehru did not accept this exchange at the time, but he was forced to do so in 1962. The contours of the state after the fateful war and territory ceded to China are shown in Map 3.

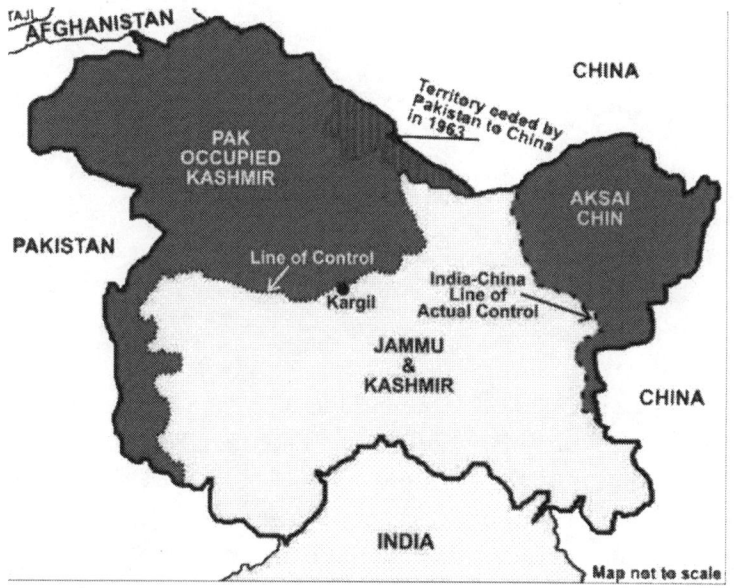

Map 3: Map of India showing Aksai Chin that was illegally occupied by China during 1950s and consolidated in 1962 War
Source: Dutta, Prabhash K., 'How China Captured Aksai Chin', *India Today*, 22 June 2020. https://tinyurl.com/3zzc2x3a. Accessed on 22 November 2023.

China built a major road across the NEFA, just north of the McMahon Line as well as several feeders to their border detachments, clearly preparing for military conflict.[17] They also engaged deeply in a narrative-building exercise to display

---

[16]Ibid.
[17]Dalvi, Brig. J.P., *Himalayan Blunder: The Curtain-Raiser to the Sino-Indian War of 1962*, Natraj Publishers, Dehradhun, 1969, p. 21.

permanent friendship with India between 1951 and 1953, with a lot of diplomatic back and forth, exchange of cultural delegations and mutual visits. We trusted this so much that the Tibetan crisis lost our attention. Within this period of prevailing camaraderie in April 1954, we signed the Sino-Indian Agreement on Trade and Intercourse between the Tibetan Region of China and India, based on 'Panch Sheel', that is, five guiding principles.[18] These were: mutual respect for each other's territorial integrity, mutual non-aggression, mutual non-interference in each other's internal affairs, equal and mutual benefit and, finally, peaceful co-existence. Till 2023, none of these commitments have been upheld by the Chinese. By signing the agreement, we basically accepted Chinese control over Tibet without extracting any benefit in exchange (that is, settlement of the McMahon border), which, in the long run, had the potential to be a source of friction. From the British, we had inherited military, communications and postal rights in Tibet, which we voluntarily gave up and agreed to withdraw our officers stationed at Yatung and Gyantse, handing these over to the Chinese.[19]

Nehru's obsession to please the Chinese was so overwhelming that he defended this agreement by stating, 'It was recognition of the existing situation there. Historical and practical considerations necessitated that step.'[20] He never made it clear what the practical considerations really were! Not only that, during Nehru's visit to the US in 1956, he pressed Eisenhower to support giving Communist China the seat in the UN Security Council that Nationalist China had been given in 1945 at the end of World War II, making it one of the five permanent members of the Council with the right to veto any resolution it did not approve. Nehru argued in China's favour, adding that 'it was only logical that any government controlling six hundred million people will sooner or later have to be brought into the council of nations.'[21] He also dismissed any

---

[18]Ibid. 22.

[19]Ibid.

[20]Ibid. 23.

[21]Halberstam, David, *The Coldest Winter: America and the Korean War*, Hyperion, New York, 2007, p. 53.

possibility that China would attack India. However, it is understood that Eisenhower did not take Nehru's proposal seriously.[22]

India was now at a massively vulnerable junction in terms of territorial security. Around this time, in 1954, Pakistan had signed a mutual defence treaty with the US and later joined the US-sponsored military alliances called Central Treaty Organization (CENTO) in the Middle East and the South Asia Treaty Organization (SEATO) in Southeast Asia.[23] Pakistan offered their territory for setting up US bases in exchange for massive military aid. By mid-1950s, Pakistan could claim to be one of the US's most important allies. Large amounts of military and economic aid followed. Even though Nehru condemned this and said that India would regard this as a hostile act, being on the southern boundary of Russia, Pakistan was an invaluable asset for the US. The US was also training Pakistani Army and Air Force officers. The massive influx of modern US arms, in addition to the US-trained force, made the Pakistan Armed Forces extremely advanced and resilient. Azad Kashmir forces were also equipped, and, thus, they no longer remained disorganized and weak, and the Indian Army could no longer treat them as 'easy to defeat'.[24]

The military balance of power had obviously tipped. With the rise in threat from Pakistan, it now faced an active threat from China as the latter began to shed its cloak of friendship by 1956. Advancing their expansionist strategy, China produced maps with large tracts of Indian land marked as Chinese territory. When the Indian government questioned them, they said these maps were old and new maps would have to be made after 'properly surveying the area'. Even after the news of them engulfing our land in Aksai Chin, no retaliatory action was taken that would dent their advance. They continued to enjoy the financial and commercial benefits of the Sino-Indian Trade Agreement.

---

[22]Ibid.

[23]Riedel Bruce, *JFK's Forgotten Crisis: Tibet, the CIA and the Sino-Indian War*, HarperCollins India, Noida, 2015, p. 29.

[24]Dalvi, Brig. J.P., *Himalayan Blunder: The Curtain-Raiser to the Sino-Indian War of 1962*, Natraj Publishers, Dehradun, 1969, p. 28.

Adding to this complacence were Nehru's informal replies on the floor of Parliament when questioned repeatedly on the issue. On the matter of sending a reconnoitring party to check how much of Aksai Chin was taken over by the Chinese, he had said on 4 February 1958,

> [M]y reaction is that we should send a reconnoitring party there in spring with clear instructions that they should not come into conflict with the Chinese. I do not think it is desirable to have air reconnaissance. In fact, I do not see what good this can do to us. Even a land reconnaissance will not be perhaps very helpful. I do not see how we can possibly protest about the alignment of the road without being much surer than we are ... It is suggested that our maps should be sent to the Chinese. Certainly they can be sent through our Embassy, but I think it would be better to do this rather informally.[25]

A large chunk of Indian territory had been occupied and our PM insisted that India remained informal about it. What is worse is that in April 1959, a question was raised in Parliament to PM Nehru by an MP of his own party, D.C. Sharma, asking if there was any dispute over any border or other kind of territory between China and India, and if not, why some parts of India, which are obviously in India, had been shown as parts of China in their maps. Characteristically, Nehru replied,

> It is rather difficult for me to answer that question. We have discussed one or two minor frontier disputes which compromise tiny tracts of territory, may be a mile this way or a mile that way, in the high mountains where no body lives and those are pending. We have discussed them and for the present no settlement has been arrived at.[26]

---

[25]Palat, Madhavan K. (ed.), *Selected Works of Jawaharlal Nehru, Volume 41*, Second Series, Nehru Memorial Museum and Library, New Delhi, 1984.

[26]Arpi, Claude, 'When Nehru Lied in Parliament', *Indian Defence Review*, 20 June 2014, https://tinyurl.com/52vwm295. Accessed on 22 November 2023.

The PM's attitude was clear. He was not willing to divulge the truth about exactly how much Indian land was captured by the Chinese. He was much rather of the opinion that the bilateral relationship with China must continue to prosper.

ᔕ

With the change in power play, India was in a tough spot. Despite recommendations by the armed forces right since 1952 to build our military capabilities, Nehru had barely acted on them. He had not allocated the necessary resources to strengthen our military and essentially relied on the promises of non-violence from the Americans and Chinese to protect India's sovereignty. In fact, when the Central Intelligence Agency (CIA) performed a top-secret post-mortem of the Sino-Indian War, the documents of which were later declassified, it was revealed that in assessing the early years of the dispute between Nehru and Mao Zedong over Tibet, China had played on 'Nehru's Asian, anti-imperialist mental attitude; his proclivity to temporize and his sincere desire for an amicable Sino-Indian relationship'. The CIA's report had concluded that the War was, 'a masterpiece of guile'.[27]

The problem was that due to his insistence on non-alignment, we did not have any strong allies who would come to our aid by supplying military equipment in our hour of need. We had Russia, which had taken our side in the UN Security Council discussions on Kashmir, but Russia was a closer ally to China and would morally stay out of an Indo-Chinese conflict. It would most certainly avoid arming India against China as Russia was helping build the military and industrial capacities for the latter. The Americans and the British were unlikely to supply us with military aid unless we compromised on the Kashmir question, which would suit their interests and legitimize Pakistan's presence in POK. And finally, we could not purchase equipment in the open market

---

[27]Directorate of Intelligence Staff Study, 'The Sino-Indian Border Dispute, 1946–63', cited in Dhar, Anuj (ed.), *CIA's Eye on South Asia*, Manas Publications, New Delhi, 2009, p. 114.

from France or Sweden because we simply did not have the funds to do so. We were in the middle of our second Five-Year Plan, and any major diversion of resources to the military would have set us back several decades.[28] India was isolated—all alone in an aggressive neighbourhood with no respite—and this was our doing. We had dug our own grave by wasting the years between 1950 and 1957 to build a respectable military force and equipping it with modern-day artillery. These were the years we could have used to build diplomatic ties that would ensure timely aid, thus readying ourselves for an eventuality of war with two of our neighbours. Thus, come 1959, a situation arose where India was forced to be in a constant state of armed readiness. This was certainly a suicidal policy for a young, developing country.

So tense and serious was the issue that, in May 1959, then US Senator John F. Kennedy, in a major foreign-policy speech, focussed on Indian and China, stating that '[No] struggle in the world today deserves more of our time and attention than that which now grips the attention of all of Asia … And that is the struggle between India and China for leadership of the East, for the respect of all of Asia, for the opportunity to demonstrate whose way of life is better.'[29] He suggested that the North Atlantic Treaty Organization (NATO) allies and Japan put together a comprehensive package of loans to strengthen the Indian economy and work to secure a foreign direct investment in India of $1 billion per year. He insisted that these loans and investment would boost Indian economic growth, enabling it to outmatch its population growth, and set the country on a path to sustainable, long-term prosperity. He said that it was the duty of the free world to help India outshine Red China.[30]

Kennedy's leanings towards India were present despite the inauspicious start to the relationship with Nehru during his first

---

[28]Dalvi, Brig. J.P., *Himalayan Blunder: The Curtain-Raiser to the Sino-Indian War of 1962*, Natraj Publishers, Dehradun, 1969, p. 35.
[29]Kennedy, John F., 'Remarks of Senator John F. Kennedy, Conference on India and the United States, Washington, 4 May 1959,' *John F. Kennedy Presidential Library and Museum*, https://tinyurl.com/ms6zwctm. Accessed on 23 November 2023.
[30]Ibid.

meeting with the latter in 1951. Back then, the former had been a Congressman and the US embassy had convinced Nehru to give him an audience. Jacqueline Kennedy recounted that while briefing them, the embassy staff had told Kennedy that 'whenever Nehru gets bored with you, he taps his fingertips together and looks up at the ceiling'. She added that after only 10 minutes with Kennedy, 'Nehru started to look up at the ceiling' and 'began tapping his fingertips'.[31] Despite Kennedy's clear leanings demonstrated by helping India against China, Nehru showed no intention of altering his basic policy of non-alignment. Kennedy's promised aid came through in April 1961—half-a-million dollars in development loans and the other half-a-million in food assistance. Despite this, Nehru maintained a stoic distance from the US. It is at this time that he visited Washington, D.C., along with Indira and his cousin Braj Kumar Nehru, who was made India's first ambassador to the US. The visit turned out to be a disaster. Even as President Kennedy tried to engage him in conversation, Nehru responded in monosyllables or said nothing at all. The US ambassador to India, John Kenneth Galbraith, recounted, 'Nehru simply did not respond. Question after question he answered with monosyllables or a sentence or two … The President found it very discouraging.' The American opinion was that 'the meeting convinced him [Kennedy] that Nehru would never be a strong reed on which to rely'.[32] Kennedy also told Galbraith later that 'it was the worst state visit of his presidency'[33] and that 'Nehru seemed more interested in talking with Jackie than with him'.[34]

In this mix, the issue of Goa sprouted. For years, Indians had been pressing Lisbon for Goan independence. In late 1961, Nehru

---

[31] Kennedy, Jacqueline, *Historic Conversations of Life with John F. Kennedy*, Hyperion, New York, 2011, p. 238; Schlesinger, Arthur, *A Thousand Days: John F. Kennedy in the White House*, Houghton Mifflin, Boston, 1965, p. 522.
[32] Galbraith, John Kenneth, *Ambassador's Journal: A Personal Account of the Kennedy Year*, Houghton Mifflin, Boston, 1969, p. 248.
[33] Ibid.
[34] Wolpert, Stanley, *Nehru: A Tryst with Destiny*, Oxford University Press, Oxford, 1996, p. 480.

decided to take it by force. While Washington assured Nehru that in six months, they would be able to diplomatically press Lisbon into giving up Goa,[35] Nehru didn't wait and, on 20 December 1961, ordered the Indian Army to seize it. 'Operation Vijay' was a success since they barely faced any resistance and were able to take control over Goa pretty easily. This did two things: it assured Nehru and the Indian leaders of the Indian Army's invincibility (despite not having adequate gear and artillery) and it exposed Nehru's hypocrisy. Given that he was a leading spokesman for the settlement of all international disputes peacefully, his use of unilateral military action certainly alerted the international community of his dual personality. Thus, combined with the disastrous state visit of 1961, ties between Nehru and Kennedy were seriously strained.[36]

1962

And then came the fateful war of 1962 where India conceded the Aksai Chin territory to China. While it may not be within the scope of this book to discuss military strategy in detail, there are a few points I wish to make. China began to increase the frequency of localized instances of violence at the border after 3 April 1962, when the Dalai Lama fled to India and was granted political asylum. Three such skirmishes had also taken place between August and October 1959, which had compelled Nehru to, for the first time, admit to Parliament that there was considerable strain on the Sino-Indian relationship. He had also admitted at the time that the Chinese had built a highway across our territory in addition to establishing a camp within our lands in Spanggur. He had then proceeded to state the action that his government had taken in face of such an explosive situation, which included placing border areas of the NEFA under direct military control.[37] In November

---

[35]Riedel, Bruce, *JFK's Forgotten Crisis: Tibet, the CIA and the Sino-Indian War*, HarperCollins India, Noida, 2015, p. 74.

[36]Ibid. 75.

[37]Dalvi, Brig. J.P., *Himalayan Blunder: The Curtain-Raiser to the Sino-Indian War of 1962*, Natraj Publishers, Dehradun, 1969, pp. 41–2.

1959, China had formally laid claim to 50,000 sq. miles of the Indian territory in Ladakh and the NEFA.[38] However, it wasn't until 1961, two years later, that our government considered it necessary to take 'limited defence measures to contain Chinese incursions into Indian territory'.[39] Many primary sources recall that the PM treated recurring Chinese aggression at the border as isolated incidents and did not find it necessary to contemplate or order any serious military response.

In addition to the military under-preparedness was the tension between the army and the leadership. Gen. Thimayya, the army chief, had informed the government of the requirements in terms of men and material to combat the Chinese. He was easily one of the ablest Indian generals and very loved by his colleagues. He had already led two important missions: he had commanded the Punjab Boundary Force in the wake of the violence that Partition had unleashed and he had commanded the Indian forces in the Kashmir Valley to defend it against the Pakistani tribals. However, Defence Minister Krishna Menon kept underplaying Gen. Thimayya's demands and insisting to not lose focus on the fact that Pakistan was still our number one enemy. In contrast, Gen. Thimayya believed that enemies should not be ranked. He knew that the army had been spread thin and that the defence minister had been interfering too much with senior army postings and petty procedural matters. There was also considerable tension between the two on strategy to counter the Chinese threat.[40] This prompted him to offer his resignation, which, like a true statesman, Nehru persuaded him to withdraw. Later, the PM dismissed the General's charges against Menon of focussing on defence strategies against Pakistan instead of China as trivial and, in fact, publicly

---

[38]Patranobis, Sutirtho, 'China Makes It Official, Wants to Revert to 1959 LAC India Has Rejected Many Times', *The Print*, 29 September 2020, https://tinyurl.com/39wur68x. Accessed on 22 November 2023.

[39]Nehru, Jawaharlal, *Chinese Aggression in War and Peace: Letters of the Prime Minister of India*, Government of India Publication, Delhi, 1962.

[40]Dalvi, Brig. J.P., *Himalayan Blunder: The Curtain-Raiser to the Sino-Indian War of 1962*, Natraj Publishers, Dehradun, 1969, pp. 48–9.

reprimanded Gen. Thimayya for threatening to quit in the face of the Sino-Indian border crisis. It is critical to understand that only overriding national interest could have prompted Gen. Thimayya to offer his resignation in such a time of crisis.

In this critical year, Gen. S.P.P. Thorat, General Officer Commanding-in-Chief, Eastern Command, also held the view that no further forward posts should be established along the border without adequate military arrangements. He opined that India didn't have the infrastructure to defend its forward posts in the event of an attack. The essential supplies for any military operations also would have to be airdropped.[41] This view was not palatable to the Indian leadership at the time, and, hence, they gave charge of the NEFA to Gen. B.M. Kaul (a cousin of the PM).[42] In Parliament, if Nehru was to show how the Indian government had set up a large number of forward posts as blue pins on the map, they'd certainly be able to silence the Opposition and the public opinion. However, as military men say, the McMahon Line cannot be defended by 'sitting on it'. Perhaps this is the thinking that led them to design and execute the disastrous Forward Policy, which eventually gave the Chinese an excuse to launch a full-scale attack in 1962.

Let us understand what this controversial Forward Policy was and who really was responsible for devising it. Speaking of the time when Nehru proposed it, Gen. Kaul has stated that Nehru was being subjected to mounting criticism for allowing Chinese incursions and was anxious to show results without going to war, which would appease the media and the people. On 2 November 1961, in a meeting attended by Defence Minister Krishna Menon, Foreign Secretary M.J. Desai, Intelligence Bureau Chief B.N. Mullick and Gen. P.N. Thapar, while studying the map of the Chinese incursions, Nehru declared that whoever succeeded in establishing a post would establish control over that territory, as possession was nine-

[41]Ibid. 69.
[42]Ibid.

tenths of the law.[43] Gen. Thapar informed the PM that India would not be able to match the Chinese pace in inducting more posts and maintaining them. After further discussion, the PM allegedly developed this new policy based on his own assumptions that China was unlikely to wage war on India and, thus, there was no need to have a battle of wits with them. He recommended erecting and maintaining a few of our posts in the Indian territory (not disputed) and that if the Chinese advanced in one place, we should advance in another.[44] Although there is no record of the Defence Committee of the Cabinet having a hand in this decision, it is very hard to believe that such a policy proposed by the PM would have been put in place without the agreement of our top army officers. What transpired was that India set up a post in a sensitive, disputed area that the Chinese had refused to concede to us on more than one occasion. This triggered the Chinese to counter the Indian forestall and, in frustration, launch a combustible situation in October 1962. This policy led several scholars to argue that 'It was Nehru, not the Chinese, who declared war.'[45]

Not only did we make mistakes with our military and diplomatic strategy but also the battle of narratives. On establishing a number of forward posts, Nehru had boasted, 'It would be wrong to call them check-posts and they were in fact military outposts.'[46] The Chinese seized this off-the-cuff remark and provided evidence that India had built 43 'strong points', signalling an intention to launch an attack against them. Technically, these posts were militarily useless. They were nothing but flag-posts and were easily overrun by a well-prepared and advancing Chinese army.[47] However, in the international community, it was India that came

---

[43]Ibid. 70.

[44]Ibid.

[45]Rautela, Parakram, 'It Wasn't China, but Nehru Who Declared 1962 War: Australian Journalist Neville Maxwell', *The Times of India*, 2 April 2014, https://tinyurl.com/ykevfdz8. Accessed on 22 November 2023.

[46]Dalvi, Brig. J.P., *Himalayan Blunder: The Curtain-Raiser to the Sino-Indian War of 1962*, Natraj Publishers, Dehradun, 1969.

[47]Ibid.

across as the aggressor and China that was compelled to defend itself against India's advanced war preparations. In addition to these grave mistakes, the attitude of the men involved remained questionable at best. The Border Roads Organisation, which was created in 1960 to build roads in these terrains, had Gen. Kaul as a permanent member of the board in his private capacity—a position he continued to hold even after being promoted from quarter master general to chief of general staff. Defence Minister Menon, along with his aides, also made play of the expansion of our ordnance factories, assembly of aircraft and other major projects. Menon deliberately kept the private sector out of defence production despite India being critically short of most essential items of equipment.[48]

☙

In May 1962, Mullick provided two important, alarming reports that should have been a dire warning for the Indian PM. One was that 'the Chinese had made up their minds to attack India and were giving out propaganda feelers'[49] and the other that Pakistani President Ayub Khan was considering a grand strategy to force India to cede Kashmir via an onslaught on the western border while the Chinese were attacking India in the north and east.[50] The prospect of a two-front war alerted the leadership, and the army headquarters decided to let the troops in western India stay in place instead of pulling them to the east and the north.

By mid-1962, the Indian Army was outnumbered in the Aksai Chin part of Kashmir by five to one, yet it was trying to staff 60 new forward posts. While the Indian soldiers were equipped with Lee-Enfield rifles that had first entered service in 1885, the Chinese had modern automatic weapons, artillery and other equipment. On 20 October 1962, China made two major simultaneous attacks

---

[48]Ibid. 77.

[49]Mullick, B.N., *The Chinese Betrayal: My Years with Nehru*, Allied Publishers, Bombay, 1971, pp. 332–3.

[50]Ibid.

on the border, 1,000 km apart. In the western part of the border, the People's Liberation Army (PLA) fought to expel the Indians from the Chip Chap Valley in Aksai Chin, whereas in the NEFA, they attacked near the McMahon Line.[51] Indian forces were quickly outnumbered and our 'posts' were conquered in a matter of hours, teaching us the valuable lesson that no nation should allow itself to fight a war for which it is not prepared. Despite reports from the ground that we were very underprepared (the Chinese soldiers had winter clothing and a supply depot immediately behind their frontlines while the Indian troops were dressed in summer uniforms and depended on airdrops for supplies),[52] Nehru and Menon ordered the army to move further and take control of the Thag La ridge.[53] The PLA took control of the border region near Bhutan in the NEFA and quickly drove the Indian Army south. At the same time, they swept the Indian Army out of Aksai Chin. Within eight days, the PLA forces overran all the posts established as part of the Forward Policy.[54]

On 24 October, the Chinese halted their offensive and offered India a three-point deal in a diplomatic gesture. The deal was: 1) India and China would agree to settle their dispute peacefully; 2) both would withdraw their troops to 20 km behind the previous Line of Actual Control (LOAC) along the McMahon Line; and 3) the two PMs would meet to negotiate a final border deal.[55] Nehru rejected this offer immediately.[56] In the meantime, the Soviets had cancelled their deal to supply MiG-21 aircraft to India, clearly indicating that they were siding with Mao[57] (despite the fact that

---

[51]Riedel, Bruce, *JFK's Forgotten Crisis: Tibet, the CIA and the Sino-Indian War,* HarperCollins India, Noida, 2015, p. 110.

[52]Ibid. 111.

[53]Ibid.

[54]Hoffman, Steven A., *India and the China Crisis,* University of California Press, 1990, p. 163.

[55]Riedel, Bruce, *JFK's Forgotten Crisis: Tibet, the CIA and the Sino-Indian War,* HarperCollins India, Noida, 2015, p. 119.

[56]Ibid.

[57]Ibid. 120.

Nehru's family friend and international fugitive Jayanti Dharma Teja had made 14 trips to the Soviet Union during the 1962 War to seek their support against China, on Nehru's behalf[58]). The Soviet Union had failed India and so had the non-aligned world. But the Americans and the UK took another step forward towards India by playing a decisive role in forestalling a simultaneous Pakistani attack on India. President Kennedy and PM Harold Macmillan, on no uncertain terms, let Ayub Khan know that an attack from Pakistan on India would be perceived as hostile and inconsistent with SEATO and CENTO treaties.[59]

On 17 November, the PLA led another offensive attack and outnumbered the Indian troops by two to one. They took control of the entire Aksai Chin region of 14,380 sq. miles and appeared ready to move further towards the city of Leh.[60] On the east, the first blow came at Waling, and the entire western portion of the NEFA fell into Chinese hands. The Indian Army was so badly outnumbered that there were no reservists to stop the PLA from moving south into Assam.[61] All of the territory that Beijing had claimed was theirs in the eastern sector south of the McMahon Line. More than 32,000 sq. miles was lost to the PLA here.[62] In addition, there was very little resistance by the Indian military to prevent further Chinese advances. India was in shock seeing the speed at which the Chinese had taken over most of the NEFA. In his memoir, the US Ambassador Galbraith wrote that 'not only Assam but also Bengal and Calcutta were at risk'.[63] Nehru had accepted the situation, and this is evidenced by the conversation he

---

[58]Menon, Vandana, Raghav Bikhchandani and Humra Laeeq, 'How Nehru's Friend Jayanti Dharma Teja Went from Lutyens' Darling to International Fugitive', *The Print*, 12 March 2022, https://tinyurl.com/2jsn33k8. Accessed on 22 November 2023.

[59]Riedel, Bruce, *JFK's Forgotten Crisis: Tibet, the CIA and the Sino-Indian War*, HarperCollins India, Noida, 2015, p. 119.

[60]Ibid. 132.

[61]Ibid. 133.

[62]Ibid.

[63]Galbraith, John Kenneth, *Ambassador's Journal: A Personal Account of the Kennedy Year*, Houghton Mifflin, Boston, 1969, p. 434.

had with Mullick on 19 November, agreeing to an idea of people's resistance after the PLA takeover of Assam. In short, Nehru and his intelligence chief were fully expecting to lose control over all of the northeastern India, east of the Siliguri neck to China.[64]

Prime Minister Nehru's non-alignment policy fell flat like a house of cards as he began to feverishly negotiate with Washington and London for arms aid to tackle the Chinese threat. On the same day, in a last desperate attempt, Nehru is believed to have written two letters to President Kennedy. In the first one, he expressed gratitude for all the help from him since the PLA attack began on 20 October. He added, 'The Chinese are, by and large, in possession of the greater part of the North East Frontier Agency and are poised to over-run CHUSHUL in Ladakh. There is nothing to stop them [...] till they reach LEH, the headquarters of the Ladakh Province of Kashmir [...] we are facing a grim situation in our struggle for survival....'[65] He further demanded 'air transport and jet fighters [...] to stem the Chinese tide of aggression' in the letter, adding that '[a] lot more effort from both of us and our friends will be required to roll back this aggressive tide'.[66] Nehru's second letter was hand-delivered to President Kennedy on the same evening, wherein he wrote, 'Within a few hours of dispatching my earlier message of today, the situation in the N.E.F.A. Command has deteriorated still further ... [T]he entire Brahmaputra Valley is seriously threatened and unless something is done immediately to stem the tide, the whole of Assam, Tripura, Manipur and Nagaland would also pass into Chinese hands.'[67] Nehru added that the Chinese had massive forces north of Sikkim and Bhutan, and another invasion from that direction appeared imminent. He wrote, 'The situation is really desperate. We have to have more

---

[64]Mullick, B.N., *The Chinese Betrayal: My Years with Nehru*, Allied Publishers, Bombay, 1971, pp. 434–5.

[65]JFKNSF-111-016-p0018, India: Subjects: Nehru Correspondence, November 1962: 11-19, Papers of John F. Kennedy, Presidential Papers, National Security Files, John F. Kennedy Presidential Library and Museum, Boston, USA, p. 10.

[66]Ibid.

[67]Ibid, p. 18.

comprehensive assistance if the Chinese are to be prevented from taking over the whole of Eastern India.'[68] And suddenly, on the morning of 21 November, the Chinese government declared that a unilateral ceasefire along the entire Sino-Indian border would begin within 24 hours and that the Chinese forces would withdraw to positions 20 km behind the LOAC between China and India. This meant that China was unilaterally imposing the settlement offer they had made to Nehru even before the war in 1959—that China would keep Aksai Chin and the strategic inhabited land to the west of Ladakh and, in the eastern part of India, retain its claim to the NEFA.

However, as the heady days of war ended, the Western powers asked India to 'renew efforts to settle the Kashmir issue'.[69] It was no secret that since Pakistan was their creation, they were committed to maintaining a power balance between Indian and Pakistan.

∽

Even though, right from the first few days of the war, it became absolutely clear that with the existing army troops, we would get completely wiped out by the Chinese, the PM didn't sanction the use of the Indian Air Force until China threatened to take over our entire Northeast and Ladakh. While it may be understandable that he hesitated putting the full force of the Indian Armed Forces in the eastern and northern areas, leaving the western border vulnerable to a Pakistani attack, he could have certainly realigned his strategy once he has assurance from President Kennedy and PM Macmillan that they had thwarted Ayub Khan's plans. However, the PM was unfortunately ill-advised. Consider the people around him who were making critical decisions in the war—all of them were his family and friends. The Indian ambassador to the US, Braj Kumar, was his cousin, defence Minister Krishna Menon was his friend, Gen. Kaul was another cousin of his and the person who advised

[68]Ibid.
[69]Riedel, Bruce, *JFK's Forgotten Crisis: Tibet, the CIA and the Sino-Indian War,* HarperCollins India, Noida, 2015.

him to trust Mao, Vijayalakshmi Pandit, was his sister. Obviously, he had left no place in his inner circle for realistic, neutral and difficult advice.

The use of the Indian Air Force at strategic points in the war could have been a game changer. India has a natural advantage, which is the fact that the slope of the Himalayas is gentler on the Indian side, whereas the slopes are rather steep on the Chinese side. This makes it more convenient for the Indian Air Force to deploy aircraft as compared to the Chinese. The Nehru government perhaps understood the strategic importance of deploying aircraft, which is why, in his second desperate letter to President Kennedy, he had requested 'a minimum of 12 squadrons of supersonic all-weather fighters'.[70] He had noted that India's only hope was to counter the Chinese gains on the ground with the use of airpower, but India lacked 'air and radar equipment to defend against the retaliatory action by the Chinese'.[71] Nehru had added in his letter:

> The United States Air Force will have to man these fighters and radar installations while are personnel are being trained ... The US Fighters and transport planes manned by the US personnel will be used for the present to protect our cities and installations. American pilots and fighters would assist the Indian Air Force in air battles with the Chinese air force over Indian areas.[72]

To summarize, in his letter, Nehru essentially asked for some 350 combat aircraft and crew, 12 squadrons of fighter aircraft with 24 jets in each and two bomber squadrons. At least 10,000 personnel would be needed to staff and operate the jets and provide radar support and conduct logistical support for the operation.[73] Of course, if the Indian Air Force shared the task with the Americans, the American numbers would come down, but it would still be a

---

[70]JFKNSF-111-016-p0018, India: Subjects: Nehru Correspondence, November 1962: 11-19, Papers of John F. Kennedy, Presidential Papers, National Security Files, John F. Kennedy Presidential Library and Museum, Boston, USA, p. 19.
[71]Ibid.
[72]Ibid.
[73]Ibid.

substantial force. It is understood that around this time, Nehru wrote similar letters to PM Macmillan too; the latter makes a reference to them in his memoirs, recalling them as 'agitated'.[74]

Essential learnings and observations emerged after India's first two wars, both of which we did not win—these helped frame our military strategy for decades to come. In the first India–Pakistan War in Kashmir, where India fought to push back the Pakistani tribesmen and recapture Indian territory in 1947–48, in what could have been a decisive victory, the Indian military efforts were halted when we were at a point-of-strength as PM Nehru withdrew and referred the matter to the UN. During the second war, which was the Sino-Indian War of 1962, India was not adequately prepared, yet took actions that forced the Chinese to launch an offensive. These are crucial lessons for us as a country; however, they came at a huge cost. We ceded miles and miles of sovereign Indian territory to the aggressors. We let Pakistan take control of about 30 per cent of our land in Jammu and Kashmir, and China another 15 per cent. India's crown had been significantly mutilated due to the mistakes of a few.

We may recall that recently, after the border incidents in Galwan and Tawang, the Modi government took immediate action by banning Chinese apps and making policy decisions that would need Chinese companies to declare their holding value if they wanted to operate in India or fund Indian companies. The PM also visited the regions of friction as a show of solidarity with the Indian Army's efforts to protect our border, sending a tough message that incursions of this nature will be dealt with at the highest priority. Despite the Chinese government's insistence that Indians treat these incidents as localized ones, Dr S. Jaishankar, India's external affairs minister, has made it clear that India–China bilateral relations cannot continue as they are in face of such border aggression. When China renamed 11 places in Arunachal Pradesh, India strongly rejected this claim. Home Minister Amit Shah also

---

[74]Macmillan, Harold, *At the End of the Day, 1961–1963*, Harper and Row, London, 1973, p. 229.

visited a village that was one of these 11 places and launched the Vibrant Villages Programme, sending a strong message that not even an inch of India's land is overlooked or dispensable. This approach is in total contrast with the Nehru government's tactic. In fact, back then, a government spokesman had even dismissed the claimed Aksai Chin territory and said that 'the entire area was a wasteland and not a blade of grass grows there'.[75]

---

[75]Dalvi, Brig. J.P., *Himalayan Blunder: The Curtain-Raiser to the Sino-Indian War of 1962*, Natraj Publishers, Dehradun, 1969, p. 44.

SECTION III
ECONOMY

6

THE BOMBAY PLAN

In the 1930s and the 1940s, when the whiff of Indian independence began to get stronger, the discussions on how India's economy should be once the British left began to take place. Economic issues took centre stage in Congress's discussions as well, and an economic programme was adopted in 1931, followed by an agrarian one in 1936.[1] In the Wardha session of the All-India Congress Committee (AICC) in 1937, a need for economic planning was brought up, followed by a resolution in favour of the same. The next year, in the Haripura session of the AICC, a resolution was passed to appoint a national planning committee under the chairmanship of Jawaharlal Nehru.[2] An advisory planning board set up by the interim government of 1946 was the successor of this National Planning Committee. While it was constituted in 1938, it took a whole decade to publish any research or even communicate its line of thought.

Meanwhile, a group of eight prominent industrialists, academicians, thinkers and technocrats—J.R.D. Tata, G.D. Birla, Sir Ardeshir Dalal, Lala Shri Ram, Kasturbhai Lalbhai, D. Shroff, John Mathai and Purushottamdas Thakurdas—collaboratively published a proposal in two parts in 1944 and 1945 titled 'A Brief Memorandum Outlining a Plan of Economic Development for India', also famously known as the Bombay Plan.[3] Over the

[1]Sanyal, Aman, 'The Industrialists behind India's First National Economic Plan', *Quartz*, 15 November 2018, https://tinyurl.com/5h5hxkwh. Accessed on 22 November 2023.

[2]Ibid.

[3]Chikermane, Gautam, *Reform Nation: From the Constraints of P.V. Narasimha Rao to the Convictions of Narendra Modi*, HarperCollins India, 2022, p. 43.

decades, many generations of experts have debated if the Bombay Plan was guided in anyway by the Nehru-led National Planning Committee, especially since parts of the plan had selectively made its way into the three subsequent Five-Year Plans of the Nehru government (1951–66). However, since there was no published material available by the National Planning Committee by the time the Bombay Plan was announced, it is now popularly believed that the Bombay Plan was an independent, original document versus a reactionary one. However, there certainly are two aspects that seem to have influenced this group of creators: first, their interactions, formal and informal, with the members of the National Planning Committee, which informed them of the government's plans for industrialization; and second, the violence unleashed after the Quit India movement pointing to the fact that the Nehru–Gandhi group of the Congress may be losing hold over the people. The first proof that this plan formed the basis of India's economic policy is the fact that many parts of it found space in the government's Statement of the Industrial Policy, 1945, and the first Five-Year Plan.[4] Regrettably, there were also significant parts that were left out. The second proof is that the Bombay Plan was influential in the creation of the Planning Commission.[5]

The Statement of the Industrial Policy, 1945, was indeed the first time that the federal British Indian government (akin to the central government of India today) intervened in matters of provinces. Until 1945, as per the provisions of the Government of India Act of 1935, industry and commerce were the domains of provinces. It would not be far from truth to say that the Statement of the Industrial Policy, 1945, on which subsequent economic policies have been based, had its roots in the Bombay Plan, which infused much needed intellectual vigour into India's economic discourse.

---

[4]Kudaisya, Mesha, 'The Promise of Partnership: Indian Business: The State, and the Bombay Plan of 1944', *The Business History Review*, Volume 88, Issue 1, 2014, pp. 97–131.
[5]H.V.R Iengar, 'A Look at the Bombay Plan in the Light of Today', *The Bombay Plan and Other Essays*, A.D. Shroff Memorial Lectures, 2, Lavani Publishing House, Bombay, 1968.

While critics of the plan have questioned how industrialists and senior executives would expect to form economic policies for the state, it is prudent to recollect that for countries like India, which got out of World War II and became newly independent, private enterprises simply did not have the resources to negotiate their future. Hence, they had to rely on the power of the State, which would inherently become the driver of the economy through its chosen policies and political will. Yet, even though there was a conflict of interest, it may be immature to assume that only profits motivated these folks to propose this exhaustive plan and wise to accept that these corporate leaders were equally passionate towards the cause of nation building as any other politician and civil servant. This is a stereotype that we see even today—that many a businesspersons provide policy suggestions, albeit driven by their own experiences, towards building a stronger, more resilient Indian economy. However, they almost always have been viewed from a distrustful lens.

So now, let us deep dive into what the Bombay Plan really was. It was divided into two parts. The first part essentially looked at wealth creation and the second, wealth distribution. With both parts, it is a truly exhaustive document with the following salient points which may be interesting to consider even today:

1. It envisioned doubling India's per capita income in 15 years.
2. It aimed for a minimum standard of living that would include food, clothing and shelter on the basic side and provisions for medical relief and education in addition. The plan goes into great detail to explain the steps that would be needed in each of the above, for instance, vaccinations and sanitation as well as structure of primary and secondary university and technical education in addition to scientific education and research.
3. It detailed designs for the country's infrastructure—transport and communication, railways, roads, shipping and so on.

4. It classified industries into two groups—basic and consumption goods. Basic goods included power (electricity); mining and metallurgy (iron and steel, aluminium, manganese); engineering (machinery and machine tools); chemicals (fertilizers, dyes, heavy chemicals, plastics, pharmaceuticals); armaments, transport (railway engines and wagons, ships, automobiles, aircrafts); and cement under the basic goods category. Consumption goods included but were not limited to textiles (cotton, silk, wool); glass; leather goods; paper tobacco; oil and so on.

5. The plan specified the need for small-scale industries as income generators but missed specifying details about their placement.

6. It contained a detailed section on India's financial health at the time while making no reference to foreign direct investment, clearly indicating the need to minimize it in order to boost local businesses/industry.

7. It laid the foundation for free enterprise and how it should be diverted towards ensuring collective good.

8. It also envisioned economic equality as a powerful tool for growth, and it is in this context that it suggested the idea of industry being controlled by the public sector. It states, 'Control by the State, accompanied in appropriate cases by State ownership or management of public utilities, basic industries etc, will also tend to diminish inequalities of income.'[6]

9. It strongly argued for a balance between economic freedom and state intervention to prevent abuse of that freedom.

10. It envisioned the role of the State as centred on ownership, control and management of economic enterprises, placing the highest emphasis on 'control', such that it explicitly clarified the role that private enterprises should play in delivering social welfare.[7]

---

[6]Thakurdas, Purshotamdas, et al., *Memorandum Outlining a Plan of Economic Development of India: Parts One and Two*, Penguin Books, India, 1945.
[7]Ibid.

Manmohan Singh, who also is looked upon as the architect of the economic liberalization reforms of the 1990s, along with P.V. Narasimha Rao and Atal Bihari Vajpayee, summarized it appropriately:

> The Bombay Plan laid great emphasis on public investment in social and economic infrastructure, in both rural and urban areas, it emphasised the importance of agrarian reforms and agricultural research, in setting up educational institutions and a modern financial system. Above all, it defined the framework for India's transition from agrarian feudalism to industrial capitalism, but capitalism that is humane, that invests in the welfare and skills of the working people. In many ways, it encapsulated what all subsequent plans have tried to achieve.[8]

The Plan caught popular interest instantly after publication, so much so that it became impossible for any major group to ignore. An author at the time had written, 'The reception accorded to the plan was unique. Within a few days of its publication the demand for copies was so great that it had to be reprinted for several successive months ... The plan has been translated in other languages than English for publication both in India and abroad and has been read by millions of people.'[9] While the British viceroy at the time, Viceroy Wavell, initially heaped praises and hailed the novel approach to the country's economic problems,[10] the stance of the British government changed as the British industry expressed concerns on their continued businesses in and with India.[11]

The popularity of the plan was so high that the British Indian

---

[8]Singh, Manmohan, 'PM's Address at ASSOCHAM's JRD Tata Birth Centenary Celebration', *Former Prime Ministers of India*, 24 August 2004, https://tinyurl.com/2cubwn7x. Accessed on 22 November 2023.

[9]Lokanathan, P.S., 'The Bombay Plan', *Foreign Affairs*, 1 July 1945, https://tinyurl.com/mrwtky69. Accessed on 22 November 2023.

[10]Ibid.

[11]Correspondences in File 13 (2), Finance Department (1905–1947), National Archives of India, New Delhi, p. 45.

government made an active effort to delay its publication, so as to delay implementation, and came under attack. A journalist at the time examined:

> So widespread was the public interest stirred by the initiative of these private planners that for a while New Delhi tried to delay the publication of their report in an attempt to steal their thunder. Despite this, the sponsors succeeded in releasing the plan at an appropriate time and the report attracted considerable attention and aroused controversy shared strangely by the conservative British Government on one hand and the extreme left-wing elements on the other.[12]

Another reason why the Congress could not embrace the plan and had to pretend like it didn't exist was because

> [T]he closeness of Mr Birla to Mahatma Gandhi and a faction of the Congress remained a point of embarrassment and a reminder that the party was close to the industry and business. Congress as a party would like to wipe out these sources of embarrassment and distance itself from the Plan and its authors … the Congress was in a position where it could neither accept the Plan nor reject it. To be seen as towing the line of big industrial houses at this point would seriously damage its claims at home and abroad.[13]

While the Nehru government didn't publicly give the plan its due credit, some of its elements inevitably informed its future policies.

Sadly, as the politics of the day played out, socialism and wealth redistribution took centre stage and were selectively adopted, whereas the capability of private partnership in nation-building was desperately ignored. As Gautam Chikermane observed:

---

[12]Lokanathan, P.S., 'The Bombay Plan', *Foreign Affairs*, 1 July 1945, https://tinyurl.com/mrwtky69. Accessed on 22 November 2023.

[13]Sanyal, Amal, 'The Curious Case of the Bombay Plan', *Contemporary Issues and Ideas in Social Sciences*, June 2010.

However, while the First Five Year Plan in form seems like the Bombay Plan, it ran contrary to the spirit of the Bombay Plan, which lay in the idea of a partnership between state and business. As the Nehruvian regime secured political legitimacy through the national elections of 1952 and 1957, the autarchic features of economic policy-making became more pronounced. Private enterprise became increasingly wary and defensive, no longer looked upon by the state as stakeholders in nation-building. The promise of partnership receded, only to see a revival in the 1990s post-liberalization, when India faced the overwhelming challenges of integration into the global economy.[14]

---

[14]Chikermane, Gautam, *Reform Nation: From the Constraints of P.V. Narasimha Rao to the Convictions of Narendra Modi,* HarperCollins India, 2022.

7

NEHRUVIAN SOCIALISM

INDUSTRIAL POLICY RESOLUTION, 1948

Post the Bombay Plan of 1944–45 and the pre-Independence Statement of the Industrial Policy, 1945, the first major document outlining the newly formed government's economic policy was the Industrial Policy Resolution, 1948. This document was the final nail in the coffin that broke the relationship between Nehru and the private industry. But before we dive into the reasons behind it, let us look at why the core structure of the government that formed policies was dysfunctional and, in fact, counterproductive, so much so that it spun even the good ideas into rubbish.

As several intellectuals and economists have recounted time and again, Nehru, who shaped socialist policy after Independence, was greatly influenced by Fabian ideas, that is, gradual implementation of goals to implement socialism versus revolutionary means, which in turn were rooted in the traditions of English utilitarianism, empiricism and classical economic thought. After his visit to Russia in 1927, Nehru was euphoric. Observing how the Soviets managed the economy, he wrote, 'Russia thus interests us because it may help us to find some solution for the great problems which face the world today. It interests us specially because conditions there have not been, and are not dissimilar to conditions in India.'[1] But the political counterpart which went hand in hand with Fabian

---

[1] Mironov, Leonid, 'Nehru's First Visit to Soviet Union', *Mainstream*, Volume 46, Issue 47, 8 November 2008, https://tinyurl.com/4wtchaue. Accessed on 22 November 2023.

principles was the adoption of a parliamentary, constitutional democracy so that socialist legislation could be conceived. This is essentially the direction we see Nehru family-led Congress taking in crafting India's future.

In the 1940s, the Planning Commission was sketched out by London School of Economics alumni K.T. Shah, Gulzarilal Nanda and Shankarrao Deo. Their original vision was to have a body that would not only suggest which paths to take but also have the power to allocate resources and enforce its recommendations.[2] When this matter came up during one of the cabinet discussions, Sardar Patel opposed it, and, eventually, the Planning Commission found itself without enforcement powers. It also didn't have any resources that it could allocate and, hence, basically remained confined to being an 'advisory' body.[3] In addition, due to scarce resources to dispense in general, there was rivalry between administrative departments, which played out especially in the developmental administrative machinery. As Taylor Sherman recounted in his book titled *Nehru's India*:

> In New Delhi, individual ministries not only refused to cooperate with the Planning Commission, but also held the purse strings. As a result, separate divisions of government gathered their own data, set their own targets and allocated funds through ad hoc bargaining. In the context of scarcity, the planning dynamic between the centre and the states was tense and complex. In the first two plans [Five-Year Plans], the planning commission tried to incentivise states to raise revenues themselves and to fund their own plan projects ... Rather than raising revenues, however, states tended to run up debt to pay for projects with matching central grants. Because they were able to raise less revenue, poorer states fared worse

[2]Newbigin, Eleanor, 'Accounting for the Nation, Marginalizing the Empire: Taxable Capacity and Colonial Rule in the Early Twentieth Century', *History of Political Economy* Volume 52, Issue 3, 2020, pp. 455–72.

[3]Chibber, Vivek, *Locked in Place: State-Building and Late Industrialization in India*, Princeton University Press, Princeton, New Jersey, 2003.

under this system, increasing inequalities between states. The predominant dynamic within government was one of suspicion and competition over scarce resources, rather than of collaboration, let alone widespread coordination towards a since purpose [development].[4]

However, we see the full force of Fabian–Nehruvian ideology trickle down in the consequent Five-Year Plans. In the second Five-Year Plan, the share of the public sector in total investment was estimated at 54 per cent, 58 per cent in the third and 63.7 per cent in the fourth.[5]

While nationalization was a small feature during economic discourse at the time, the seeds of it had already been sown into the Statement of the Industrial Policy, 1945. The 1945 policy had listed 'twenty industries that would be centralised, subject to consultations with the Provinces and leading Indian States'; these included iron and steel, automobiles and tractors, heavy machinery, cement, electric power and coal amongst others.[6] Subsequently, in January 1948, before the Resolution was declared, the Congress released a report prepared by their Economic Committee, which called for progressive nationalization of the Indian economy. The report was such a shock to the private sector that 50 of the country's most prominent industrialists convened a meeting in Bombay and voiced 'grave apprehensions' about the proposals enlisted in the Congress's report.[7] They warned that 'this kind of large-scale nationalisation would reverse the industrial progress achieved so far'.[8] Around the same time, Gandhi was assassinated and that took away a lot of public and media attention from the complaints of the

---

[4]Sherman, Taylor C., *Nehru's India: A History in Seven Myths*, Princeton University Press, Princeton, New Jersey, 2022.
[5]Bhagwati, Jagdish and Padma Desai, 'Socialism and Indian Economic Policy', *World Development*, Volume 3, Issue 4, 1975, pp. 213–21.
[6]Chikermane, Gautam, *Reform Nation: From the Constraints of P.V. Narasimha Rao to the Convictions of Narendra Modi*, HarperCollins India, 2022, p. 60.
[7]*The Times of India*, 3 February, p. 1, cited in Sherman, Taylor C., *Nehru's India: A History in Seven Myths*, Princeton University Press, Princeton, New Jersey, 2022.
[8]Ibid.

industrialists. However, despite that, the report managed to cause a storm big enough for the Nehru government to drop its hard stance.[9] It is in this context that the 1948 Resolution should be looked at. The final 1948 Resolution published by the Government of India in April that year reserved only three areas of economic activity for the exclusive purview of the State: defence, railways and atomic energy.[10]

Another key problem with the Resolution was that the government felt comfortable using excessive control on businesses as a tool to curtail economic freedom. While the 1948 Resolution followed the post-War reconstruction trends then prevalent in the West, it missed out on one major difference—that the West as well as its opponent, the Soviet Union, went about their government-led, government-managed reconstruction on the strength of affordability. However, India had to operate from a position of poverty. While adopting a policy that mindlessly mimicked economic giants without comparable financial, institutional or human capital to manage, it showed an acute lack of political and intellectual grasp on the part of the Nehru government. Writer Gautam Chikermane draws an analogy for the situation stating, '[I]t's like a weakling attempting to lift a mace, which would obviously crush the lifter.'[11]

The Resolution set a condescending tone towards entrepreneurs and businessmen with the live threat that they could be nationalized anytime of the government's choosing while also maintaining an ivory-tower view that if that were to happen, the businesses should consider it a favour by the government. Here are the exact words from the 1948 Resolution to this effect:

> The Government would always have the power to take over any industry vital for national defence. While the inherent right of the State to acquire any existing industrial undertaking

[9]Chibber, Vivek, *Locked in Place: State-Building and Late Industrialization in India*, Princeton University Press, Princeton, New Jersey, 2003.
[10]Ibid.
[11]Chikermane, Gautam, *Reform Nation: From the Constraints of P.V. Narasimha Rao to the Convictions of Narendra Modi*, HarperCollins India, 2022.

will always remain, and will be exercised whenever the public interest requires it, Government have decided to let existing undertakings in these fields develop for a period of ten years, during which they will be allowed all facilities for efficient working and reasonable expansion. At the end of this period, the whole matter will be reviewed and a decision taken in the light of circumstances obtaining at the time.[12]

India had inherited a particular type of bureaucracy from the British Raj era, one that was able to carry out instructions while also maintaining a high-handed attitude towards the citizens. If the centre was to control critical industries efficiently, a new kind of bureaucracy capable of managing these State-run enterprises would be needed—one that would have the ability to make quick decisions, carry out flexible and complex operations, take risks and possess moral courage to resist political pressure. The new Indian bureaucrat would have to be honest enough to resist 'his pound of flesh' in every contract and truly run the enterprise like a good businessman. However, there was one big problem: there simply weren't enough civil servants with these qualities to take on this work. And what India ended up with was a huge variety of state-owned enterprises run by far-from-deft, overworked and underpaid civil servants, which eventually led to a handful of them wielding immense power as they monopolized control over State-run enterprises.

To understand the Congress's thinking as to why this was done, we must recollect that we were a newly free country. After many decades of being subservient to British masters, the politicians and the babus were finally in positions where they could wield immense, unquestioned power. This, combined with the fact that they overcompensated for their servile existence in the pre-Independence era by trying to control everything that mattered, made for a deadly combination for the private sector. As a result, the union government basically controlled every aspect of citizens'

---

[12]Resolution, Ministry of Industry and Supply, *The Gazette of India*, Government of India, 6 April 1948, Section 4, p. 534.

lives and, most certainly, any enterprise that generated wealth. And to make matters worse, all of this was done under the guise of 'public interest'. Private businesses struggled to stay afloat and were in apathy and despair. The government totally failed to recognize the contributory role of these entities, in multiplying and scaling industry, which would add up to the economic health of the country. The Industrial Resolution, 1948, essentially placed the union government at the core of economic activity and managing large enterprises (the list of which kept expanding for decades thereafter). What this led to was that government interference grew so large that it began to choke enterprises. This excessive State control led the politicians and bureaucrats, who had no business being in business, as they did not have the ability, experience or knowledge of the sector, to suddenly become bosses of industries and businesses.[13]

Now, let's get to the topic of strategic industries. It may be in the nation's interest to exercise government control on industries that are of strategic importance to the nation such as defence, energy, public transport, and so on. However, what the Industrial Resolution, 1948, did was that it infused these important industries with non-competent, entitled bureaucrats with little to no accountability, who were protected by permanent employment with inflation indexed pensions.[14] Instead of encouraging domestic manufacturers to build defence equipment, innovate and manufacture new railway apparatus or aircraft, India ended up importing all of the above along with other strategic products from foreign manufacturers.[15] Thereafter, for decades, with respect to most of the above sectors, India remained at the mercy of countries that could choose at any time to stop supplies, attach embargos and dictate speed of supplies of products vital for India's growth. In addition to these, the 1948 Resolution also placed 18 industries, including textiles,

---

[13]Chikermane, Gautam, *Reform Nation: From the Constraints of P.V. Narasimha Rao to the Convictions of Narendra Modi*, HarperCollins India, 2022.

[14]Ibid.

[15]Ibid.

sugar, tools, etc., under central regulation and added air transport as the exclusive monopoly of the State to the list of the already established three sectors—manufacturing of arms and ammunition; production and control of atomic energy; and railway transport.[16] Additionally, it identified six industries for which the State would be exclusively responsible for setting up new units: coal, iron and steel; aircraft manufacturing; ship building; telephone manufacturing; wireless apparatus (excluding radio receiving sets); and mineral oils.[17]

---

[16]Resolution, Ministry of Industry and Supply, *The Gazette of India*, Government of India, 6 April 1948, Section 4, pp. 533–8.
[17]Ibid.

8

LICENCE RAJ

For decades to come, several Bills, Acts and resolutions followed, which had the same anti-industry, anti-wealth and anti-entrepreneurship stance. To this extent, in 1949, the Nehru government put forward the Industrial Development (Regulation) Bill. Its initial drafts indicated that the central government would be able to direct firms' investment decisions, step in and manage firms or revoke licences when firms acted in a manner that, according to the government, was reducing the value of the venture.

This spooked the industrialists and businessmen, who then created a pressure group and ensured that the Bill was revised and watered down. They also went on an investment strike until the government committed to do so. The government caved in but a crocodile only goes so far from his waterhole. Therefore, while the Industrial Development (Regulation) Act, 1951, was cut down from its original, which included rather dangerous and ambitious powers over businesses, the final version too required large enterprises to acquire a range of permissions, licences and permits if they wanted to continue doing business in India while retaining a few levers by which the government could potentially shape investment decisions. Under this Act, a licence was required to establish a new industrial unit, increase production or even change location of business. This, combined with the complex web of further controls, resulted in the creation of a vast, power-wielding bureaucracy that tended to get the job done when pressed and courted by middlemen. Such a web of bureaucracy was spun that when a production unit needed to obtain a licence or a permit, the businessmen would have to go through a control officer, assistants and inspectors at every level. Now imagine this ecosystem for each permit to be acquired: mountains of forms would need to be submitted by businesses only to remain in compliance. For instance, a single mill in Bombay had to fill out approximately 577 forms each year. Year on year, more State control took ground.

In 1955, the AICC, at its Avadi session, committed itself to pursuing a 'socialistic' pattern of society.[1] To justify themselves and to pacify the already cross business community, then Minister of Revenue and Civil Expenditure M.S. Shah told them that 'the field left open to the private sector was a vast one'.[2] He also made assurances that the Government of India would encourage and assist private enterprise during the second Five-Year Plan (which certainly did not happen).[3] So miffed was the private sector that Nehru had to assure India's most influential industrialists that 'for the private sector, planning would not be so precise and definite' while also urging them to 'make themselves part of the plan', to coordinate their efforts with the government's and above all, 'to think what is good for the people as a whole'.[4] While this sounded fabulous ideally, in reality, what it meant was that companies were simply not left alone. The government expected to exhort an extremely high tax from them, so that the wealth collected in the government's coffers could be redistributed. The government also expected the companies to look after the welfare of their employees and designed interventionist labour laws, which eventually ended up increasing inequality.

The idea that government revenue should be increased through high taxation on businesses had been on the Nehru government's radar since the interim government of 1946. To prod businesses

---

[1]Chikermane, Gautam, *Reform Nation: From the Constraints of P.V. Narasimha Rao to the Convictions of Narendra Modi*, HarperCollins India, 2022, p. 81.
[2]*The Times of India*, 15 February 1955, p. 4, cited in Sherman, Taylor C., *Nehru's India: A History in Seven Myths*, Princeton University Press, Princeton, New Jersey, 2022.
[3]Ibid.
[4]Sherman, Taylor C., *Nehru's India: A History in Seven Myths*, Princeton University Press, Princeton, New Jersey, 2022, p. 97.

to do so, they had established the Income Tax Investigation Commission. While the Commission did its work, the government simultaneously ran 'disclosure drives'. Three years later, in 1950, *The Times of India* reported that there was 'no evidence' that the drive had attracted any cooperative response.[5] Where there was no willingness to cooperate, the Income Tax Investigation Commission undertook 'dramatic raids on businesses and private residences, carrying away cartloads of materials to sift through to make its case'.[6] The tax structure was so unfriendly to businesses that companies tended to hide their income by opening a large number of subsidiaries for a short time, closing them again while shifting money through these, maintaining false account books and resorting to under-invoicing and fictitious entries, thus making the commission's investigation exhausting and, in most cases, non-conclusive.[7]

Frustrated, in 1955, the government decided to hire an expert to advise them on how the tax base may be expanded. This tax expert was Nicholas Kaldon, famous for his work on wealth redistribution at Cambridge University. After spending two months studying the field, Kaldon recommended that the government move away from high-income taxes and moderate taxes that could be levied on a broader base of people. He recommended that the top rate of income tax should be lowered to 45 per cent from the existing appalling 80 per cent.[8] However, over the next two years, the Nehru government, under Finance Minister T.T. Krishnamachari, introduced a bunch of new taxes that included, but were not limited to, an excess dividends tax, a bonus tax, a wealth tax, a

[5] *The Times of India*, 25 October 1950, p. 5, cited in Sherman, Taylor C., *Nehru's India: A History in Seven Myths*, Princeton University Press, Princeton, New Jersey, 2022.

[6] Shankar, T.R., 'Handling the Tax Dodger–The Tughlakian Way', *Economic and Political Weekly*, Volume 1, Issue 25, 18 June 1949.

[7] Sherman, Taylor C., *Nehru's India: A History in Seven Myths*, Princeton University Press, Princeton, New Jersey, 2022, p. 98.

[8] Ibid.

capital gains tax, an expenditure tax and a gift tax.[9] This was the final nail in the coffin for India's upper and middle class. Not only did the government completely ignore Kaldon's recommendation of slashing the top rate of income tax to 45 per cent but let it stay at 80 per cent in addition to the others.[10] So crushing was this blow for businesses that new forms of tax evasions spawned as the government clearly began to look at wealth creation as a pie, from which it would take the largest chunk.

The Industrial Policy Resolution, 1956, followed, which continued to increase and justify the involvement of the State in business. It classified industries in to three categories: ones whose future development would be exclusively the responsibility of the State; ones that would be progressively State-owned and in which the State would take the initiative to establish new undertakings while also expecting private industry to supplement efforts of the State; and ones whose future development would be left to the private sector.[11] From the six industries that were identified in the 1948 Resolution, for which new units would be set up only by the State, the list of industries was expanded threefold in the 1956 Resolution, totalling 18 sectors.[12] By 1959, India had over 50 entities that were State-run and whose management arrangements were absolutely baffling, ranging from banks, statutory corporations, control boards, commodity boards, boards with commercial functions, limited companies, cooperatives and companies running on an operating-contract system. These complex, opaque establishments ran a gamut of industries ranging from finance to fertilizers and hotels to antibiotics.[13]

While this licensing structure got overly complicated and burdensome for business entities, there emerged little evidence

---

[9]Ibid.

[10]Ibid.

[11]'Industrial Policy Resolution', *The Gazette of India: Extraordinary*, Part I– Section I, Cabinet Secretariat, Government of India, 30 April 1956, pp. 137–44.

[12]Ibid.

[13]Sherman, Taylor C., *Nehru's India: A History in Seven Myths*, Princeton University Press, Princeton, New Jersey, 2022.

that the licensing was successful in bending them to the wishes of the government.[14] Loopholes emerged. Firms applied for multiple, overlapping licences to increase their chances of success, making it impossible to gauge how much investment was really planned.[15] Even though one of the stated aims of this overwhelming licence raj structure was that it would allow the government to distribute businesses through the country and correct for concentration of industry in particular areas, a great number of licences were, in fact, doled out to already industrialized states.[16] For businesses, obtaining a licence to start a new undertaking did not guarantee that all the other requirements would be lined up for the licence holder. Many projects stalled at the point of obtaining foreign exchange, for which the licence had to be obtained from another authority. Within this confusing, tangled system, corruption reigned. Instead of a scientific approach to the allocation of licences, industrialists pushed their contacts in the government to obtain licences. Middlemen with 'connections in New Delhi' emerged as go-to people for business to ease the licencing burden.[17] The way the system operated basically boiled down to this: '[A] licence was only a permit which entitled the holder to apply for numerous other sanctions and permissions.'[18]

In 1966, the Government of India employed the services of Rabindra Kishen Hazari, an economics professor (who later became deputy governor of the Reserve Bank of India only to be fired during the Emergency due to his non-compliance with

---

[14]Chibber, Vivek, *Locked in Place: State-Building and Late Industrialization in India*, Princeton University Press, Princeton, New Jersey, 2003, pp. 136–42, 155–7.

[15]Das Gupta, Chirashree, *State and Capital in Independent India: Institutions and Accumulations*, Cambridge University Press, New Delhi, India, 2016.

[16]Banerjee, Debdas and Anjan Ghosh, 'Indian Planning and Regional Disparity in Growth' *Economy, Society and Polity: Essays in the Political Economy of Indian Planning in Honour of Professor Bhabatosh Datta*, Oxford University Press, New Delhi, 1988, pp. 104–65.

[17]Arthagnani, 'Growth of the House of Birlas: Lessons for Licensing Policy', *Economic and Political Weekly*, Volume 2, Issue 16, pp. 748–50.

[18]Sherman, Taylor C., *Nehru's India: A History in Seven Myths*, Princeton University Press, Princeton, New Jersey, 2022.

Sanjay Gandhi's Maruti project) to enquire into the working of the licencing structure. As he went about understanding and breaking down the complex web, Hazari explained in his findings in 1967 that 'applications went through multiple agencies' where they were considered and reconsidered 'without improving the feasibility of the projects concerned'. Those in the licencing authority and correlated departments worked 'without clear and definite criteria' by which to judge each application. And with so many applications sloshing around the system, and so many different offices that had to review them, 'even the authorities concerned were not fully aware of the total investment and foreign exchange commitments of licences issued or those under implementation at any particular period of time.'[19] Overall, Hazari concluded that the success of licencing in channelling investment appeared to be 'extremely doubtful'.[20]

Now let us look at some statistics that prove that this licence raj arrangement had begun to choke business enterprise. A total of 10,016 business licences were issued between January 1956 and December 1966; 7,477 applications were rejected.[21] Notably, between 1956 and 1960, the number of licences granted tripled from 585 to 1,890. However, in the following six years, it fell from 1,388 in 1961 to 423 in 1966—a 70 per cent drop from 1961 and 28 per cent lower than the number in 1956.[22] The fall in the grant of licences signifies the long-term negative impact that the licence raj had begun to have on the industry.

---

[19]Hazari, R.K., *Industrial Planning and Licensing Policy*, Interim Report to Planning Commission, University of Bombay, Bombay, 1966, https://tinyurl.com/yc8xvavx. Accessed on 29 November 2023; Hazari, R.K. *Industrial Planning and Licensing Policy*, Final Report, Planning Commission, Government of India, 1966.
[20]Ibid.
[21]Dutt, S., *Report of the Industrial Licensing Policy Inquiry Committee*, Main Report, Department of Industrial Development, Ministry of Industrial Development Internal Trade and Company Affairs, New Delhi, July 1969, p. 45.
[22]Chikermane, Gautam, *Reform Nation: From the Constraints of P.V. Narasimha Rao to the Convictions of Narendra Modi*, HarperCollins India, 2022, pp. 85–6.

INDIRA'S SOCIALISM

On Nehru's passing, the reins of government passed on to Lal Bahadur Shastri for a short period of time, followed by the former's daughter Indira Gandhi. Now, it may be critical here to recollect that Indira was inexperienced, hadn't really held any important portfolio in the government or proved her mettle to qualify as the PM of India. Just the fact that she was Nehru's daughter was enough to get the senior Congress leadership to rally behind her. When she took over command in 1966, her inexperience began to manifest in dangerous ramifications for the Indian economy.

Worried that she may be just a temporary puppet in the hands of Congress leaders, she schemed with her closest coterie to carve out a niche, for which she may become a cult personality. Therefore, on the advice of P.N. Haksar, her principal secretary, she sought to mark her own identity by presenting herself as a socialist.[23] In May 1967, she presented a 10-point programme of reform to the party, which included the 'social control' of banking, the abolition of privy purses of princes and guaranteed minimum wages for rural and industrial labour.[24]

Here, let us go back into the history of the policy for labour equality in her father's era. From pre-Independence times, Indian statute books have had plenty of legislation for improving lives of workers. This body of legislation encompasses several sectors, ranging from factories, mines, plantations, transport and commercial establishments and consist of rules for wages, safety welfare and social security (including maternity compensation). There were even special Acts that provided for the protection of children and relief from indebtedness and predatory contractors.[25] However, after 1947, a plethora of new laws were passed. According to the data from Ministry of Labour and Employment, by 1961,

---

[23]Guha, Ramchandra, *India after Gandhi: The History of the World's Largest Democracy,* Pan Macmillan India, 2007, p. 433.

[24]Ibid.

[25]Ministry of Labour and Employment, 'Appendix 1: List of Labour Acts', *Employers' Obligations,* Government of India.

there were about 30 new laws at the central level and about 82 in various states.[26] The basic gist of these laws was that the private sector was entrusted with the responsibility of improving the lives of Indians. However, a closer look at the operations of individual companies in the private sector presented a disturbing situation— that these enlisted legislative benefits were mostly doled out to higher-ranking employees, skilled employees and middle-level management. For the rest of the working-class folks, industries would mostly just erect *bastees* (informal settlements) where conditions were extremely unhygienic and poor. In conclusion, what the unnecessarily complex legislation on labour laws achieved was a more differentiated workforce with an intricate arrangement of privileges.[27] And eventually this led to counterproductive effects, that is, increased inequality. Sadly, Indira's socialist bent was equally counterproductive for India. In fact, on problems of landless labour as well as of the public sector losing money, she defended herself by saying, '[T]he public sector didn't need to make money since it was building a base for economic development.'[28] Ironically, absolving herself of all blame with regard to the injustice to labour, Indira, in her 1968 Independence Day speech, singled out 'industrialists and businessmen' who spoke of worker indiscipline while continuing to 'make big profits and draw fat salaries'.[29]

Between 1951 and 1979, India's economy grew at a snail's pace of 3.1 per cent annually. On 6 June 1966, Indira took the drastic step of devaluing the Indian rupee by a sharp 57 per cent in order to counter India's significant balance of payments crisis.

[26]Sherman, Taylor C., *Nehru's India: A History in Seven Myths*, Princeton University Press, Princeton, New Jersey, 2022, p. 99.

[27]Ahuja, Ravi, 'A Beveridge Plan for India? Social Insurance and the Making of the Formal Sector', *International Review of Social History*, Volume 64, Issue 2, 2019, pp. 207–48.

[28]Guha, Ramchandra, *India after Gandhi: The History of the World's Largest Democracy*, Pan Macmillan India, 2007, p. 434.

[29]*The Years of Challenge: Selected Speeches of Indira Gandhi—January 1966–August 1969*, second edition, Publications Division, New Delhi, 1985, pp. 25–8, 34–9, 172–4, 268–9.

The rupee fell from 4.76 per US dollar to 7.50 per US dollar. Due to India's alienation of foreign investments and neglect of the exports sector, there were constant trade deficits. The devaluation aimed to boost exports amid limited access to foreign exchange. Instead, it accelerated inflation and drew criticism. Despite that, Indira thought that it was in her best interest politically to promote nationalization. Indian industry was continuously undermined due to a spate of government actions in that era, which included, but were not restricted to, nationalization of banks in 1969; nationalization of coal mines in 1971, 1972, 1973 and 1974; nationalization of general insurance in 1972 and enacting Foreign Exchange Regulation Act in 1973. As Gautam Chikermane puts it, 'The Nehru–Gandhi ideological stronghold on the economic freedom of India, at a time when it needed it the most, bordered on the criminal.'[30]

When questioned in Parliament on the fact that the public sector was not making money, she had replied, '[I]t did not need to, since it was building a base for economic development.'[31] The fact that her policies created a troublesome impact on the Indian economy began to catch the public eye. Historians have liberally written about how frustrated Indira was in the period between 1968 and 1969, noting that 'she was not strong enough to defy the Congress organisation and not rash enough to quit'.[32] She was obviously on the lookout for opportunities where she could exert more power. Such an opportunity presented itself when Dr Zakir Husain passed away in the middle of his term as the president of India. While the Congress wanted to field their own man, N. Sanjiva Reddy, Indira decided to put her weight behind V.V. Giri, with whom she enjoyed very good relations. In an effort to further her control over the party, she decided to make the struggle for political control over the Congress into an ideological one. This

---

[30]Chikermane, Gautam, *Reform Nation: From the Constraints of P.V. Narasimha Rao to the Convictions of Narendra Modi*, HarperCollins India, 2022.
[31]Vasudev, Uma, *Indira Gandhi: Revolution in Restraint*, Vikas Publishing House, New Delhi, 1974, p. 502.
[32]Ibid.

was followed by several missteps in that direction, the first of which was the nationalization of 14 major banks. When Finance Minister Morarji Desai disagreed with the move because he believed that the State's takeover of the banks would reduce the resources available for economic development and increase bureaucracy and red tape, she relieved him of his post. On All India Radio, she justified her decision by stating that India was a young democracy and had to remain vigilant to prevent the domination of a few of over the social, economic and political systems.[33] Indira Gandhi used excessive economic control over businesses and industries to enhance her personal political fiefdom. Through industrial licensing, she harnessed the financial power of the private sector to aid her in sustaining her voting base. For instance, she got Gujarati oil barons to fund the Congress Party's 1974 election campaign in Uttar Pradesh in exchange for industrial deregulation.[34] She used money from the nationalization of commercial banks for the establishment and expansion of protected industries, an act that was very attractive for her voter base. On returning to power in 1980, she nationalized six additional banks and further tightened import controls. In combination with the US policy of isolating India, the country was driven into absolute economic isolation. As Prof. Aravind Panagariya wrote, 'By the mid-1970s, India's trade regime had become so repressive that the share of non-oil, non-cereals imports in GDP fell from an already low 7 per cent in 1957–58 to 3 per cent in 1975–76.'[35] After her death, Rajiv Gandhi, too, continued on a spree of perverse policy-making by using too little of our rich labour and inefficient allocation of our poor resources.

[33]Zaidi, A. Moin, *The Great Upheaval, 1969–1972*, Orientalia India, New Delhi, 1972, pp. 103–6.

[34]Frankel, Francine, *India's Political Economy, 1947–1977*, Princeton University Press, Princeton, 1978.

[35]Panagariya, Aravind, 'India's Trade Reform', *Indian Policy Forum 2004– Volume 1: Editors' Summary*, edited by Suman Bery, Barry P. Bosworth and Arvind Panagariya, The Brookings Institution, Washington, D.C., 2004, https://tinyurl.com/25euvu4u. Accessed on 22 November 2023.

NEHRUVIAN SOCIALISM'S IMPACT ON EDUCATION

Many great minds in the field of economics have made parallels between a country's economic growth and literacy and education. After Independence, our leadership recognized the need for the country to be educated and wrote Article 45 into the Constitution, which makes it obligatory for the government to provide free and compulsory education for children up to the age of 14. They earmarked the year 1960 as the deadline for this countrywide school network to be set up. For the first few years, there persisted mostly disinterest on the part of the central government on fulfilling this responsibility.[36]

However, some southern states like Madras (presently Tamil Nadu), which, from pre-Independence times, had one of the most forward and elaborate education programmes, including the mid-day meals scheme. They had to be paused due to budget cuts during the War. In 1955, states took the initiative to relaunch the education system by building their own institutions. To fund this, they devised the innovate strategy of holding School Improvement Conferences, which were essentially crowdfunding opportunities for communities to come together and contribute towards their local schools. By 1955, they had held over 130 such conferences and had thus amassed huge contributions, which then funded construction and electrification of school buildings, provision of books, staffing, stationery and first-aid materials required.[37]

Let's take some data to illustrate the point. In 1949, India's literacy rate was 14 per cent[38] and, by 1961, it stood at only 28.3 per cent,[39] which was an increase only possible by local-level,

---

[36]Sherman, Taylor C., *Nehru's India: A History in Seven Myths*, Princeton University Press, Princeton, New Jersey, 2022, pp. 114–15.

[37]*National Seminar on Compulsory Primary Education, 23 January 1961 to 9 February 1961*, Ministry of Education, Government of India, pp. 37–8.

[38]'Efforts to Eradicate Illiteracy in India', *Ministry of Human Resource Development*, 1 September 2008, https://tinyurl.com/5av57e96. Accessed on 22 November 2023.

[39]Singh, Hemant, 'Census 2011: Literacy Rate and Sex Ratio in India Since 1901 to 2011', *Jagran Josh*, 17 October 2016, https://tinyurl.com/7ez2f34w. Accessed on 22 November 2023.

community efforts. While the Nehru government was desperate to meet the 1960 deadline set by the Constitution for fulfilling its responsibility of setting up schools, it could only organized the National Seminar on Compulsory Education in 1961. The seminar concluded that constructing or finding feasible buildings for schools countrywide would cost the centre ₹330 crore, which was termed by them as a 'colossal problem'.[40] The seminar had studied some of the models that states like Madras and some smaller districts had adopted and recommended that the whole country adopt this 'self-help model' to set up education systems. This recommendation of crowd-funding resources to set up basic primary education systems across the country found its way into the third Five-Year Plan. In 1964, the Kothari Commission was appointed, which recommended the introduction of a common public education system and a gradual increase in government investment in education from the then 2.9 per cent of GDP to 6 per cent by 1985–86.[41] None of these recommendations were heeded by the government.

As it became clear that the centre was not interested in funding primary education, the burden to educate their children fell on communities. Obviously, communities with greater literacy rates and funds had a better idea of how local schools should function and were able to collect resources for the same. Communities that had leaders 'with connections in New Delhi' were able to tap into programmes of the government for assistance.[42] However, India's most marginalized communities, which lacked resources or simply didn't know how to set up and run local schools, remained without such a primary school structure. There were also communities that desperately wanted to educate their next generation but were

---

[40] *National Seminar on Compulsory Primary Education, 23 January 1961 to 9 February 1961*, Ministry of Education, Government of India, p. 12.

[41] Meshram, Tanoj, 'In 75 Years, India's Education Policies Have Failed to Eradicate Inequality', *The Wire*, 21 August 2022, https://tinyurl.com/y8t6xvfs. Accessed on 22 November 2023.

[42] Subramanian, Ajantham, *Shorelines: Space and Rights in South India*, Stanford University Press, Palo Alto, 2009.

simply too poor to cough up the money to set up schools for themselves.

Economist Jagdish Bhagwati, who devised principles of rescuing India's economic downward trajectory (much of those which found space in policies in the 1991 reforms), and Prof. Aravind Panagariya have time and again articulated very clearly that it is indeed the glacial economic growth that was the reason for poor education and healthcare indicators. In their book *Why Growth Matters*, they stated, 'A lack of awareness of the importance of health and education or the absence of good intentions was not behind the slow progress in these areas. Instead...progress was inhibited by slow growth.'[43] Several other programmes—the National Education Policy (NEP) issued in 1986, Operation Blackboard in 1988, revision to the NEP in 1992—remained merely superficial changes. In 1994, the Government of India, with the help of funds from the World Bank, initiated the District Primary Education Programme (DPEP). However, it was an even bigger failure and became a smokescreen to hide the pitfalls of structural adjustment that India embarked on in 1991. It failed to meet even the lowered (compared to international benchmarks) expectations of minimum levels of learning. In fact, the effect was counterproductive because the DPEP damaged the Indian education system by lowering the quality and stature of teachers by hiring temporary para-teachers and encouraging substandard alternative schools.[44]

Today, we see the Congress take great pride in the fact that Nehru envisioned and set up Indian Institute of Technology (IIT). In his terms as the PM, he had set up five IITs, with a vision that these institutes would be cornerstones in building the industrial, scientific and technological support system of the nation. However, the reality was that, back in the day, in the absence of all-round

---

[43]Bhagwati, Jagdish and Aravind Panagariya, *Why Growth Matters: How Economic Growth in India Reduced Poverty and the Lessons for Other Developing Countries*, Hachette Publishers, New Delhi, 2013, p. 18.

[44]Kumar, Krishna, Manisha Priyam and Sadhna Saxena, 'Looking Beyond the Smokescreen: DPEP and Primary Education in India', *Economic and Political Weekly*, Volume 37, Issue 7, 2001, pp. 560–8.

primary education and lack of competitive job opportunities, these institutions essentially served the rich and the wealthy—families who could fund private education for their children and send them abroad. The much talked about 'brain drain'—the attrition of skilled scholars from India in the search for better, higher paying opportunities—seems to be catalysed by these institutions.

Even with the Right to Education reform in the 2000s during the United Progressive Alliance (UPA) eras, we still see the spillover effects in educational inequality. Private primary schools, which are concentrated in Tier I and II cities and demand higher fees, are the go-to centres for quality education. Primary schools remain run-down, understaffed and under-resourced, which aggravates the substandard quality of education for children of poor families.

P.V. NARASIMHA RAO'S ECONOMIC POLICIES

When PM P.V. Narasimha Rao came to power after Rajiv Gandhi's assassination, he inherited an economy that was in shambles. As per budget reports, the inflation rate stood in double digits at 16.3 per cent, second only to the highest ever number of 28.6 per cent in 1974 (during Indira's term). The annual GDP growth rate was just 1.2 per cent. Almost half the population was under the poverty line, spending less than $1.90 per day in purchase power parity terms. Worse, life expectancy remained at 58 years as compared to the global average 65 years.[45] However, it was at this point that the World Bank and the International Monetary Fund (IMF) stepped in, cajoling PM Narasimha Rao and Finance Minister Dr Manmohan Singh to change India's approach to pro-market and pro-free trade. Several reforms for liberalization were announced, which opened the Indian economy to the world and put the country on a systematic path of growth.

Unfortunately, after announcing the reforms, Dr Singh was reprimanded by the Congress and had to take the flak for it at a

---

45'India Life Expectancy 1950–2023', *Macrotrends*, https://tinyurl.com/msp4ddyk. Accessed on 30 November 2023.

Congress meeting eight days later for his departure from the party's socialist agenda.[46] These reforms also led to a rift between the party and Narasimha Rao. There was so much bad blood between them that despite the PM overseeing transformational reforms for India, when he died, Sonia Gandhi didn't even allow for his body to enter 24 Akbar Road, the Congress Party headquarters (customary for all senior party leaders). When the body reached the gate of 24 Akbar Road, she refused to give the order to open the gate.[47] She also insisted that the funeral take place in Hyderabad instead of in Delhi, going against the norm held for previous PMs. Despite meting out this kind of treatment, the Congress now tries to take credit of the 1991 reforms and, in turn, Rao's legacy.

[46]Vikraman, Shaji, '25 Years On, Manmohan Singh Has a Regret: In Crisis We Act. When It's Over, Its Back to Status Quo', *The Indian Express*, 24 July 2016.
[47]Sitapati, Vinay, *Half Lion: How Narasimha Rao Transformed India*, Penguin Viking, India, 2016.

9

SCAMS AND SCANDALS

The pattern of siphoning money off government coffers is alleged to have first started under Nehru's prime ministership.[1] Over the years, it has been reported that over ₹4,800 billion have been looted from the Indian treasury by politicians of the INC.[2] In the 75 years of independent India, the country has had a Nehru–Gandhi family member or chosen man in the PM's post for 53 years. So, wouldn't it be natural to attribute this loot to the Nehru–Gandhi-led Congress Party? While there have been innumerable scams of all sizes, which continue even today in the Congress-led states, in this section I'd like to talk about some of the biggest scams which rocked the nation.

JEEP SCAM, 1948

The Jeep Scam was the first scam to come into the public eye after India's independence. Krishna Menon, Nehru's friend and India's high commissioner to the UK (a post he had lobbied to Mountbatten for, in exchange for 'convincing' Nehru on sensitive topics during the latter's viceroyalty) purchased 2,000 refurbished Jeeps for the Indian Army.[3] The Jeeps and the spare parts were to be

---

[1]Sharma, Vibha, 'BJP Targets Nehru, Rakes Up "Jeep Scandal of 1948"', 28 May 2017, *The Tribune*, https://tinyurl.com/3hnun74r. Accessed on 24 November 2023; Aitharaju, Ved, 'The First Corruption Scandal of India', *Medium*, 6 October 2020, https://tinyurl.com/7zdcx2ez. Accessed on 24 November 2023.

[2]Biswas, Sayantani, 'BJP Releases "Congress Files" ahead of 2024 Polls, Says "They Looted ₹48,20,69,00,00,000..."', *Mint*, 2 April 2023, https://tinyurl.com/2hwzu5zk. Accessed on 24 November 2023.

[3]Ray, Jayanta Kumar, *India's Foreign Relations, 1947–2007*, Taylor & Fracis, New Delhi, 2011.

delivered immediately since India was in the midst of the 1947–48 Indo-Pak War in Kashmir. Because the need was urgent, normal procurement procedure was not observed. The Jeeps were to be delivered by a company called M/s Anti-Mistantes (which had paid-up capital of only £605) at a price of £300 per vehicle, which would total up to £600,000.[4] Menon devised suspicious terms for the deal, in which he agreed to pay 65 per cent of the money for the jeeps on inspection, 20 per cent on delivery and the remaining 15 per cent a month after delivery. He also clarified that only 10 per cent of the jeeps that are totally delivered will be inspected. This meant that after inspecting only 10 per cent of the refurbished jeeps, a payment of US $172,000 was made. After the payment, only 155 out of 2,000 Jeeps arrived, which were in such a bad condition that the Ministry of Defence refused to accept them. As the first consignment was rejected, there was no further supply from M/s/ Anti-Mistantes, despite advance payment having being made for all 2,000 Jeeps.[5]

Now, the need for Jeeps for the Indian Army was still standing, and Menon signed another contract with a new company called S.C.K. Agencies for 1,007 Jeeps at a higher price of £458.10 (as compared to £300 offered by Anti-Mistantes). The delivery terms were that 68 Jeeps would be delivered monthly.[6] When questioned about onboading a new company, Menon explained that since these companies were only delivery agents, he got S.C.K. Agencies to agree to pay the ₹1.9 million owed by the old supplier to the Indian government. However, only 49 Jeeps were supplied over two years by S.C.K. Agencies, and no money was compensated to the Indian government.[7] Nehru not only forced the Indian government to accept the substandard Jeeps sent by Anti-Mistantes but also refused to demand a resignation from Menon. There was a huge

[4]Ibid.

[5]Bhargava, G.S., *India's Watergate: A Study of Political Corruption in India*, Arnold-Heinemann Publishers, New Delhi, pp. 198–201.

[6]Ray, Jayanta Kumar, *India's Foreign Relations, 1947–2007*, Taylor & Fracis, New Delhi, 2011.

[7]Bhargava, G.S., *India's Watergate: A Study of Political Corruption in India*, Arnold-Heinemann Publishers, New Delhi, pp. 201–2.

uproar over this issue, and various reports such as the *First Report of the Estimates Committee, 1950–51*; *Ninth Report of the Public Accounts Committee, 1954*; *Fourteenth Report of the Public Accounts Committee, 1954*; as well as the Congress Party Parliamentary Committee 1951 report, indicted Krishna Menon.[8] Despite this, Nehru inducted him into the union cabinet on 3 February 1956 and later made him the defence minister in 1957.

In a rather abhorring revelation, it came to light that Krishna Menon was being groomed by the KGB to perpetrate Soviet propaganda in India. In fact, so much was the involvement of the Soviet deep state in India's affairs that Krishna Menon orchestrated the shift of India's arms imports from the West to the Soviet Union during his tenure. In the summer of 1962, Krishna Menon also dubiously changed his decision to purchase British Lightnings and bought MiG-21s instead due to the KGB's active-measures operations.[9]

MUNDHRA SCANDAL, 1958

The Life Insurance Company (LIC) was nationalized in 1956 on the grounds that it wasn't managed well. A Calcutta-based businessman, Haridas Mundhra, lobbied then Finance Minister T.T. Krishnamachari to purchase shares worth ₹1.24 crore across six troubled companies owned by him. On the instructions of the finance minister, the LIC bypassed its own investment committee to do so. In turn, Mundhra bled these companies dry, manipulated their share prices and forged share certificates.[10]

The issue was first brought to light by the media, after which it was raised in Parliament by Indira's estranged husband and MP Feroze Gandhy (later Gandhi), who produced the confidential

---

[8]Ray, Jayanta Kumar, *India's Foreign Relations, 1947–2007*, Taylor & Fracis, New Delhi, 2011.

[9]Andrew, Christopher and Vasili Mitrokhin, *The Mitrokhin Archive II: The KGB in the World*, Penguin Random House, UK, 2005, p. 315.

[10]Tyabji, Nasir, 'Chapter 6', *Forging Capitalism in Nehru's India: Neocolonisation and the State 1940–1970*, Oxford University Press, New Delhi, 2015.

correspondence between T.T. Krishnamachari and the then finance secretary. This led to a nationwide furore, after which Nehru prepared to set up a one-person commission headed by Justice M.C. Chagla to look into the charges, if at all it became evident that there was a prima facie case in the first place. However, as the scandal grabbed more headlines, Mundhra was sentenced to 22 years in prison and T.T. Krishnamachari resigned as the finance minister, not without aggressively justifying his actions that he only forced the LIC to buy these shares in order to 'stabilize the markets'.[11]

TEJA SCANDAL, 1966

Jayanti Dharma Teja was a scientist and shipping magnate who enjoyed a very close relationship with the Nehru–Gandhi family.[12] He was first introduced to Nehru at a high-profile party in Delhi as someone who had returned to India after pursuing a prestigious scientific career abroad. He instantly became a part of Nehru's close group of businessmen to the likes of J.R.D. Tata, G.D. Birla and Ramkrishna Dalmia. Teja promised Nehru to revolutionize the Indian shipping industry, for which he was given a huge loan of ₹20 crore.[13] It may be interesting to note that so far, Teja had no demonstrable experience or even any particular interest in shipping. As per a report, when the loan was requested, Nehru had allegedly instructed his cabinet, '*Thoda kuch de do*', and the little something translated into the Indian government investing ₹20 crore as 'loan' to him.[14] Teja brought on board Dutch engineers and the Japanese giant Mitsubishi, and, by late 1962, Jayanti

[11]Ibid.

[12]Menon, Vandana, Raghav Bikhchandani and Humra Laeeq, 'How Nehru's Friend Jayanti Dharma Teja Went from Lutyen's Darling to International Fugitive', *The Print*, 12 March 2002, https://tinyurl.com/2jsn33k8. Accessed on 24 November 2023.

[13]Ibid.

[14]Kidwai, Rasheed, 'Jayanti Dharma Teja: Nehru-Era Crony Capitalist India Chased across Three Continents', *India Today*, 2 March 2021, https://tinyurl.com/ye229ep5. Accessed on 24 November 2023.

Shipping controlled 40 per cent of India's shipping.[15] Following the success, Teja made attempts to diversify into the thermal power industry but failed. He and his business partners in Jayanti Shipping Corporation absconded, evading taxes worth crores of rupees, leading the Indian government on a wild goose chase around the globe to recover the money.[16] Even as this went on, Teja's relationship with the Nehru–Gandhi family grew stronger; in fact, he was entrusted with top-secret diplomatic missions. On one such crucial mission, he was sent to Russia some 14 times during the 1962 Indo-China War to seek support against China and press the Soviets for timely delivery of the MiG-21s.[17] He failed at both. Teja had also bragged about funding Sanjay's and Rajiv's education in the UK as well as their living expenses.[18]

It is believed that after Nehru's death in 1964, he lost his pull with Lal Bahadur Shastri (who, as Nehru's junior, would comply with his instructions), and an inquiry against him for evasions first started during this time.[19] In 1966, Indira continued to investigate Jayanti Shipping's affairs and the Shipping Corporation of India, and the inquiry was headed by Shastri's private secretary. However, it soon became clear that the laundering was so extensive that even

[15]Menon, Vandana, Raghav Bikhchandani and Humra Laeeq, 'How Nehru's Friend Jayanti Dharma Teja Went from Lutyen's Darling to International Fugitive', *The Print*, 12 March 2002, https://tinyurl.com/2jsn33k8. Accessed on 24 November 2023.

[16]Kidwai, Rasheed, 'Jayanti Dharma Teja: Nehru-Era Crony Capitalist India Chased across Three Continents', *India Today*, 2 March 2021, https://tinyurl.com/ye229ep5. Accessed on 24 November 2023.

[17]Menon, Vandana, Raghav Bikhchandani and Humra Laeeq, 'How Nehru's Friend Jayanti Dharma Teja Went from Lutyen's Darling to International Fugitive', *The Print*, 12 March 2002, https://tinyurl.com/2jsn33k8. Accessed on 24 November 2023.

[18]Kidwai, Rasheed, 'Jayanti Dharma Teja: Nehru-Era Crony Capitalist India Chased across Three Continents', *India Today*, 2 March 2021, https://tinyurl.com/ye229ep5. Accessed on 24 November 2023.

[19]Menon, Vandana, Raghav Bikhchandani and Humra Laeeq, 'How Nehru's Friend Jayanti Dharma Teja Went from Lutyen's Darling to International Fugitive', *The Print*, 12 March 2002, https://tinyurl.com/2jsn33k8. Accessed on 24 November 2023.

Indira as the PM wasn't going to be able to protect her family friend.[20] He was a symbol of wealth and privilege, and Indira, to carve out her socialist image, needed to distance herself from him. He had projected himself as a diplomat, and the Indian government had to send telegrams across Europe to clarify that he was not an accredited diplomat and that if he uses the charge that he was on a diplomatic mission to the UK, he would be doing so to avoid arrest. The problem here was that Teja was allowed to hobnob with powerful world leaders on Nehru's behalf and strike diplomatic deals. It was only when the tax evasion figures came to light that he lost favour and was stripped of his powers. More importantly, this goes to show how Nehru had built an extensive, unofficial network with the likes of Teja to cut deals around the world,[21] putting India's reputation at stake when these 'assets' went rogue.

MARUTI SCAM, 1974

The Indian government first began to think of developing an affordable people's car in 1959, and, to advance this thought, formed two committees in 1959 and 1960. These committees, under the chairmanship of L.K. Jha and G. Pande, were to assess the feasibility of such a project and if such an inexpensive passenger car could be produced.[22] The committees made recommendations that included taking foreign technical and manufacturing assistance since the existing Indian auto-manufacturing industry did not have the capacity or scale. However, due to the crunch in foreign exchange, the government

---

[20]Kidwai, Rasheed, 'Jayanti Dharma Teja: Nehru-Era Crony Capitalist India Chased across Three Continents', *India Today*, 2 March 2021, https://tinyurl.com/ye229ep5. Accessed on 24 November 2023.

[21]Menon, Vandana, Raghav Bikhchandani and Humra Laeeq, 'How Nehru's Friend Jayanti Dharma Teja Went from Lutyen's Darling to International Fugitive', *The Print*, 12 March 2002, https://tinyurl.com/2jsn33k8. Accessed on 24 November 2023.

[22]Celestine, Avinash, 'The Origins of the Indian Small Car Dream', *The Economic Times*, 31 March, 2011.

stalled the idea. Meanwhile, Sanjay Gandhi, Indira's younger son who had a passion for automobiles, set his eyes on the project. He had been able to use his family friend and international fugitive Jayanti Dharma Teja's relationship to bag a three-year apprenticeship at Rolls Royce in London.[23] He left it midway and returned to India. He revived the project to produce the affordable Indian car. By then, the committees had estimated a demand of 50,000 cars per annum and suggested that they should be priced at ₹6,000 per unit. At first, on Krishna Menon's insistence, it was agreed that the car would be made in Indian defence-material manufacturing factories. But after Sanjay arrived in India in 1968, he was able to influence the government decision on where the car can be manufactured and got the law changed for the private sector to be allowed to manufacture them. Immediately on his return, he set up two private limited companies in quick succession. One was Maruti Technical Services Private Limited (MTSPL), which was registered on 19 November 1970 with a paid-up capital of ₹200. The other was Maruti Motors Limited on 4 June 1971. The MTSPL, of which Sanjay and Sonia Gandhi were the first and permanent directors, was responsible for rendering the technical know-how for a sum of ₹5 lakh and a technical fee of 2 per cent on the net sales of the cars to be made by Maruti Motors Limited.

Thus, proposals were sought for the best price and quality for a small Indian car, to which 13 manufacturers, both Indian and foreign responded. Among Indian firms, Hindustan Aircraft, the public company, was said to have had the most attractive proposal. Among the rest, Renault had proposed to make the car at a price of ₹11,190 and Toyota at ₹6,000. Sanjay threw into the mix the proposal from Maruti Motors Limited, matching the Toyota price of ₹6,000. His quote was based on a suspicious prototype he had developed with a car mechanic he had come across called Arjun

---

[23]Menon, Vandana, Raghav Bikhchandani and Humra Laeeq, 'How Nehru's Friend Jayanti Dharma Teja Went from Lutyen's Darling to International Fugitive', *The Print*, 12 March 2002, https://tinyurl.com/2jsn33k8. Accessed on 24 November 2023.

Das.[24] It was said that since this was to be a completely indigenous car, the parts would have to be Indian. Sanjay didn't have those and had instead arranged for two engines to be smuggled into the country to fit into the prototype, the specifications of which were listed by the Government of India. Since he didn't even have the indigenous engines, an accurate estimation of the cost of the car was impossible to arrive at.

What happened next was a blatant abuse of the system. Bypassing all requirements, Maruti Motors Limited, which had no prior experience of building a car, a working prototype or even a tie-up with a reputed car maker, was given the contract and an exclusive production licence. The Opposition called out this act as one of nepotism and disgrace, as a 22-year-old with no manufacturing experience and declared income as ₹748 for the year 1969–1970 was duly granted the manufacturing licence in a cabinet discussion presided over by his mother, thus making him the head of a huge car manufacturing industrial complex involving an investment of $10 million.

After being criticized by Parliament, media and the public at large, the Congress and the MTSPL showcased the test model of the car, which was so bad that it angered the people even more. However, with the help of Bansi Lal, Congressman and then CM of Haryana, Sanjay was able to procure land in Gurgaon to build a factory at a throw-away price of ₹10,000 an acre when the rate was ₹35,000.[25] The land he had bought was agricultural land next to an airfield as well as an air force ammunition dump. Both these factors would have made it impossible for the land to be set up for an automobile manufacturing unit. Conveniently, then Defence Minister V.C. Shukla moved both the airfield and the air force ammunition dump out of the area, so that Sanjay's plan could move

---

[24]Suryesh, Saket, 'The Making of Maruti: A Sordid History of Congress Scams', *OpIndia*, 29 December 2018, https://tinyurl.com/mprc7emd. Accessed on 24 November 2023.

[25]Kapoor, Coomi, *The Emergency: A Personal History*, Penguin Books, New Delhi, 2015, p. 209.

forward without any hindrance.[26] The government had acquired the land from the farmers who were given barely eight hours to file grievances or raise objections. In November 1972, after raising funds via dealerships, Sanjay declared that the prototype was ready and had increased the quoted price from ₹6,000 rupees to ₹11,300 rupees. Government banks that were nationalized by Indira gave loans to Sanjay's companies to the amount of ₹7.5 million, with significantly reduced interests and no collateral. Deputy director of the RBI R.K. Hazari, along with the chairman of Central Bank, Dharam Vir Taneja, raised an alarm of unaccounted loans being given to Sanjay, refusing to give him any more money. Both were dismissed from their posts by Indira during the Emergency. The governor of the RBI, S. Jagannathan, too, was removed and so was the chairman of the SBI, both of whom had resisted the demands of overdrafts and further loans, and were replaced by more compliant folks within the ecosystem.

The engine issue of the prototype remained a problem, and so, the consultant company MTSPL imported refurbished Perkins and Ford engines as well as refurbished old rollers and sold them to Maruti Motors Limited as new. And then the period of the Emergency came, where Sanjay temporarily redirected his attention to politics. After the Emergency, the Congress lost the general elections to Janata Dal, and Maruti was liquidated in 1977. Crores of rupees from the public exchequer had gone into supporting Sanjay's venture, and yet, no people's car was made available. *India Today* ran a piece that read, 'Maruti Ltd turned out to be a huge land grab and financial scam...a sycophantic loan mela by nationalised banks, extortion and blackmail to squeeze funds from business groups and traders. Bankers, cabinet ministers and captains of industry who opposed or resisted Sanjay's muscle-flexing were sent packing.'[27] A commission headed by Justice A.C.

---

[26]Gandhi-Mody, Priyam, 'Opinion | Indian Prime Ministers and Cases of Corruption: Nehru and the Birth of Scams', *News18*, 13 August 2023, https://tinyurl.com/59578ak7. Accessed on 23 November 2023.
[27]Sethi, Sunil, 'If Sanjay Gandhi Had Lived', *India Today*, 9 December 2016, https://tinyurl.com/5n9754bd. Accessed on 24 November 2023.

Gupta was set up to investigate the Maruti scandal. In its report released on 31 May 1979, it was stated:

> The affairs of Maruti [Companies] ... appeared to have brought about a decline in the integrity of public life and sullied the purity of administration. From the interest taken in Maruti's progress by men from the Prime Minister's Secretariat and the way even matters connected to the country's defence were subordinated implicit obedience, one is left in no doubt as to the origin of the power that made such a state of affairs possible. Sanjay Gandhi exercised only a derivative power; its source was the authority of the Prime Minister.[28]

BOFORS SCANDAL, 1987

In 1985–86, it came to light that agents during the Indira Gandhi regime had allowed for a bribe in the purchase of German Howaldtswerke-Deutsche Werft AG (HDW) submarines, amounting to 7 per cent that is, ₹330 crore (₹7,000 crore in today's calculation) of the total amount. These agents also made concessions in the technical specifications and requirements in the submarines mandated by the Indian Navy. For example, the Indian Navy needed submarines whose diving depth was 350 metres, but the HDW submarines could only achieve a diving depth of 250 metres. The cost of the submarines mysteriously increased to ₹465 crore as well. Such a sudden rise pushed then Defence Minister V.P. Singh to order that attempts be made to renegotiate the price and bring it down, since it was clear that the Germans were overcharging. In a response to his order, the Indian ambassador in Germany clarified that the HDW officials were unwilling to renegotiate the price since the 7 per cent commission given to Indian agents was included

---

[28]Sethi, Sunil and Prabhu Chawla, 'Maruti Commission Report Documents the Story of Sanjay Gandhi's Dream of Building an Automobile Empire Gone Awry', *India Today*, 22 January 2015, https://tinyurl.com/2cyusjpx. Accessed on 24 November 2023.

in the full cost and already paid. This submarine purchase deal carried over to Rajiv's tenure and, despite all the efforts of his party and ecosystem to paint him as the honest technocrat thrown into the corridors of power, he seemed adept at playing the power game just like previous members of his family. As the HDW submarine scandal broke, V.P. Singh ordered an inquiry into the accusations of Indians having taken a 7 per cent commission. This led to differences between him and Rajiv Gandhi, and the former had to resign from the union cabinet within three days of the investigation being ordered.

Around the same time, the Indian Army was looking to acquire field guns that could neutralize the fleet of F-16 fighters, which Pakistan had acquired from the Americans. A committee under the then defence secretary S.K. Bhatnagar was formed to identify manufacturers that could deliver the same. AB Bofors (Sweden) and Sofma (France) were shortlisted by this committee. The Army then chose Bofors after further evaluation, post which negotiations for the purchase of 400 155-mm Howitzer guns began on 13 December 1985. Even before the official negotiations began, Arun Nehru was speaking closely with the Swedes to work out the deal. However, suddenly, in July 1985, Rajiv pulled him out of the talks. Nehru testified this information to the Central Bureau of Investigation (CBI), stating, 'In July 1985, Rajiv Gandhi told me not to bother futher about the Swedes and that he would deal with Mr Palme [then PM of Sweden].'[29] A little over a year later, on 23 March 1986, these negotiations concluded, and within 24 hours, the Rajiv Gandhi government endorsed the recommendation, finalizing the procurement. On 18 March 1986, the Rajiv Gandhi government signed a ₹1,437 crore procurement contract with the Swedish arms company called AB Bofors for the supply of 400 155-mm Howitzer guns for the Indian Army.

On 16 April 1987, about a year after the deal was signed, the

---

[29] Chowdhary, Neerja, *How Prime Ministers Decide: An Unprecedented, Explosive Look at How Decisions are Taken at the Very Top of the Indian Political Establishment*, Aleph Book Company, New Delhi, 2023, p. 148.

news that middlemen in India had been paid a large commission for this deal first broke on the Swedish national radio. Pressure built on Rajiv to investigate and name these middlemen and, perhaps in an instantaneous moment, he announced in Parliament that neither he nor anyone close to him had received any kickbacks for the Bofors deal. This outright lie was one that compromised him—no one had pointed fingers at him before his impulsive outburst.[30]

Meanwhile, the Indian ambassador in Sweden learned that even while the negotiations were ongoing with the two shortlisted companies (Sofma and AB Bofors) for the arms purchase, Rajiv Gandhi, while on a visit to Sweden to condole Swedish PM Olaf Palme's death, had assured the incumbent PM Ingvar Carlsson that the purchase order will go to the Swedish firm. This was eight days before the negotiations officially concluded and a purchase order was issued.[31]

As further pressure built, Rajiv Gandhi was forced to allow his government to press the Swedish government to conduct an investigation about the recipients of kickbacks given by Bofors were. However, Rajiv stalled this investigation by assuring the Swedish PM that Bofors had already clarified that no money was paid to middlemen in India, and, thus, no investigation was necessary. On Rajiv's insistence, the Swedish government stalled the inquiry. However, as pressure continued to mount on Rajiv, he accused people of his own party of conspiring with 'international forces' to bring down his government, using the Bofors deal as an excuse. Following this, he expelled several Congress leaders who had begun to point fingers at him from the party.

Meanwhile, further investigations and journalistic reports revealed that three firms had been paid in their Swiss bank accounts—two of which were owned by Hinduja brothers and one by Vin Chaddha.[32] It was the third firm, AE Services, owned by

[30]ABP News, 'Rajiv Gandhi And Bofors Scandal, An Unsolved Mystery | ABP News', *YouTube*, 12 May 2019, https://tinyurl.com/4n632zd9. Accessed on 24 November2023.
[31]Ibid.
[32]Chakravarty, Sayantan, Saba Naqvi Bhaumik and Farzand Ahmed, 'Bofors Case:

Vin Chaddha, which linked Rajiv and the Nehru–Gandhi family directly with this deal. The investigations and a personal diary of the CEO of AB Bofors eventually revealed that AE Services paid money to Ottavio Quattrocchi, an Italian businessman with close links to Sonia and Rajiv Gandhi. The two families were so close that even the children had reportedly grown up playing together.[33] Quattrocchi was stationed in India for several years before the Bofors deal and had been acquiring large government contracts, starting with fertilizers. By the time the Bofors deal was closed, it was well known in the corridors that Quattrocchi was the man for big-ticket procurements in the Rajiv Gandhi government. As the investigation continued and more and more details of the deal began to emerge, the public sentiment against Rajiv Gandhi grew. There was immense anger and slogans like, *'gali gali mein shor hai, Rajiv Gandhi chor hai'* and *'ab yeh spasht hai, Rajiv Gandhi bhrasht hai'* began to echo on the streets. Rajiv and the Congress lost the forthcoming elections due to this mass public anger. However, even after Rajiv's death, his wife Sonia Gandhi as well as the subsequent Congress governments reportedly went out of their way to protect Quattrocchi, whether it was by allowing him to leave India despite orders of his passport to be impounded, by hiding the fact that the Interpol had arrested him for weeks to win some state elections, or Priyanka and other family members meeting Quattrochhi's son at a party thrown by a Congressman.[34]

2G SPECTRUM SCAM, 2008

Second-generation (2G) spectrum is essentially a range of radio waves that are monitored, sorted into 'bands' by the government

---

CBI Files Chargesheet, Italian Businessman Ottavio Quattrocchi under Scanner', *India Today*, 24 January 2013, https://tinyurl.com/mrymp9pk. Accessed on 24 November 2023.

[33] Kidwai, Rasheed, 'Man Who Knew the Truth about Bofors', *The Telegraph*, 14 July 2013, https://tinyurl.com/y546ejuh. Accessed on 24 November 2023.

[34] Gandhi-Mody, Priyam, 'Indian Prime Ministers and Cases of Corruption', *News18*, 13 August 2023, https://tinyurl.com/yx245ayp. Accessed on 24 November 2023.

and managed by assigning the bands to different 'telecom circles' across the country. This means that for a company to provide telecom access across India, they would have to bid for a spectrum licence in the 22 existing bands. A spectrum is treated as a natural resource by the government and is typically auctioned to companies that then provide a number of services. The gist of the 2G scam is the misappropriation of kickback payments for these spectrum allocations made to the information technology (IT) minister A. Raja of the UPA era.

A. Raja became the union minister for communications and IT on 16 May 2007 in the Manmohan Singh cabinet. In order to make way for new players in the industry, A. Raja's ministry decided to grant new licences and allocate spectrum to new players in the market. The ministry reminded A. Raja that in addition to the cabinet decision of October 2008, the Telecom Regulatory Authority of India (TRAI) insisted on an auction to allocate spectrum to telecom providers. However, A. Raja stood firm in his wish to grant licences on the basis of a first-come-first-served policy, that is, those who paid the licence fee first would be allocated the spectrum. He also insisted that the spectrum should be allocated at the fixed price that was arrived at in 2001. This was already a problem since, in 2001, there were only 4 million mobile subscribers in India and, in 2007, at the time of the spectrum allocations, the number of subscribers had risen to 350 million. Obviously, there was room for the government to raise the price of the spectrum and, thus, make the allocation process competitive. A. Raja waited for telecom secretary D.S. Mathur to retire in order to begin the allocation procedure. When a compliant secretary (Siddharth Behura) took over, within 10 days, he issued a press release stating that the cut-off date for applications for spectrum allocations was brought forward by a week.[35] The press release also asked the new players to remit the fees (which typically ran in the range of ₹1,000–1,700 crore) within an hour, between 3.30 and 4.30 p.m., the same day. Nine

[35]Kumar, Sharad, '2G Spectrum Scam: Chronology of Events', *Economic Times*, 20 May 2011.

companies were able to remit these huge amounts at such short notice of barely 45 minutes from the time of the press release![36] Later, a Comptroller and Auditor General of India (CAG) report revealed that all these nine companies were aware that such a press release was to be issued and were ready with their demand drafts a few days prior to the release.

The two companies favoured by Raja—Swan and Unitech—were granted licences without seeking recommendations of the TRAI (which was the norm), among others.[37] Unitech, after allotment, formed eight companies. In order to help Unitech merge all of these licences and waive the mandatory three-year lock in period, an order was issued by Secretary Behura permitting them to do so. Raja also forced BSNL to enter into a memorandum of understanding with Swan (known as the Intra-Circle Roaming Agreement), by which Swan would be able to use all the infrastructure of BSNL. A week later, Swan entered into a deal worth ₹4,500 crore with the UAE-based Etisalat, giving the latter 45 per cent shares. Swan's shareholding pattern was dubious, as shares were held by a multitude of shell companies and also primarily by Anil Ambani, who then assigned his shares to Shahid Balwa and Vinod Goenka under Raja's instructions. Later, Swan allotted ₹380 crore worth of shares to a newly floated company called Genex Exim (which is believed to be a kickback from Swan to Raja).[38] The CAG report later revealed that of the 122 licences meted out by Raja, Swan (13), Unitech (22), Loop (21), Datacom (21), STel (6) and Allianz Infra (2) were illegal and not in accordance with the guidelines of the Department of Telecommunication.

This extensive, elaborate scam resulted in a loss of $25 billion

[36]'A Comprehensive Timeline of 2G Scam: How It All Started and as It Happened', *Swarajya*, 21 December 2007, https://tinyurl.com/5u9wj8yx. Accessed on 24 November 2023.
[37]'A Raja Threatened Staff to Favour Swan, Unitech: CBI', *The Indian Express*, 9 June 2011.
[38]'A Comprehensive Timeline of 2G Scam: How It All Started and as It Happened', *Swarajya*, 21 December 2007, https://tinyurl.com/5u9wj8yx. Accessed on 24 November 2023.

revenue to the Indian government.[39] A. Raja resigned when the scam came to light but the lost revenue never made it back into the Government of India coffers.

COMMONWEALTH GAMES SCAM, 2010

India was the host country for the 2010 Commonwealth Games (CWG). After the conclusion of the event in October 2010, the Central Vigilance Committee (CVC) unearthed a major financial scam. Even while the event was going on, allegations of corruption and mismanagement plagued the Organising Committee. The committee explained that 'since the target date was immovable, such delays could only be overcome by seeking, and liberally granting, waivers in laid-down governmental procedures. In doing so, contracting procedures became a very obvious casualty. Many contracts were then entertained based on single bids, and in fact, some of them were even awarded on nomination basis.'[40] Such liberties made the organizing committee eliminate competition and grant contracts to individual bidders. The truth is that they had more than enough time to plan in advance; the right to host the CWG in 2010 was awarded to Delhi in November 2003, a full seven years before the games were to take place. However, the organizing committee was registered only at the end of 2005.[41] The poor infrastructure as well as unexplained high prices paid for items like chairs, umbrellas and toilet paper led to a public outcry, after which the UPA government appointed a high-level committee to investigate the allegations. To give an example of exactly how severe the misappropriation was, one roll of toilet

---

[39]Sengupta, Subhajti and Suhas Munshi, '2G Scam Explained', *News18*, https://tinyurl.com/45dx35ys. Accessed on 24 November 2023; A Comprehensive Timeline of 2G Scam: How It All Started and as It Happened', *Swarajya*, 21 December 2007, https://tinyurl.com/5u9wj8yx. Accessed on 24 November 2023.

[40]Kumar, Naveen, 'Major Scams in India since 1947: A Brief Sketch', *Journal of Emerging Technologies and Innovative Research*, Volume 2, Issue 7, 2015, pp. 158–96, https://tinyurl.com/4zw3udpc. Accessed on 24 November 2023.

[41]Ibid.

paper was purchased at ₹4,000.[42] During the probe by CVC, the IT department, the CBI and the ED, it was found that Suresh Kalmadi, a Congress politician and member of the organizing committee, was at the helm of the financial fraud. Kalmadi had paid ₹141 crore to a Swedish firm to buy timing-scoring-result (TSR) systems. This amount was ₹95 crore more than what another bidder, MSL Spain, had offered for the same systems.[43] Kalmadi and his aide had eliminated the competition in return for kickbacks.

As the investigation in the financial misappropriations progressed, it was revealed that the CWG organizing committee had initially estimated a budget of ₹296 crore, but the final expenditure had amounted to ₹28,000 crore—100 times more than the budgeted amount![44] In its 700-page audit report on CWG 2010, tabled in Parliament on 4 August 2011, the CAG stated: 'The modus operandi observed over the entire gamut of activities leading to the conduct of the Games was: inexplicable delays in decision-making, which put pressure on timelines and thereby led to the creation of an artificial or consciously created sense of urgency.'[45] The CWG scam cost the country about ₹2,000 crore[46] and cases linked to the CWG scam are still pending in the courts and amount to over ₹700 crore.[47]

---

[42]'As Team India Shines in 2022, Read about the CWG Scam of 2010 Where One Toilet Paper Roll Was Purchased for Rs 4,000', *OpIndia*, 9 August 2022, https://tinyurl.com/9nennbef. Accessed on 24 November 2023.

[43]Ibid.

[44]Comptroller and Auditor General of India, *Report of the Comptroller and Auditor General of India for the Year Ended 31 March 2011 (Report No. 4) on XIX Commonwealth Games – 2010*, Government of the National Capital Territory of Delhi, 2011–12, https://tinyurl.com/4pzse2bw. Accessed on 24 November 2023.

[45]Kumar, Naveen, 'Major Scams in India since 1947: A Brief Sketch', *Journal of Emerging Technologies and Innovative Research*, Volume 2, Issue 7, 2015, pp. 158–96, https://tinyurl.com/4zw3udpc. Accessed on 24 November 2023.

[46]Ibid.

[47]Vasavda, Mihir, '10 Years on, CWG Mess: 50 Payment Cases, Rs 40-Crore Aerostat Idle', *The Indian Express*, 3 October 2020, https://tinyurl.com/572tnh52. Accessed on 24 November 2023.

AGUSTAWESTLAND HELICOPTER SCANDAL (CHOPPER GATE), 2013

Leading up to the year 2010, Indian officials and ministers were paid millions of dollars as bribe to purchase 12 AgustaWestland helicopters (AW101) for the use of top politicians from the manufacturing giant Finmeccanica at an estimated cost of ₹3,600 crore.[48] These helicopters were to be used to ferry VVIPs like the president, PM and others. The bribe amount totalled about $31 million as per the CBI.

In February 2013, Bruno Spagnolini, the CEO of AgustaWestland, was arrested by Italian authorities on the charges of the company bribing middlemen to secure a deal with the Indian Air Force. Italian prosecutors alleged that Ahmed Patel, Congress president Sonia Gandhi's then political secretary, received kickbacks from the deal.[49] The day following the arrest of Bruno Spagnolini, amidst protests from then Opposition parties, then defence minister A.K. Antony was forced to order a probe into the contract.

Accepting that corruption has taken place in the deal, Antony stated in March 2013, 'Yes, corruption has taken place in the helicopter deal and bribes have been taken. The CBI is pursuing the case very vigorously.'[50] However, after the scandal came into public domain, the UPA government cancelled the deal.

NATIONAL HERALD CASE, 2012

The *National Herald* was a newspaper started in 1938 by Jawaharlal Nehru and was published by Associated Journals Limited (AJL).

---

[48]Tripathi, Rahul, 'CBI Gets Michel Custody: Bank Linked to Payoff Taken Over, Account Details Are Missing', *The Indian Express*, 6 December 2018, https://tinyurl.com/4w8n9ta3. Accessed on 28 November 2023.

[49]Pubby, Manu, 'Does AP Mean Ahmed Patel, Asks Prosecutor in Italy Court; Middleman Says Don't Know', *The Indian Express*, 3 May 2016.

[50]A. Harikumar, 'Bribes Were Taken in the VVIP Helicopter Deal, Admits AK Antony', *India Today*, 25 March 2013, https://tinyurl.com/37hws2n5. Accessed on 24 November 2023.

The AJL was founded in 1937 with 5,000 freedom fighters as shareholders.[51] Apart from the *National Herald*, it published two other dailies—the *Qaumi Awaz* in Urdu and *Navjeevan* in Hindi. As a consequence of being founded by the top freedom fighters of the country, the *National Herald* acquired a reputation of being a legitimate voice of India's freedom struggle, thus becoming the most popular newspaper of the country in the years leading up to Independence. Nehru was the chairman of the board and frequently wrote strong-worded columns in it, as did other strong voices. The British government banned it in 1942, and the newspaper had to shut down. However, it restarted three years later. In 1947, after Independence, when Nehru became the PM, he resigned as the chairman from the board of the newspaper. The Congress continued to play a major role in shaping the newspaper's ideology and essentially controlled the information published. It also groomed several journalists and experts who would be loyal to the Congress ideology, as the paper continued to be funded by the party.[52]

In 2008, the newspaper ceased operations due to 'unavailability of adequate funds'. At the time of shutting down, the AJL owed the Congress an accumulated debt of ₹900 million.[53] In 2010, the Congress assigned this debt to Young India Private Limited, a not-for-profit company, newly created with Sonia and Rahul Gandhi as directors on the board and owning 38 per cent of it.[54] Another 24 per cent was owned by Congress leaders Sam Pitroda, Suman Dubey, Motilal Vora and Oscar Fernandes. Young India Private Limited acquired complete control over AJL and its real estate in Delhi, Mumbai, Lucknow and other cities. [55]

The matter is in the Supreme Court for hearing as it is alleged that the Gandhis used subterfuge to 'take over' assets worth millions

---

[51]Mateen, Zoya, 'Rahul and Sonia Gandhi: What Is the National Herald Case?', *BBC News*, 21 June 2022, https://tinyurl.com/5x46r98m. Accessed on 24 November 2023.
[52]Ibid.
[53]Ibid.
[54]Ibid.
[55]Ibid.

in a 'malicious manner'. The Congress maintained that the AJL became debt-free when it swapped its debt for equity and assigned shares to Young India Private Limited.

As with most scams, this case too is complex, making it difficult to gather complete evidence on the web of international networks involved, to even get a realistic estimate of the worth of assets being 'taken over'. However, the matter is currently sub-judice and, therefore, no conclusions can be arrived at with certainty.

THE GARIBI HATAO EYEWASH

If there is one campaign that marches ahead in terms of cheating, lies, amount of money looted, manipulation, deceit and outright misuse of government machinery for personal gain, it is Indira Gandhi's 'Garibi Hatao'. She coined this term sometime in 1970 when she had managed to split the Congress into two factions—her faction named Congress (R), where 'R' stood for 'requisitionist', and Congress (O), where 'O' stood for 'original'. The evidence lies in the data: despite running a high-decibel PR campaign on the slogan 'Garibi Hatao', the fact remains that the poverty ratio in India did not fall at all after 1947 until 1983.[56] More than half the population faced poverty.[57] Around the mid-1970s, India ranked 102nd among the nations of the world in terms of per-capita income.

The Garibi Hatao campaign first began when 14 banks were nationalized. While economists over the years have maintained that without accompanying measures to kickstart growth, it only remained a powerful political tool. Before 1969, banks were fiefdoms of big businesses and after nationalization, they became Indira's fiefdom. Let me explain: if Indira Gandhi's aim was to help the poor, she could have just ordered the banks to provide loans

---

[56]Bhalla, Surjit, *Not as Poor, Nor as Unequal, As you Think – Poverty, Inequality and Growth in India 1950-2000—for The Myth and Reality of Poverty in India*, Planning Commission, Government of India, 4 December 2003, https://tinyurl.com/w3vfzcre. Accessed on 24 November 2023.

[57]Chikermane, Gautam, *Reform Nation: From the Constraints of P.V. Narasimha Rao to the Convictions of Narendra Modi*, HarperCollins India, 2022, p. 138.

to them at lower rates and less collateral and offered government collaterals and government guarantees in cases of default. However, it seemed that her true motive behind the bank nationalization was to bankrupt the Opposition and cut off supply of funds, thus checkmating her political detractors. She justified her policies to be pro-poor and portrayed herself as a lone tigress standing up to big corporations. As a result, there was a wave of public affection towards her efforts. But her economic policies were such a failure that inflation stood at 34.7 per cent in 1974. At one point, the government attempted to lower market demand by freezing wages—an entirely anti-working class, anti-poor move. She kept looking to expand the public sector with increasingly strict regulation on the private sector, and almost completely rejecting foreign aid (which was coming at the cost of economic reforms). There was an extensive amount of policy and ideological confusion in 1973—the Indira government even took over the wholesale trade of food grains! The country panicked. Food stocks 'disappeared' and food trucks were looted. These shortages resulted in the need to import massive quantities of food grains, because of which cost of food went up, which hit the poor the most. Widespread labour and rural unrest against her began to grow, and this policy was reversed with haste.[58]

However, this didn't stop her from implementing her licence raj blackmail system even more forcefully. The permit-licence-quota raj was used to procure vast funds, on which Stanley A. Kochanek wrote, '[T]he period after 1969 was characterized by one member of the Indian parliament as the era of "briefcase politics", a phrase used to describe the transfer of vast amounts of black money in the form of cash into the coffers of the Congress party.'[59] Another description offered by C.S. Pandit states:

Often representatives of trade and industry were called up by

---

[58]Ghose, Sagarika, *Indira: India's Most Powerful Prime Minister*, Juggernaut Books, New Delhi, 2017, p. 148.
[59]Kochanek, Stanley A., 'Briefcase Politics in India: Congress Party and the Business Elite', *Asian Survey*, Volume 27, Issue 12, 1987, pp. 1278–301.

him (L.N. Mishra, foreign trade minister) to Delhi and asked to produce specified amounts. Those who declined were threatened with possible raids by people of the Revenue Intelligence and Enforcement Directorate, which are now operating under the Cabinet Secretariat. In Bombay financial circles stories started circulating of the amounts secured by the foreign trade minister under such threats. Others who came forward willingly with whatever was asked for, received concessions beyond their imagination to expand their business and amass further resources. A number of new stars were born on the industrial firmament of India during this time.[60]

Yet another description of the licence raj is offered by Indira's biographer Krishan Bhatia, who opined that donations had become more like extortions. He stated:

[T]he money that Indira's senior cabinet colleagues collected for the parliamentary elections in 1971 and state elections the following year allegedly amounted to millions of rupees and usually changed hands on the basis of a quid pro quo. At times, ministers deliberately talked about non-existent government plans to nationalize or regulate a particular industry or trade with the intention of creating nervousness among the people concerned. This naturally encouraged the flow of contributions, especially as the apparent threat ceased once the interest concerned had paid up.[61]

By the time the Emergency was imposed in 1975, Sanjay Gandhi had become the unconstitutional PM, the supreme authority of the country, with Indira rendered simply a figurehead, often indulging in Sanjay's illegal activities, excesses and loot. Wherever he went, people were allegedly forced to collect money and give purses. Millions of rupees were given to him in this way. This has been described by Kuldip Nayar perfectly in his book:

---

[60]Pandit, C.S., *End of an Era*, Allied Publishers, New Delhi, 1977, p. 70.
[61]Bhatia, Krishan, *Indira: A Biography of Prime Minister Gandhi*, Angus and Robertson, London, 1974, p. 267.

The Directorate and the Income Tax Department came in handy to raid business and the homes of leading industrialists. One purpose was to instil fear and to ensure that they would not support, financially or otherwise, her (Indira's) opponents and critics. The other was to extort money, which her son, Sanjay Gandhi needed to run a parallel force of roughnecks and goons. Many Congressmen too acquired wealth arranging the release of 'economic offenders.[62]

Indira's own uncle B.K. Nehru recounts the excesses of extortion at the time, citing an incident which took place on the day after Sanjay Gandhi's funeral, 'I asked Rajiv whether the money Sanjay had collected allegedly for the Congress was safe. He said all they found in the almarihs of the Congress office was 20 lakh rupees. I asked how much Sanjay had. He held his head in his hands and said, "Crores and uncounted crores."'[63]

It is very clear from a multitude of accounts that while the people of India remained in abject poverty, almost all government policies were formed wither for political gain or the Congress and the Nehru–Gandhi family's personal profiteering.

This attitude of pressuring industrialists and businessmen to extort money continued across subsequent Congress governments. Even during the Manmohan Singh government, Sonia Gandhi ran a parallel government that made the decisions—financial and otherwise—and businessmen were expected to bow to that structure, so that that they could be left alone. The Niira Radia tapes released during the time demonstrate a web between media editors, businessmen and the Congress leadership so as to pick 'favourable' union ministers of choice in exchange for truckloads of money, so that, in return, these ministers would provide 'benefits'.[64]

---

[62]Nayar, Kuldip, 'Emergency: Thuggery in Disguise', *Hindu Business Line*, 23 June 2000.

[63]Nehru, B.K., *Nice Guys Finish Second: An Autobiography*, Penguin Books India, New Delhi, 1997, p. 582.

[64]'The X-Tapes', *Open Magazine*, 20 November 2010.

SECTION IV

GOVERNANCE

10

DEMOCRATIC CORRUPTION

As we have already seen, during Nehru's prime ministership, he surrounded himself with and gave important power positions to friends and family members such as B.K. Nehru, Vijayalakshmi Pandit and Krishna Menon (who was promoted to the position of defence minister of India despite his involvement in the Jeep Scam). At the same time, Nehru also kept Indira close, even more so after she separated from her husband Feroze. She even accompanied him on state visits abroad, becoming privy to private, secretive conversations. Unsurprisingly, she negotiated her way into becoming the Congress president on 2 February 1959.[1] During her tenure, she overturned her father's disapproval at state divisions on linguistic agitations and separated the Bombay State into Gujarat and Maharashtra. For her, it was all about political calculations, a trend she would maintain for the rest of her life. On her decision to divide the Bombay State, she said, 'I was positive we would lose the elections in Gujarat and Maharashtra and parties who were committed to separation would come in and vote for separation. What would we have gained?'[2]

Another show of her undemocratic means was on display when the Communist Party of India (CPI) won the elections in Kerala in 1957. Photos of Gandhiji in offices and classrooms came to be replaced by Marx and Stalin. Indira could not tolerate being upstaged, and, hence, set in motion a plan to dismiss a democratically elected government.[3] This was a precedent—a dangerous one at

---

[1]Jayakar, Pupul, *Indira Gandhi: A Biography*, Penguin India, New Delhi, 2000.
[2]Ghose, Sagarika, *Indira: India's Most Powerful Prime Minister*, Juggernaut Books, New Delhi, 2017, p. 68.
[3]Ibid. 69.

that—she set for independent India. This was also a demonstration of the fact that the Congress under the Nehru–Gandhi ideology used secularism only as a tool of convenience. When it came down to politics, they did not hesitate being in bed with the most radical religious forces. In Kerala, too, the Indira-led Congress tied up with the Muslim League and joined protests being carried out by the Church against E.M.S Namboodiripad government's new education Bill on the grounds that it was hurting Muslim and Christian sentiments.[4] It is widely believed that she orchestrated the unrest from Delhi, with the help of AICC workers on ground in Kerala, hand in hand with the Muslim League. Indira weighed down heavily on her father to dismiss the CPI government in Kerala owing to the protests. And, of course, Nehru obliged. He dismissed a democratically elected government that enjoyed the support of the people for the very first time on the behest of his daughter's undemocratic machinations. While dismissing democratically elected governments would continue as part of the Congress's pattern of governance for years to come, soon after, on 30 October 1959, Indira resigned from the post of the Congress president.

It is a popular perception that when there are unconstitutional authorities influencing decisions of the highest public office, the democracy of that nation would likely be on sale. Even in Nehru's and Indira's cases, global powers were watching closely, waiting to get hold of a low-hanging fruit as an opportunity to ascertain their influence over the newly independent India. And Indira's access to unbridled power despite not holding any official post was the perfect opportunity to influence their way into India's top-decision making. Let me give you an instance—the Soviet KGB began to first court Indira during her visit to the Soviet Union in 1953.[5] Much to her liking, they ensured that she was surrounded by handsome, attentive, male admirers and had planned an elaborate holiday on the Black Sea for her. She was also kept under

---

[4]Ibid.

[5]Andrew, Christopher and Vasili Mitrokhin, *The Mitrokhin Archive II: The KGB in the World*, Penguin, UK, 2005, p. 316.

continuous surveillance. She was so overwhelmed with the excessive attention that, in a letter to her father, she wrote, 'Everybody—the Russians—have been so sweet to me ... I shall be horribly spoilt by the time I leave. Nobody has ever been so nice to me ... I don't think I have had such a holiday for years.'[6] In later conversations to Nehru, she had also described this Soviet visit with the exact words that she was 'wallowing in luxury'.[7] A couple of years later, she had accompanied Nehru, once again to the Soviet Union, during his official State visit in which they were carefully exposed to the successes of Soviet planning and economic modernization by staged visits to Russian factories. She was also presented a very expensive mink coat by Khrushchev, a piece which became one of her favourites in her wardrobe.[8] Ironically only a few years before, she had criticized the Indian ambassador for accepting a similar gift.[9] But, different rules seemed to apply to the first family versus the public at large. The father–daughter duo came away overwhelmingly impressed with the Soviets. The Soviets have admitted that their attempts to 'cultivate' Indira Gandhi during the 1950s were motivated mostly by the desire to influence her father.[10] However, looking at how deeply they were able to influence her, the Soviets involved themselves through her, in the years to come, in many sensitive, internal matters of the country.

INDIRA THRONED AS PRIME MINISTER

In January 1964, while addressing a Congress session in Bhubaneshwar, Nehru suffered a paralytic stroke and collapsed.

[6]Gandhi, Sonia (ed.), *Two Alone, Two Together: Letters between Indira Gandhi and Jawaharlal Nehru*, 1940–1964, Hodder, London, 1992, pp. 592–4.

[7]Ibid.

[8]Andrew, Christopher and Vasili Mitrokhin, *The Mitrokhin Archive II: The KGB in the World*, Penguin, UK, 2005, p. 317.

[9]Frank, Katherine, *Indira: The Life of Indira Nehru Gandhi*, HarperCollins, London, 2001, p. 93.

[10]Andrew, Christopher and Vasili Mitrokhin, *The Mitrokhin Archive II: The KGB in the World*, Penguin, UK, 2005, p. 317.

While Nehru was recuperating, Indira wielded utmost power, and the extent of her power was 'feverishly speculated on in Delhi's durbars at this time'.[11] She quite enjoyed being perceived as the 'power behind the throne'.[12] In fact, it is widely believed that she, along with the new Congress president Kumaraswami Kamaraj, an ex-CM of Tamil Nadu, orchestrated a manipulative plan, which is popularly known as the Kamaraj Plan, to ensure that all thorns between her inheriting Nehru's legacy, and, hence, the prime ministership, were adequately disposed.[13] As part of the plan, which had Nehru's blessings, those leaders holding high offices for an extended period of time, CMs and cabinet ministers, had become distanced from the grassroots and were required to resign from their posts and work for the party in the field. The Machiavellian plan was implemented at breakneck speed to ensure that no single person from the Congress party could put himself forward as Nehru's successor. As part of it, six cabinet ministers and six of the Congress party's strongest CMs were made to resign. Stalwarts like Kamraj, along with Morarji Desai, Lal Bahadur Shastri, Jagjivan Ram, S.K. Patil, Biju Patnaik and others, renounced their positions for party work, thus putting them all on a level playing field, washing out any individual advantage one or the other leader may have.[14] For now, this arrangement worked in Indira's favour.

Four months after his stroke, on 27 May 1964, Nehru passed away, and as an inheritor of his legacy, Indira organized a funeral fit for a king, leaving no doubt about succession. She did this despite Nehru's instructions in his will that he didn't want a religious funeral. She was convinced by her advisors that the people of India would not accept a non-religious funeral for Nehru.[15]

---

[11]Norman, Dorothy, *Indira Gandhi: Letters to an American Friend 1950–1984*. Harcourt Brace Johanovich, New York, 1985, p. 103.

[12]Ibid.

[13]Kapoor, Coomi, *The Emergency: A Personal History*, Penguin Books, New Delhi, 2015, p. 166.

[14]Ghose, Sagarika, *Indira: India's Most Powerful Prime Minister*, Juggernaut Books, New Delhi, 2017, pp. 84–5.

[15]Chowdhary, Neerja, *How Prime Ministers Decide: An Unprecedented, Explosive Look at*

Nehru's deputy, the unassuming Lal Bahadur Shastri, became the second PM of India. There was clamour from the party to include Indira in the cabinet, and Shastri complied by giving her the less significant information and broadcasting (I&B) portfolio. While announcing to the press Shastri's elevation to the post of the PM, Kamaraj had made it clear that the loss of an 'undisputed role of a great man' would now be replaced by 'collective leadership' of the party. This position of collective leadership seemed to be in contention of Indira's preference of becoming a power centre herself, continuing her father's legacy. So, when Shastri attempted to move into the PM residence, the Teen Murti House, Indira checkmated him and proposed to turn it into a museum that would conserve her father's memories.

In less than two years of becoming PM, Shastri died under mysterious circumstances in Tashkent, where he had gone to sign the Tashkent Agreement. The Tashkent Agreement was mediated by Soviet PM Alexei Kosygin, by which India was to give up the claim to Haji Pir Pass in exchange for international arbitration of the Kashmir dispute. In 1965, Pakistan had launched Operation Gibraltar, by which groups of infiltrators trained in the use of arms, had crossed the ceasefire line into Kashmir and blown up bridges and bombed government buildings. The hope was to create enough confusion among the local people so that there would be widespread unrest. However, the locals seemed disinterested and even began to work with the police and the armed forces to turn in the invaders. When this plan failed, Pakistan launched Operation Grand Slam, as a part of which their troops crossed the ceasefire line in Jammu, making swift progress with the use of heavy artillery and arms. Indian troops fought back most courageously, succeeding in capturing Haji Pir Pass in the Uri sector, a strategic point in the high mountains, which gave India a position of advantage to look out for infiltrators. After this, the Pakistani Army, using American Patton tanks, occupied 30 sq. miles of the Indian territory with the

How Decisions are Taken at the Very Top of the Indian Political Establishment, Aleph Book Company, New Delhi, 2023, p. 62.

purpose to capture the bridge at Akhnoor, which would sever links between Jammu and Kashmir. In response, several tank regiments and supporting infantry of the Indian Army opened a new front and crossed the international border in Punjab, heading for Lahore. Pakistan hastily redeployed their tanks from the operation in Kashmir and a deadly battle of tanks followed in the middle of the fields of Punjab. Although poised to, Lahore never fell.[16] This eventuality seemed consistent with all our previous wars, wherein at critical junctures of war, when our armed forces have been in a position of strength, they have been asked to suspend operations and retract by the Congress leadership.

The Tashkent Agreement was signed on the 10 January 1966 in the afternoon; just a few hours later, Shastri was found dead in his room.[17] The KGB was still running active operations in India and their preferred candidate after Nehru's death was either then Home Minister Gulzarilal Nanda[18] or Lal Bahadur Shastri. However, as Shastri showed more will and determination and, more importantly, an independent mind, the KGB once again turned its focus on cultivating Indira. You see, even though the Congress's thought process prevailed on Shastri in many decisions like giving up the Haji Pir Pass, there were other decisions that he had made outside of the Congress's standard operating procedure. For instance, unlike during the Indo-China War of 1962 when the Nehru government had essentially brought the whole country to a state of collapse, during this 1965 India–Pak War, Shastri ensured that the trains ran and the armed forces made adequate advances with adequate preparations (as opposed to the 1962 War where Nehru had refused to deploy the aircrafts), which made him popular among the people. More importantly, there was decisiveness in the leadership that was fully lacking

---

[16]Guha, Ramchandra, *India after Gandhi: The History of the World's Largest Democracy*, Pan Macmillan India, 2007, pp. 394–6.

[17]Srivastava, C.P., 'Chapter 31', *Lal Bahadur Shastri: Prime Minister of India 1964–1966 —A Life of Truth in Politics*, Oxford University Press, New Delhi, 1996.

[18]Andrew, Christopher and Vasili Mitrokhin, *The Mitrokhin Archive II: The KGB in the World*, Penguin Random House, UK, 2005, p. 316.

during the 1962 War when Nehru essentially lost Aksai Chin and Northeast India (the Chinese could have had it, if they wanted it—Nehru was not in a position to stop it as we have seen earlier in the book). With deep disdain for Shastri's growing popularity and success, which Indira believed was undeserved, she wrote to Sanjay, 'Shastri was weak but we have made him a national hero.'[19] It may be a co-incidence that the KGB operations aligned with Indira's forceful assertion of being the only capable Indian to lead the country, going over Shastri's head every opportunity she got; or perhaps alternatively it may all be perfectly planned to be in sync. It is believed that after Shastri's death, a friend who visited her found her 'holding her excitement in check'.[20] Although she seemed calm from the outside, she burst out, 'No one can be Prime Minister without my support.'[21]

With Shastri's death, Indira was back in action. Gulzarilal Nanda was sworn in as interim PM while Kamaraj began to find a way to bring in Indira as the PM and worked towards building a consensus in the party. To Kamaraj, Indira was the best choice as he believed that due to her inexperience, the Syndicate will be able to control her and essentially act as her 'remote control'. Little did they know that Indira had other ideas. Technically, it was Morarji Desai, Nehru's most trusted after Shastri, who deserved the top job. Desai and Indira lobbied the Congress heavyweights for days, and forceful horse-trading became commonplace. However, when the time came for the party to cast their vote, Kamaraj had persuaded even the state leaders to support Indira under the pretext that she was harmless and would allow the senior Congress leaders to continue their activities with minimal interruption.[22] The elections

---

[19]Kapoor, Coomi, *The Emergency: A Personal History*, Penguin Books, New Delhi, 2015, p. 166.

[20]Ghose, Sagarika, *Indira: India's Most Powerful Prime Minister*, Juggernaut Books, New Delhi, 2017, p. 92.

[21]Ibid.

[22]Ibid.

of 1967 were only 13 months away, and they needed a wave of emotion to capture popular sentiment.

She was sworn in as the PM. Almost immediately, as if to establish her 'divide for appeasement' policy, her government conceded to the Sikh demand of a separate state of Punjab with two chunks of it separated—the hilly areas in the west became Himachal Pradesh and the Hindu-dominated belt in the east became Haryana. The new Punjab was now Punjabi-speaking and dominated by Sikhs.[23] Around the same time, she also went to the US to persuade President Lyndon Johnson to give India food and foreign exchange, attracting headlines in the US media like 'New Indian Leader Comes Begging'.[24] The American President agreed to sanction 3 million tonnes of food and $9 million in aid in exchange of economic reforms demanded by the IMF, World Bank and the US administration, such as measures to increase private investment, more foreign direct investment (FDI), reducing public sector undertakings and substantially devaluing the rupee. Indira accepted most of these reforms, including devaluing the rupee by 36.5 per cent.[25] She came under attack from not only the Opposition, which was weighing down on the Congress for giving away the Haji Pir Pass in the Tashkent Agreement, but also from her own party for going against the socialist ideals prescribed by her father.[26] To save face, when Hindu groups came to Parliament in strength of thousands demanding an immediate ban on cow slaughter, she ordered the police to open fire.[27] Several protestors were killed, sparking communal disturbances. Shops and buildings were lit on fire. Indira ordered the army to be out on the streets—the very first time since Independence.[28] Peaceful protests

[23]Guha, Ramchandra, *India after Gandhi: The History of the World's Largest Democracy*, Pan Macmillan India, 2007, p. 406.
[24]Ibid. 407.
[25]'Rupee Devalued by 36.5 per cent', *The Times of India*, 6 June 1966.
[26]Ghose, Sagarika, *Indira: India's Most Powerful Prime Minister*, Juggernaut Books, New Delhi, 2017, p. 96.
[27]Ibid. 97.
[28]Guha, Ramchandra, *India after Gandhi: The History of the World's Largest Democracy*, Pan Macmillan India, 2007, p. 411.

are a fundamental right in a democracy. To establish her secular credentials, after giving up her socialist ones by allying with the capitalist US for aid, she attacked Hindu protestors, many of them being sadhus and holy men. She declared boisterously that she had 'no intention to be cowed down by cow savers'.[29] She even forced Gulzarilal Nanda, a devout Hindu whom she disliked, to resign in light of these events, transferring the blame from her to him.[30] In addition, she made a hasty decision to bash America by condemning American bombing in Vietnam, which obviously did not go down well with the Americans, who, in turn, delayed food shipments and the promised monetary aid. Having failed on all fronts, she was alone. Regardless of her tough 'secular' stance, the Congress Syndicate was displeased, and Kamaraj severed ties with her, later confessing his error at assessing her and giving her the PM post, using the tough words 'a big man's daughter, small man's mistake'.[31]

Finding her alone once again, the KGB's activities caught speed. In the 1967 General Elections, they pumped in so much money to ensure that Indira won that after the results, they claimed that they had been able to influence 30 to 40 per cent of the new Parliament.[32] They had funded several agents and confidential contacts within the Congress.[33] The Congress vote share and seats had plummeted drastically and people were generally disenchanted—they only had a 44-seat majority. Without the KGB's intervention, there would have been a 40 per cent reduction in the already reduced number of seats, in which case, the Congress would have lost power, making way for the right-wing Opposition parties—the Swatantra Party and the Bhartiya Jana Sangh—to form a government. Owing to the

[29]Ghose, Sagarika, *Indira: India's Most Powerful Prime Minister*, Juggernaut Books, New Delhi, 2017, p. 97.

[30]Ibid.

[31]Chowdhary, Neerja, *How Prime Ministers Decide: An Unprecedented, Explosive Look at How Decisions are Taken at the Very Top of the Indian Political Establishment*, Aleph Book Company, New Delhi, 2023.

[32]Andrew, Christopher and Vasili Mitrokhin, *The Mitrokhin Archive II: The KGB in the World*, Penguin Random House, UK, 2005, p. 318.

[33]Ibid.

small margin of victory for the Congress, in order to accommodate the Syndicate's wishes, Indira was forced to install Morarji Desai as the deputy PM after taking her second prime ministerial oath on 13 March 1967.[34]

END OF DEMOCRACY WITHIN THE CONGRESS

Indira's actions over the next two years display how she manoeuvred her way to take complete authority and control over the Congress, dismissing all democratic rules. Tension between her and the Syndicate remained high when Indira chose to instil her candidate, Dr Zakir Husain, as the new president of India, when the current president, S. Radhakrishnan's term had come to an end. Her decision prevailed over the party. She would go on to boast later of her secular credentials:

> When I was Congress president and even earlier, many people felt how can a minority person be a Chief Minister because the majority is another religion and they won't stand for it [sic]. So I worked for it without any fanfare or slogan mongering and I was able to change the atmosphere, so now we've had Muslims in the highest possible places like the President of India.[35]

This move, coupled with her attack on the Hindu protestors and the early days of allying with the Muslim League in Kerala to dislodge a democratically elected CPI government, ensured that she had the Muslim minority in full confidence.

In 1969, President Zakir Husain died suddenly, and Indira, once again, went against the Syndicate's wishes. The latter wanted to make Sanjiva Reddy the president but Indira instead pushed for her independent candidate V.V. Giri. By now, she had gathered the support of the 'Young Turks' of the Congress party who had been urging for a return to the pro-poor, socialist, pro-SC, pro-

---

[34]Ibid.

[35]The India Archive 'Indira Gandhi - Interview - TV Eye – 1978', *Facebook*, 20 July 2016, https://tinyurl.com/55yb3b78. Accessed on 24 November 2023.

minority and pro-downtrodden narratives and policies. With their support, V.V Giri won the presidential election. Congress President Siddavanahalli Nijalingappa, who had replaced K. Kamaraj, had written an open letter to her, accusing her of 'creating a personality cult' and reminding her that it was the Syndicate who she was at war with, who had made her the PM. He also accused her of making personal loyalty to her as a test of loyalty to the Congress.[36]

Indira responded to this by holding a separate, parallel Congress Working Committee meeting with the Young Turks of the party, after which, in a letter, she told Nijalingappa that 'this is not a mere clash of personalities … [I]t is a conflict between those who are for socialism, for change … and those who are for status quo and conformism.'[37] She was then expelled from the Congress party, after which she formed a new party called Congress (R). Losing majority in both Houses, she sought support from the communist and regional parties and retained her government. She deinstitutionalized the party and sought absolute control over its organs like the working committee and parliamentary board. As a journalist put it eloquently, 'She destroyed inner-party democracy by making herself the supreme leader of the Congress. She really came into her own when she broke the party but it was the end of the Congress, the beginning of autocracy. The split laid the ground for the consequent establishment of dynastic rule.'[38] For as long as she lived, elections were never held in the party.

THE STATE OF INNER-PARTY DEMOCRACY IN THE CONGRESS OF 2023

The Congress of 2023 remains the exact same: undemocratic and dynasty-ruled. After the 2004 Congress victory, Sonia stated that she listened to her inner voice and gave up the post of the

[36]Malhotra, Inder, *Indira Gandhi: A Personal and Political Biography*, Hay House India, New Delhi, 2014, p. 122.

[37]Nayar, Kuldip, *India: The Critical Years*. Vikas Publications, New Delhi, 1971, pp. 2–3.

[38]Ghose, Sagarika, *Indira: India's Most Powerful Prime Minister*, Juggernaut Books, New Delhi, 2017, p. 111.

PM to nominate Dr Manmohan Singh instead. However, she remained very much a power centre. She bypassed constitutional processes and the Prime Minister's Office (PMO) when it came to policy-making, procurements as well as allocation and selection of bureaucrats and ministers. A standout example was the creation of the National Advisory Council (NAC), for which she hand-picked members, left Dr Singh out, chaired it herself and made decisions that the UPA government had to implement. An unconstitutional body, such as the NAC, provided immense power to its members to make decisions that would be subject to zero accountability. It became a 'politically fatal combination', as described by Sanjaya Baru, former advisor to Dr Singh, further adding that 'responsibility without power and governance without authority meant that Dr Singh was unable, even when he was aware, to check corruption in his ministry to avoid disturbing the political arrangement over which he nominally presided'. Sonia's rigorous personal branding exercise continued aggressively. According to insiders, '[S]he would take credit for all the good work, project herself as the caring socialist concerned about the welfare of the poor, while all the blame for any mistake or failure would go to Dr Singh.'[39]

Even today, we see the family firmly quashing any inner-party demands to restore democratic processes. Let us take the instance of when 23 senior Congress leaders wrote an open letter demanding more democracy, transparency and accountability.[40] The leaders were shushed by the Gandhi-family lackeys, hailing Rahul as the deserving prince and Sonia as the supreme queen, indicating zero tolerance for questioning of the family dominance. Even the installation of Mallikarjun Kharge, who organized the lackeys against the 23 stalwarts, as the Congress president, remains merely superficial.

---

[39]Baru, Sanjaya, *The Accidental Prime Minister: The Making and Unmaking of Manmohan Singh*, Penguin Books Limited, New Delhi, 2014.
[40]'Group of 23: The Congress Leaders Who Wrote the Letter of Dissent and Why They Are Important', *News18*, 24 August 2020, https://tinyurl.com/ycxw8sy9. Accessed on 24 November 2023.

INSTITUTIONAL CONTROL

With the murder of democracy for the sake of unbridled power within the party, Indira now set her sights on the nation, eroding the fundamentals of democracy step-by-step in order to become the supreme, unquestioned authority in the country. In the 1967 elections, the Congress had collapsed in several Hindi-speaking heartland states of Uttar Pradesh and Bihar, in addition to Kerala, Punjab, West Bengal, Rajasthan, Tamil Nadu and Kerala. By 1969, she dismissed democratically elected state governments in Bihar, Uttar Pradesh, West Bengal and Punjab by imposing President's Rule.[41] This seemed like a replication of her tactics in Kerala during her stint as the Congress president in 1959. According to Article 356 of the Constitution, President's Rule can be imposed in a state 'if a situation has arisen in which the government of the state cannot be carried on in accordance with the provisions of the Constitution'. This Article was exploited and deployed as a political tool to keep Opposition out of power and dismiss elected governments in Opposition-ruled states.

After nationalizing the banks, she turned her attention to the abolition of the privy purses of the princes. When their states merged with the Union of India, the princes were given a constitutional guarantee that they would be able to retain their titles, jewels and palaces; be paid an annual privy purse in proportion to the size of their states; and be exempt from central taxes and import duties. In her quest to re-establish her socialist, anti-capitalist credentials, abolishing these privileges for the rich royalty would make people perceive her as the Robin Hood of the poor. The home ministry prepared a detailed note on how this could be done via legislation versus executive action. A decision was made to engage with the princes and arrive at an amicable settlement that could then be pushed in order to make a constitutional amendment. No settlement was reached. However, on 18 May 1970, the last

---

[41]Ghose, Sagarika, *Indira: India's Most Powerful Prime Minister,* Juggernaut Books, New Delhi, 2017, p. 107.

day of the summer session of Parliament, Home Minister Y.B. Chavan introduced a Bill calling for a constitutional amendment annulling the privileges of the princes. It was taken forward in the next parliamentary session in which the Lok Sabha adopted the Bill by the necessary two-thirds margin, but the motion failed to pass in the Rajya Sabha. Indira overruled Parliament's decision to strike down the Bill, and soon, on her behest, a presidential order was issued to her liking. Four days later, on 11 September 1970, a group of Maharajas moved the Supreme Court of India against the president's order of de-recognizing the princes.[42] The case was heard by a full bench, headed by the Chief Justice. On 11 December, the Supreme Court bench ruled that the order was arbitrary and against the spirit of the Constitution. The Supreme Court had made similar observations in the case of the bank nationalization.[43] However, being an astute politician, she knew very well that public opinion was in her favour. To stop further damage to her credibility due to the Supreme Court judgements reversing her legislative decisions, she called for fresh elections despite a full year of her government's term remaining.

Having learned a lesson that in order to have complete control, she would have to establish not only full parliamentary majority by way of popular mandate but also judicial control, she worked towards realizing both those goals diligently. With the emergence of regional parties in various states, she was worried that concurrent elections would weigh on the outcome of legislative decisions as the composition of Parliament would possibly change. Having learned her lesson from 1967, when several states also went out of the Congress's kitty, she concurred that moving the general elections ahead of schedule would help her create a wave around national issues, and, thus, make it easier for her to win. In their manifesto, the Congress (R) listed several pro-poor, socialist measures, offering a 'genuine radical programme of economic and

---

[42]Guha, Ramchandra, *India after Gandhi: The History of the World's Largest Democracy*, Pan Macmillan India, 2007, p. 439.
[43]Ibid.

social development'.[44] Meanwhile, the Opposition began to build a united front against the Congress and constituted the 'Grand Alliance' that brought together Jana Sangh, Swantantra Party, Congress (O) and several regional parties. They came up with the slogan 'Indira Hatao'. In response, she roared, '*Woh kehte hai Indira hatao, hum kehte hai garibi hatao*', thus coining the term for the biggest and longest-running election campaign in the history of independent India—Garibi Hatao. The people were enamoured and swayed by her narrative, and she was voted back to power in a thumping majority. It is a different matter that the poverty rate remained the same until 1983 and the destitute found no help from her government. A major study concluded that 40 per cent of the rural population and 50 per cent of the urban population did not enjoy even a 'minimum level of living' by the year 1970. The incidence of poverty had grown over the decade, and economists agreed that over 40 per cent of the Indian population were poor. They noted that close to 200 million people spent 80 per cent of their income on food and 10 per cent on fuel, leaving a mere 10 per cent for clothing and other necessary items.[45]

As discussed earlier, schemes that Indira's government formulated in the name of Garibi Hatao became means to extort money from the rich, to fill the Congress's coffers. There was rampant abuse of central agencies, like the Enforcement Directorate (ED) and the Income Tax Department, to threaten the rich to cough up huge sums for the party, and in the event they did not, they would be raided and put behind bars. Ironic as it is, the Congress party frequently accuses the BJP government today of the same. The Gandhi grandchildren seem to have forgotten about Indira's tactics of subverting democratic processes by suspending democratically elected governments by using central agencies at her disposal. The state governments were administered from Delhi as well by keeping

---

[44]Ibid. 444.
[45]Bhalla, Surjit, *Not as Poor, Nor as Unequal, As you Think – Poverty, Inequality and Growth in India 1950-2000—for the Myth and Reality of Poverty in India*, Planning Commission, Government of India, 4 December 2003, https://tinyurl.com/w3vfzcre. Accessed on 24 November 2023.

the looming sword of the President's Rule imposition over their heads. Despite such control, effective legislation was kept suspended, so that the Opposition was completely blocked from challenging the Congress. In another shocking statistic, during Nehru's time between 1950 and 1964, Article 356 of the Constitution, which dismissed state governments, was invoked nine times. From 1966 to 1977, during Indira's first tenure, the President's Rule was imposed in several states, totalling to 36 times![46] Taking a longer period of Congress rule, between 1971 and 1990, it was imposed 63 times, and 49 of those times were during Indira's subsequent tenures. Even Congress CMs who got too popular were quickly switched out from their posts[47] to include more conforming men.

So desperate was she to remain in power—by hook or by crook—that it prompted tall Opposition leaders like Dr Ram Manohar Lohia to comment that the Nehru family members would work under the garb of democracy until it suited them and when it did not, they would discard it.[48]

DEALING WITH PROTESTS

The environment in the country in the early 1970s was charged with dissatisfaction with the government's strong-arm tactics, and there were protests erupting all over the country. In Gujarat, students had taken to the streets to protest against uncontrolled inflation and rising prices. Out of these protests arose a powerful movement—the Nav Nirman movement—that demanded the resignation of Gujarat's then Congress CM Chimanbhai Patel. There was rampage across the state—buses were burned, property looted, and the mood across was of radical rebellion. Within a month, over a hundred people were killed in riots, 300 injured and 8,000 arrested. The protests would have much likely remained

---

[46]Maiorano, Diego, *Autumn of the Matriarch: Indira Gandhi's Final Term in Office*, HarperCollins India, New Delhi, 2015, p. 183.

[47]Ibid.

[48]Goyal, Rama (ed.), *Saving India from Indira: Untold Story of the Emergency*, Rupa Publications India, New Delhi, 2019, p. 3.

peaceful had it not been for the government's heavy-handed, violent handling of the protestors, who, in a democracy, had every right to put forth their demands. However, President's Rule was imposed on the state, and the government struck back at protestors with an unprecedented use of force.[49]

The same model of government's aggressive response to dissenting voices was seen even in West Bengal and Uttar Pradesh.[50] In the latter, in May 1973, the state's Provincial Armed Constabulary (PAC) had revolted against shortages of basic commodities, demanding better pay and working conditions. However, CM Kamalapati Tripathi from the Congress called in the army, which led to violent aggression on both sides. Thirty protesting policemen were shot dead, and the Uttar Pradesh CM was forced to resign due to public outcry.

Adding to this fray was the Jana Sangh's student movement under the outfit Akhil Bhartiya Vidyarthi Parishad (ABVP), which took the Nav Nirman movement to student cadres across the country. It started from Bihar, which led to the notable Bihar movement, in which Indira's nemesis, 72-year-old Jayaprakash Narayan, a freedom fighter who had chosen to retire from public life after Independence to lead one devoted to social reform, rose and claimed leadership of the anti-Indira movement across the country.

Born in Sitab Diara, Bihar, in a lower middle-class home, Jayaprakash Narayan was the antithesis to Indira with her privileged pedigree. At one point, he was even considered as a successor to Nehru instead of Shastri—when an offer to lead the country was made to him, he had declined,[51] disappointing several Congressmen. He was a figure of immense moral authority. His involvement boosted the student movement—*yuvashakti*, he'd call it—which began to spread across the country like wildfire. It even began to be called the JP movement.

---

[49]Ghose, Sagarika, *Indira: India's Most Powerful Prime Minister*, Juggernaut Books, New Delhi, 2017, p. 151.
[50]Ibid. 151–2.
[51]Ibid. 153.

He became the messiah of the anti-Indira group in the country and a moral rallying point around whom all forces, from the Jana Sangh and the Rashtriya Swayamsevak Sangh (RSS) to the Communist Party of India (Marxist) (CPIM), united to dislodge the Indira government. Realizing that only a united Opposition could dislodge Indira, JP, along with Morarji Desai (then president of Congress (O), Jana Sangh and the socialists, formed the Janata Morcha or Janata Front, which was the precursor to Janata Party. Several other non-communist student groups joined the movement in Bihar, and the resultant united front was called the Chatra Sangharsh Samiti (CSS). On 18 March, the CSS marched to the state assembly in Patna to put forth their demands. The state police used physical force to push back the protestors, as was the common practice in Indira's handling of dissents.[52] The police and the mob clashed; at least three students died and several were injured. The public responded positively to the dissent, sympathetic to the students and JP's leadership, and the Congress lost seats in their stronghold in by-elections, that is, Jabalpur. After more wins in the by-elections followed, the student protestors became charged and encouraged. The Indira government, once again, quelled these protests by sheer physical force. Protestors were lathi-charged and tear-gassed, after which JP called for 'sampurna kranti' (total revolution). In Gujarat, Morarji Desai went on an indefinite hunger strike in support of the Nav Nirman movement, demanding fresh elections. Worried about the possible death of Desai and the public outcry it would create, Indira agreed to fresh elections in Gujarat in June 1975, in which the Janata Party ousted the Congress.[53]

At the same time, India was also dealing with a railway strike led by socialist leader George Fernandez. The government staff working in the railways demanded better wages and housing conditions. The strike went on for three weeks, paralysing movement of people and goods. Over a million railway workers participated in the strike. There were several militant demonstrations in many towns and

---

[52]Ibid. 159.
[53]Ibid. 163.

cities. Indira's response to this, as per norm, was to bring in the army to maintain peace instead of arriving at a consensus and chalking out acceptable solutions.[54]

The wave was real. It was spreading across the country and wasn't fitting into the Nehru–Gandhi family's autocratic model of governance. Indira was desperate to act fast and reclaim her unquestioned authority on the country. The scientists had been pressing Indira to conduct an atomic test for a while. Developing nuclear arms fit neither into Nehru's narrative of non-violence nor into Gandhi's peaceful existence. Hence, to test an atom bomb would be akin to throwing away Gandhi's legacy, which the Congress so desperately tries to hold on to even today, or even Nehru's, for that matter. But, in a desperate attempt to divert attention away from the violence and protests sweeping the country, she finally agreed to the demands of the scientists on 18 May 1974.[55]

JUDICIAL INTERFERENCE

In the 1971 Lok Sabha elections, Indira won from the Raebareli constituency in Uttar Pradesh, defeating the Samyukta Socialist Party candidate Raj Narain. Elections are an expensive affair in India and large amounts of funds are mobilized to run election campaigns. With the nationalization of banks and threatening the private sector from donating to opposition parties, Indira had ensured that her political Opposition was financially weak. However, she didn't hesitate to use government funds in various states to cover her campaign expenses. In 1969, as PM, she had gotten instructions in the 'Blue Book' titled 'Rules and Instructions for the Protection of the Prime Minister When on Tour or Travel' changed, wherein the word 'except' was replaced by the word 'including' in Section 71 (6). It originally read:

It has been noticed that the rostrum arrangements are not always properly made because the hosts are sometimes

---

[54]Ibid. 156–7.
[55]Ibid. 157.

unable to bear the costs. As the Prime Minister's security is the concern of the State, all arrangements for putting up the rostrum and barriers at the meeting place will be borne by the state whatever may be the occasion for which the public meeting is called, except election meetings.[56]

With the replacement of the word 'except' with 'including', Indira Gandhi placed the financial onus of her security arrangements on state funds, by which states were compelled to spend huge sums of money for her election meetings that were clearly not for government functions or public purposes but rather for per personal benefit or for the benefit of the Congress.

In Raebareli, after her victory, Raj Narain filed a petition in the Allahabad High Court, challenging her election by alleging that she had won through corrupt practices, spending more money than was allowed and using the official government machinery and officials in service to aid her campaign. In such cases, an election petition is a plea filed directly before a High Court challenging the election of a particular candidate within 45 days of declaration of the election results. The Representation of People (RP) Act of 1951 lists the grounds on which the election of a candidate can be called into question. Section 123 of the RP Act lists certain corrupt practices, which, if proven in court, can be grounds to declare the election of a candidate void.

It is on these grounds that Narain challenged Indira's election. In his judgement, Justice J.M.L. Sinha invalidated Indira's election on two grounds: using government machinery for setting up public events, which is classified as a corrupt practice under Section 123(7) of the RP Act; and second, using a gazetted government officer as her election agent.[57] Yashpal Kapur, under Indira's instructions, delivered election speeches on 7 January 1971 at Munshi Ganj and another speech at Kalan on 19 January 1971. It was concluded that

---

[56]Goyal, Rama (ed.), *Saving India from Indira: Untold Story of the Emergency*, Rupa Publications India, New Delhi, 2019, p. 19.
[57]Bhushan, Prashant, *The Case that Shook India*, Vikas Publishing House, New Delhi, 1978, p. 98.

Gandhi obtained and procured the assistance of Kapur for the furtherance of her election prospects when Kapur was serving as a gazetted officer with the government.[58] Yashpal Kapur had been in the PM's secretariat since 1966, first as her Officer on Special Duty and later as her political advisor. Even in the election of 1967, he had resigned from government service just before elections to become Indira's election agent. After the election, he was reinstated to his post. After 1971, he would have most likely been reinstated immediately if it wasn't for Raj Narain's case. However, he was adequately compensated a year later in 1972, when he was nominated as a member of the Rajya Sabha by the Congress from Uttar Pradesh.[59] After dragging on for two odd years, on 12 June, Justice J.M.L. Sinha found Indira Gandhi guilty on two counts out of the 14 mentioned in the petition. The order of Justice J.M.L. Sinha stated that the stay order would continue for 20 days or till the time the appeal was filed in the Supreme Court by Indira Gandhi, whichever took place earlier.[60]

On 24 June, a vacation bench of the Supreme Court allowed a partial stay of the judgement after Indira had appealed against the High Court verdict. The Supreme Court's interim order passed by the vacation judge Justice V.R. Krishna Iyer said that she could continue as Member of Parliament (MP) in the Lok Sabha and could attend the House but could not participate in its proceedings, vote as MP or draw any remuneration. Later, Justice V.R. Krishna Iyer revealed how he and his wife were pressurized and under duress to decide the case in favour of Indira Gandhi.[61] It may be noted here that this wasn't the only time that the Congress leader had interfered in judicial processes. In April 1973, she had superseded three eminent judges to bring in

---

[58]Sharada Prasad, H.Y., *The Book I Won't Be Writing and Other Essays*, Chronicle Books, New Delhi, 2003, p. 113.

[59]Goyal, Rama (ed.), *Saving India from Indira: Untold Story of the Emergency*, Rupa Publications India, New Delhi, 2019, p. 12.

[60]Ibid. 28.

[61]T.R. Andhyarujina, 'Justice for the Helpless', *The Indian Express*, 6 December 2014.

Justice A.N. Ray as the Chief Justice of India, particularly at a time when crucial cases against her government and herself were to be listed.[62] It is said that Justice Ray used to have private dinners with Indira Gandhi at her residence.[63] In such circumstances, how logical would it be to believe that he would act in neutral discretion? Indira tried every trick in the book to influence the appeal of the case in Supreme Court in her favour. At that time, the Election Bench was different, of which the Chief Justice was not a member. However, rules were bent, and to grant himself jurisdiction in the matter, Justice Ray constituted a five-judge bench presided over by him.[64] The three superseded judges resigned and voices of Indira trying to corrupt the judiciary got louder. Hers was a serious, deliberate attempt to undermine the independence of the judiciary of India.

Raj Narain had raised several electoral offences against Indira. Several of those got quashed through clearly unconstitutional means. Let us take the example of Narain's charge that Indira had spent more funds than permitted for her electoral campaign. He contended that Indira and her election agent Yashpal Kapur incurred or authorized expenditure in excess of the amount prescribed by Section 77 of the RP Act (limit of ₹35,000), read with Rule 90 of the Conduct of Elections Rules, 1961. If the funds spent exceeded the prescribed limit, it amounted to a corrupt practice under Section 123(6) of the RP Act. Indira claimed that the election expenses incurred by her amounted to ₹12,892. However, Narain alleged that she had spent ₹128,700 as hiring charges of vehicles; ₹43,230 as vehicle fuel and ₹9,900 as payments to the drivers of the vehicles. He also claimed that Gandhi spent ₹132,000 for construction of rostrums for public meetings. In this context, on 3 October 1974, the Supreme Court, in another case (*Kanwar Lal Gupta* vs *Amar Nath Chawla & Ors*), held that the expenses incurred by a political

---

[62]Goyal, Rama (ed.), *Saving India from Indira: Untold Story of the Emergency*, Rupa Publications India, New Delhi, 2019, p. 20.
[63]Ibid.
[64]Ibid.

party for a candidate would also be considered to be the expenses incurred by that candidate. This judgement would negatively affect Indira's election case. Therefore, in order to undo the effect of this judgement and protect herself from the charges, the Congress party got the RP (Amendment) Act, 1974, passed by Parliament, which gave retrospective operation to the Amendment.[65]

The new Amendment provided therein that the expenses incurred by a political party for a candidate will not be treated to be the candidate's expenses. The Opposition protested heavily. However, owing to majority, the legislation was passed by Parliament, solely for the purpose of shielding Indira in her election case against use of excessive funds over the prescribed limit.[66] This mattered because the finances of the Opposition were wiped out due to the Indira government's draconian control over the banks. The fact that the PM of the country had the means within the limited period allotted for election campaigning to address, say, 10 or 20 meetings in a day due to the opportunity of using government planes without any cost to herself or the party was against the fundamentals of equality. It may be important to note that the means of election campaign during the election period prescribed cannot be minimized. If the PM, the high office of the ruling party, was given facilities at the expense of the government exchequer to have an open hand in the matter of election campaign, in which even government servants and officers were used, then how was it possible for the Opposition to even try to dislodge the government of the day?

It is believed that the judgement against her would have been much more severe had she not inserted her mole in the team of lawyers representing Raj Narain.[67] This is evidenced by several instances where Shanti Bhushan disagreed with the opinions of the other prominent legal minds on the case and decided to take his own course, which turned out to be detrimental to the case.

---

[65]Ibid. 27.

[66]Ibid.

[67]Goyal, Rama (ed.), *Saving India from Indira: Untold Story of the Emergency*, Rupa Publications India, New Delhi, 2019, pp. 29–31, 35.

The order by the apex court, while not completely against Gandhi, did not satisfy her. She wanted a blanket stay on the Allahabad High Court judgement. But the salient features of the Supreme Court resolution were that Indira Gandhi had not gotten a full stay order and under the circumstances, she should not remain the PM. She was found to be guilty of corrupt practices. Even Supreme Court Justice Krishna Iyer had brought up the issue of political propriety and democratic dharma in his order.[68] There was no grey area—Indira Gandhi was morally bound to give up the prime ministership. It was also pointed out in the order that the principles and practice in democratic countries had been that if a person was under a cloud of suspicion, then he or she was bound to vacate the office held by him or her. When the verdict did not go according to her wishes, she turned to erase the very foundations of Indian democracy and declared an Emergency in India, instead of opting for a more democratic recourse of filing an appeal.

Under the goal of creating a 'cooperative judiciary', under guidance from her close colleague Mohan Kumaramangalam, also a minister in her cabinet, the government set out to limit the rights of the judicial arm of the Indian democracy.[69] The Supreme Court had ruled in the Golak Nath case in 1967 that the legislature or the government could not tamper with fundamental rights of citizens enlisted in the Indian Constitution, that is, fundamental rights could not be amended by ordinary amending processes.[70] This was inconvenient for Indira, and, thus, once again under the garb of creating pro-poor policies, Indira's government asserted Parliament's right to change the Constitution and alter even the fundamental rights. Thereby, twenty-fourth, twenty-fifth and twenty-

---

[68]*Indira Nehru Gandhi (Smt)* vs *Raj Narain & Anr,* 1975 AIR 1590, 1975 SCC (2) 159. Justice Krishna Iyer observed, 'Legality is within the Court's province to pronounce upon, but canons of political propriety and democratic dharma are polemical issues on which judicial silence is the golden rule.'

[69]Ghose, Sagarika, *Indira: India's Most Powerful Prime Minister,* Juggernaut Books, New Delhi, 2017, p. 149.

[70]Ibid.

sixth Amendments to the Constitution were passed in Parliament in quick succession with a span of one year: 1971–72. Basically, these amendments upheld bank nationalization in its entirety, upheld the abolition of privy purses that the Supreme Court had stalled and, most importantly, asserted Parliament's right to dilute fundamental rights.[71] Tampering of the Constitution was a dangerous precedent, and these amendments were challenged in April 1973 in the Kesavananda Bharati case, better known as the case that saved Indian democracy. Seven of the 13 judges on the bench constituted by Chief Justice A.N. Ray, despite pressure, agreed that Parliament did not have the unlimited power to amend the Constitution. Thus, due to majority decision (albeit a wafer-thin majority), the Supreme Court held that Parliament had no jurisdiction to pass a Constitution (Amendment) Act; it violated the basic structure of the Constitution. Imagine, if the judgement had been set aside, the Opposition at the time believed that Indira was way on her way to get even a one-page Constitution passed, declaring her as the Empress of India and giving her descendants the right to rule the country in the future. The 13-judge bench had been carefully chosen to include four minority judges and some others who could be easily persuaded. In a meeting presided by Judge N.A. Palkhivala, who represented Indira in her election case but stepped down after she declared the Emergency, addressed a room full of lawyers appearing in the Kesavananda Bharati case. In an emotionally charged speech, the noted lawyer is believed to have said that if the judgement in the case was overruled, the country was going to be destroyed further and monarchy was going to be established. It is pertinent to note here that Palkhivala worked very closely with Indira on her election case against Raj Narain and had a close view of her malicious intent and collusions.[72]

---

[71]Ibid. 150.

[72]Goyal, Rama (ed.), *Saving India from Indira: Untold Story of the Emergency*, Rupa Publications India, New Delhi, 2019.

DECLARATION OF EMERGENCY

The judgement of the Allahabad High Court and the Gujarat election results came within a span of a couple of days. Both events shook Indira. Ideally, she should have resigned, but it is believed that Sanjay weighed in heavily stating that there was no question of his mother resigning. The loyal lackeys, afraid of losing their jobs, supported her by saying, 'Indira is India and India is Indira, the two are inseparable'.[73] Sanjay blamed the Gujarat loss to the poor publicity of the rallies, which fell under the ambit of the I&B minister I.K. Gujral. He was eventually sacked and replaced by a more obliging, Vidya Charan, who complied obediently with irrational demands of the Nehru family. Indira responded as well, shocked at the disbanding of the Gujarat Assembly. Speaking to her colleague Siddharatha Ray, she said, 'We're in serious trouble. The Gujarat Assembly is dissolved. Bihar is dissolved. There will be no end. Democracy will come to a grinding halt. Some drastic emergent action is needed.'[74] Ironically, 'democracy in danger', reminiscent of the Muslim League's 'Islam in danger', was often used by her to push the most undemocratic, unconstitutional decisions in the days to come. Outside Indira's residence, Congress henchmen held rallies and demonstrations, begging her not to resign. She even addressed some of these rallies, justifying her stance and advancing spurious arguments. An effigy of the High Court judge who held her guilty, Justice J.M.L. Sinha, was burnt and even posters suggesting a link between Justice Sinha and the CIA appeared around the city.

On the night of the Supreme Court's refusal of her appeal to give her an unconditional and absolute stay, JP was scheduled to conduct a huge political rally at the Ram Lila Maidan in Delhi. At the rally, JP animatedly roared to the huge crowd, inviting loud applause, '*Singhasan khali karo, ki janta aati hai*'. JP called for the

---

[73]Guha, Ramachandra, 'India Was Indira, Indira Was India', *Himal Southasian*, 1 July 2000, https://tinyurl.com/29wbaunx. Accessed on 24 November 2023.
[74]Ghose, Sagarika, *Indira: India's Most Powerful Prime Minister*, Juggernaut Books, New Delhi, 2017, p. 169.

police and army to mutiny against an unconstitutional government as established by the Supreme Court judgement. He also warned of a peaceful satyagraha that the Opposition leaders would carry out until the time she stepped down. In fact, in a letter written to Indira on 21 June, JP had explained his planned satyagraha:

> The programme was for a selected number of persons to offer satyagraha before or near your residence in support of the demand that you should step down until the Supreme Court's judgement on your appeal. The programme was to continue for seven days in Delhi, after which it was to be taken up in the states.[75]

To an already shaken Indira, who was on the brink of losing power, JP's appeal to the crowds seemed like an attack on her government's sovereignty. Combined with the apex court's observations on the unconstitutionality of her government, this came as a strong blow to her. And, for Indira, her sovereignty was akin to India's sovereignty. Thus, that evening, Indira, along with Siddhartha Ray, met President Fakhruddin Ali Ahmed at Rashtrapati Bhavan, asking him to declare an internal Emergency, which had become necessary given that the country's sovereignty was being threatened (by the Opposition). Later that night the 'Emergency Order Proclamation' was sent to the president, which he signed just a few minutes before midnight on 25 June 1975—the darkest day in the history of independent India. The country was declared to be in a state of Emergency.

Across the country, fundamental rights were suspended. Strikes and protests, which are an integral part of a rich democratic society, were now banned. Under the notorious Maintenance of Internal Security (MISA) Act, which was enacted in 1971 into a law, activists, Opposition leaders, protestors and anyone who questioned or defied the Nehru family was hunted down and jailed. JP and Raj Narain were among the first few to get arrested

---

[75]File 2-2, JP Papers, Cultural Informatics Lab, Indira Gandhi National Centre for Arts, New Delhi, and Braj Kishore Memorial Institute, Patna.

under the MISA Act. Over the years of the Emergency, over 2 lakh people were arrested and detained without trial. Most tall political leaders and workers of the Opposition were arrested on the intervening night of 25 and 26 June. Even the relatives of the detenu were not informed of where they were taken and the detenu were not allowed to write freely to anyone. If a letter was written, it would be censured by the jail authorities, and there was no guarantee that it would reach its destination. Opposition leaders like Atal Bihari Vajpayee and Shyam Nandan Mishra are believed to have showcased great amounts of poise when witch-hunted by the police when they showed up to arrest them without warrants. The *rajmata*s of Gwalior and Jaipur were singled out and made to share cells with inmates. The treatment of the political detenus was so poor that older prisoners reminisced being jailed in the days of the British Raj when the treatment was more humane and jails much cleaner.[76]

The treatment meted out to JP in detention was mysterious. He was first detained at Sohna Rest House in Gurgaon (now Gurugram). There were rumours being circulated that he had gone into coma and was being treated at G.B. Pant Hospital. Three days later, from the Sohna Rest House, he was brought to AIIMS and admitted there for three days. It was leaked via the censored press that JP had been brought to AIIMS for treatment of an ailment.[77] What is interesting to note here is that JP was absolutely healthy on the night he was arrested after his rally at Ram Lila Maidan. After AIIMS, he was taken to PGI Hospital where an entire ward was vacated to put JP under detention. Most curiously, the floor on which JP was detained was meant for heart patients and those who needed intensive care. The corridor had police officers liberally stationed at every corner and glass panes that were never opened. JP was regularly paid visits by 'doctors' who were giving him 'treatment'.[78] In his deposition before the Alva Commission in

---

[76]Goyal, Rama (ed.), *Saving India from Indira: Untold Story of the Emergency*, Rupa Publications India, New Delhi, 2019.
[77]Ibid.
[78]Ibid. 57–61.

1977–78, when asked, he made it clear that he did not desire to be hospitalized and did not know why the government had done so. He was detained in a place where he was in solitary confinement and not even getting fresh air and sunlight. Under these circumstances, his colleagues began to fear an adverse effect on his health. To his advocates, who were allowed to interview him, JP complained that his health was deteriorating and that he was being made to take some medicines that were possibly leading to great stomach pain.[79] JP became so ill that, on 12 November, the government released him out of fear of public outcry in the event that he died in confinement. He was then admitted to AIIMS again.[80] JP believed that he was being slowly poisoned, and that something was amiss in his medical treatment.[81] It was apparent even to his colleagues, for his health deteriorated suddenly and mysteriously. He looked haggard, and his doctors were only releasing vague reports.[82] In an open letter to his supporters in February 1977, he confessed his suspicion that he had been slowly poisoned while in detention. He wrote, 'A number of my friends have expressed a doubt which I share…that my kidneys may have been deliberately damaged.'[83] There is no other record in modern, democratic India of a PM trying to wipe out their primary opponent by plotting to poison them. Nehru family's attempt to slow poison Indira's primary political opponent to death is perhaps a lone event that is very revealing of their autocratic psyche. Sadly, it wasn't just JP on whose life attempts were made during incarceration. Once the Emergency ended, members of the Nehru family boasted several times that political opponents were treated in extremely

---

[79]Ibid. 65.

[80]Ibid. 66.

[81]File 9, Minutes of Conversation between Allan and Wendy Scarfe and Shri M.G. Devasahayam—16.3.1994 in Room 419, Hilton Hotel, Melbourne Australia, JP Papers, Cultural Informatics Lab, Indira Gandhi National Centre for Arts, New Delhi. and Braj Kishore Memorial Institute, Patna.

[82]Ibid.

[83]Chowdhary, Neerja, *How Prime Ministers Decide: An Unprecedented, Explosive Look at How Decisions are Taken at the Very Top of the Indian Political Establishment*, Aleph Book Company, New Delhi, 2023, p. 41.

comfortable, humane ways. Since press was not allowed to report the truth then, their word was the only word. However, reports from multiple surviving prisoners, which came out gradually over a period of time, suggested that they were subjected to violent, inhuman treatment. For instance, Snehalata Roy, who was detained in the same prison as Lal Krishna Advani and Atal Bihari Vajpayee, was indeed kept in such absolute unsanitary conditions that she caught a deadly lung infection. And as per the Indira government's playbook, on realizing that she may not survive the infection and weakness, they released her. She died five days later.

As compared to that, let us draw a comparison to Rahul Gandhi's recent disqualification from Parliament on account of a district court judgement against him. When asked to give up his official residence, he invited the entire New Delhi press as the entire task of handing over the keys was done under full media glare, filmed and widely circulated, possibly to garner public sympathy.

DESTRUCTION OF THE CONSTITUTION

The Nehru family's impatience for democratic processes began to grow. Indira had already sent packing dissenters within the civil service, the judiciary and even from the Congress party. She had replaced them with men who would conform to the family's every wish. With the Opposition MPs locked away, she passed a series of constitutional amendments to prolong her rule. The thirty-eighth Amendment, which barred the judicial review of the Emergency, was passed on 22 July 1975; the thirty-ninth Amendment, which stated that the election of the PM could not be challenged by the Supreme Court, was passed two weeks later, effective retrospectively. This was very timely since it came in handy for her review petition. With the new Amendments, the Court now held the view that there was no case to try, as it placed her actions in 1971 outside the purview of the law of the land.[84] In anticipation

---

[84]Austin, Granville, *Working a Democratic Constitution: The Indian Experience*, Oxford University Press, New Delhi, 1999, pp. 319–24.

of a judgement in her favour, she was clad in a Kashmiri saree on the day of the judgement and had made preparations to go to Kashmir on a family vacation.[85] Sincerity died a thousand deaths when a month later, in December, Indira stated in her speech at the All India Lawyers' Conference, '[T]oday there is a great deal of talk about constitutional changes ... We certainly do not want to change anything just for the sake of changing it ... [I]f any change is required it will not be to lessen democracy.'[86]

When the jailed detenus appealed that the right of habeas corpus could not be taken away, the Supreme Court bench held that detentions without trial were legal with the new Amendments made to the Constitution. A five-member bench was constituted, out of which only one judge, Justice H.R. Khanna, argued, stating, '[D]etention without trial is an anathema to all those who love personal liberty.'[87] The others who were part of the bench were clearly pressurized and coaxed by extra-legal considerations and commitments. *The New York Times* ran an editorial after the judgement titled 'Fading Hopes in India' and noted that 'the submission of an independent judiciary to an absolutist government is virtually the last step in the destruction of a democratic society'.[88] Of course, H.R. Khanna was punished. When he was up for the job of the Chief Justice, he was forced to resign, and, in his place, Justice M.H. Beg, who was more compliant to the family's diktat, was given the top job.

As part of the forty-second Amendment, Parliament was given unprecedented powers, which included the right to extend its own term, which it immediately did. It also provided laws that gave the legislature further protection from judicial scrutiny. It basically allowed Parliament 'unfettered power to preserve or destroy the Constitution'.[89] Even the preamble of the Constitution

---

[85]Goyal, Rama (ed.), *Saving India from Indira: Untold Story of the Emergency*, Rupa Publications India, New Delhi, 2019, p. 108.

[86]Ibid.

[87]Ibid.

[88]'Fading Hope in India', *The New York Times*, 30 April 1976, https://tinyurl.com/9t34txmb. Accessed ob 29 November 2023.

[89]Goyal, Rama (ed.), *Saving India from Indira: Untold Story of the Emergency*, Rupa Publications India, New Delhi, 2019.

was changed: from being 'sovereign democratic republic', India became 'sovereign, socialist, secular democratic republic'.[90]

MEDIA CONTROL AND OTHER EXCESSES

Newspapers were censored, and guidelines that positive news had to be published were issued. Praises for the all-pervasive leader was the order of the day. Within the first week of government, the rule that editors had to submit any material that would be critical of the government for scrutiny and approval was clearly communicated to the press. Reports on occasions and strikes and political opponents or their condition in jails were disallowed to be published. The press had to write pieces that would either carry the PM's words or praise her governance. The foreign media ecosystem and their journalists were asked to leave the country. After weeks of negotiation, guidelines were framed for the foreign press if they wanted to report from India. As a mark of protest, several outlets refused to sign on the new censorship regulations. Billboards praising Indira with catchy slogans were put up all over the streets and top-notch artists were enlisted to make artworks in her praise. Shopkeepers were required to display Indira's pictures prominently on the windows of the shops. Legal judgements, too, were not allowed to be published in newspapers and law reports. Justice J.M.L. Sinha's judgement in Indira's election petition case was not allowed to be published in law reports. Thus, there was an active effort to create a sanitized narrative that would pass down over the years, favouring the Nehru family, pushing any works of criticism into oblivion.

Many of these artists and writers remained and continue to remain Congress loyalists till date. Over the years, they have been duly rewarded with luxuries and favours for falling in line with the family's dictums.

One of the worst programmes to have been forcibly run during the Emergency was Sanjay Gandhi's mass vasectomy programme under the government's National Population Policy of 1976. Sanjay

---

[90]Palkhivala, Nani, 'Reshaping the Constitution', *Illustrated Weekly of India*, 4 July 1976.

Gandhi was essentially the undeclared emperor of India with an abiding mother. This time around, his mother looked the other way as he committed cruel excesses. Wherever he went, he was given a thumping welcome by CMs. His words were as good as law in the country. During the two years between 1975 and 1977, over 1 crore sterilizations were performed according to the Shah Commission of Inquiry, which was set up by the Government of India in May 1977 to inquire into all wrongful acts committed during the Emergency.[91]

Government employees, such as policemen, doctors and teachers, would be paid salaries only after they had motivated the targeted number of people to undergo vasectomy. Millions were lured, persuaded and forced to undergo sterilization, the poor being top victims. According to a report by Marika Vicziany, over 1 million women had intrauterine devices (IUDs) inserted.[92] The sterilizations performed were in assembly-line fashion, in great haste and in unhygienic conditions. There was no follow-up care whatsoever. Many men and women died of subsequent infections, and over 1,800 families filed wrongful death lawsuits on behalf of deceased relatives, but the actual death toll was much higher.[93] Given these horrific tactics, it didn't take long for public anger over the forced sterilization campaign to result in riots.[94] To control the riots, the police resorted to firing, and there was a reign of terror everywhere in the country. People felt insecure, in shackles and as helpless as caged birds and the whole nation was demoralized.

Another example of the Indira government indulging in another one of Sanjay's fanatic acts is of the slum clearance drive at Delhi's Turkman Gate. Describing this event, Ghose writes in

---

[91]Third and Final Report, Shah Commission of Inquiry, Appointed Under Section 3 of the Commissions of Inquiry Act, 1952, 6 August 1978, p. 207.
[92]Vicziany, Marika, 'Coercion in a Soft State: The Family-Planning Program of India: Part I: The Myth of Voluntarism', *Pacific Affairs,* Volume 55, Issue 3, 1982, pp. 373–402.
[93]Ibid.
[94]Ibid.

Indira's biography of slum clearance drives that were in progress in Delhi in April 1976. While on an inspection tour, Sanjay stood at Turkman Gate and announced to Jagmogan, his loyalist and vice chairman of Delhi Development Authority, that he wanted to see Jama Masjid from where he was standing. Ghose goes on to write,

> Once the royal edict was issued, the loyalists rushed to obey. Turkman gate had to be cleared forthwith ... The Turkman Gate area was then a teeming sea of shops, jhuggis, slum colonies and markets, home to thousands of people. In mid-April 1976, the glamourous jewellery designer Rukhsana Sultana set up the Dujana House Sterilization Centre in the area to encourage Muslims to get sterilized as part of the government's family planning drive. On April 13 the first bulldozers began to arrive at Turkman Gate, demolishing walls and roofs of homes.

Residents looked to Sultana for help. But she in return asked for their help to meet a target of 300 sterilization cases per week. Tensions were escalating in the Turkman Gate area until 19 April when a van full of potential sterilization patients arrived and protests began at Dujana House Sterilization Centre. The CPRF rushed in with tear gas to control the situation. But people began to throw bricks, soda bottles and acid bulbs at the Central Reserve Police Force (CRPF) in retaliation. The CPRF opened fire, 'resorting to 14 rounds of firing... The harshness of the Turkman Gate slum clearance was a stark reminder that India had ceased to be a democracy.'[95] Jagmohan Malhotra was duly rewarded and made lieutenant governor of Delhi for his unquestioning loyalty to Sanjay.[96]

[95]Ghose, Sagarika, *Indira: India's Most Powerful Prime Minister*, Juggernaut Books, New Delhi, 2017, p. 186.
[96]Chowdhary, Neerja, *How Prime Ministers Decide: An Unprecedented, Explosive Look at How Decisions are Taken at the Very Top of the Indian Political Establishment*, Aleph Book Company, New Delhi, 2023, p. 80.

11

THE SIKH BLOODBATH

Abruptly, in January 1977, Indira Gandhi lifted the Emergency temporarily to allow for general elections to take place in less than two months, that is, in March 1977. The tag of being 'undemocratic' was washing away the Nehru legacy and she, the inheritor and protector of it, perhaps felt that she may need to revert to democratic means if she wanted any ounce of the Nehru–Gandhi Congress legacy to remain with her and her family. It is also believed that she was possibly advised that the Opposition stood no chance of winning as the senior leaders had been in jail for far too long and had no funds to run a strong campaign, in which case, the chance of her winning was high. Even with little to no resources left at their disposal, the Janata Party, which was formed by the merging of the Congress (O), the Jan Sangh and other Opposition parties, came to power, thus sending a clear message to Indira that her undemocratic ways were not acceptable. Morarji Desai became the PM. It remains a matter to discuss another time as to how the Janata Party was plagued by infighting and inexperience, which led to the fall of their government in a matter of 34 months. With no strong, united political opposition in sight, Indira returned to power in 1980.

However, in this section we shall look at what was brewing in Punjab after the Congress's 1977 loss and how the Sikhs were used by the incumbent Congress government to further their own political goals—an exercise that came at the cost of thousands of Sikh and Hindu lives. The turn of the decade of the 1980s marks a significant moment in history, after which the Congress led a vicious pogrom against Sikh interests, which continues to put national interest at risk even today.

What was different between Indira's previous terms as PM and the one following 1980 was that this time, the manifestation of Sanjay as the true power centre was complete. It was Sanjay who would control all decision-making and truly render his mother a silent spectator playing to his tunes. It may be safe to also say that the bloody experiment of inciting Sikh separatist sentiments was conceived by Sanjay and his coterie, and brought to fruition by Rajiv after the former's death. So, who were these men and what did they do that led to the Sikh genocide of 1984 and Indira's assassination?

THE CREATION OF THE KHALISTAN DEMAND AND BHINDRANWALE

When the Janata Party came to power in 1977, the Congress simultaneously lost many states including Punjab. In Punjab, the Akali Dal and Janata Party formed a coalition government that adopted moderate policies towards religious Sikh issues. Here is the origin of the problem that would kick-start a decades-long Congress-led pogrom of injustice towards the Sikhs. On losing Punjab, the former CM Giani Zail Singh was most distraught. As the defeated CM, he had lost power and a commission called the Gurdial Singh Commission, which was appointed to look into his conduct as CM, had found him guilty of misuse of power.[1] He was on the lookout for a way to return to power. However, it was Sanjay Gandhi, who was already known for his extra-constitutional methods, who suggested that some *sant* should be put up to challenge the Akali government. Zail Singh and Sanjay convinced Indira that the Akali Dal–Janata Party government could possibly be destabilized if an appropriate 'Sikh sant' was to constantly attack their moderate policies.[2] The logic was that if the government

---

[1]Nayar, Kuldip, *Beyond the Lines: An Autobiography*, Roli Books, New Delhi, 2012; Nayar, Kuldip, 'Operation Blue Star: How Congress Invented a Saint', *India Today*, 6 June 2018, https://tinyurl.com/425zkzd3. Accessed on 24 November 2023.

[2]Nayar, Kuldip, 'Operation Blue Star: How Congress Invented a Saint', *India Today*, 6 June 2018, https://tinyurl.com/425zkzd3. Accessed on 24 November 2023; Ghose, Sagarika, *Indira: India's Most Powerful Prime Minister*, Juggernaut Books, New

came under constant attack for taking a moderate stand on Sikh interests, the Akali Dal, led by Harchand Singh Longowal, G.S. Tohra (chairman of Shiromani Gurudwara Parbandhak Committee [SPGC]) and CM Prakash Singh Badal, would be forced to harden their stance and take hard-line positions, much to the discomfort of their alliance partner, the Janata Party. Cracks in the alliance would widen, which would eventually lead to the disintegration of their government. The idea wasn't novel—it had been done before. The former Punjab CM Pratap Singh Kairon had fought the Akalis by building up Sant Fateh Singh against Master Tara Singh, the Akali leader, who had been too big to defeat politically.[3]

Originally, the intent behind looking for a radical Sikh sant to do their bidding was to dislodge the existing Punjab government, but as the operation progressed, the Congress leadership realized that the issue could be abused and mobilized nationally to turn Hindus and Sikhs against each other, by creating a 'Hindus in danger' narrative. The idea was for the Congress to pitch themselves as the protectors of Hindus and thus win the next general elections as well. In fact, after the 1980 General Elections, when Indira and the Congress returned to power at the centre as well as in Punjab, Sanjay is said to have told his mother that losing the 1977 General Elections had rendered their condition pitiable. He is believed to have added that they would win the next election on the Khalistan–Bhindranwale issue.[4]

On Indira's approval, a team of Congress leaders (Kamal Nath, Zail Singh and Sanjay Gandhi, later expanding to include Arun Nehru, Makhan Lal Fotedar [political assistant to PM Indira], Arjun Singh [a member of the Kapurthala family] and Rajiv Gandhi after

---

Delhi, 2017, p. 251. See also Sidhu, G.B.S., *The Khalistan Conspiracy: A Former RAW Officer Unravels the Path to 1984*, HarperCollins India, 2020, p. 6.

[3]Nayar, Kuldip, 'Operation Blue Star: How Congress Invented a Saint', *India Today*, 6 June 2018, https://tinyurl.com/425zkzd3. Accessed on 24 November 2023.

[4]ANI News, 'EP-74| Unheard, Detailed Story of the Khalistan Conspiracy as Told by Former R&AW Official GBS Sidhu', *YouTube*, https://tinyurl.com/24925ewm. Accessed on 24 November 2023.

254 • What If There Was No Congress

Sanjay's death)[5] began a search for a suitable Sikh sant who could execute the aforementioned plan perfectly. Of the two shortlisted contenders, one was Jarnail Singh Bhindranwale, the fourteenth head of the Damdami Taksal.[6] As Kamal Nath has recounted to Kuldip Nayar, 'The first [sant] we interviewed did not look the courageous type. Bhindranwale, strong in tone and tenor, seemed to fit the bill. We would give him money off and on, but we never thought he would turn into a terrorist.'[7] Sanjay, on behalf of the Congress and his mother, approved the choice of Bhindranwale. As we shall see in this section, the aforementioned team of influential Congress leaders maintained constant contact with Bhindranwale, offering protection, funds and direction, ensuring that he walked on the line they had meticulously chalked out for him in order to achieve their political motives. However, even today, the Congress party, the Gandhi family members as well as Kamal Nath, a surviving member of the team that ran this pogrom, continue to deny charges of any association with Bhindranwale, despite ample evidence of the same.

Bhindranwale began to make political moves when he first opposed a convention held in Amritsar by the Nirankari sect, a move made to please Hindu traders and businessmen. Sikhism had been sceptical of the Nirankari movement in general due to significant differences with religious Sikh practices. Bhindranwale made fiery speeches and led a charged agitation against the Nirankari convention, leading to a scuffle in which 13 Sikhs and three Nirankaris were killed.[8] The Congress made every possible attempt to credit the anti-Nirankari sentiment to Bhindranwale. Even though Bhindranwale was willing to follow political directions from the Congress leadership, the fact remained that he was a

[5]Sidhu, G.B.S., *The Khalistan Conspiracy: A Former RAW Officer Unravels the Path To 1984*, HarperCollins India, 2020.
[6]Ibid, p. 34.
[7]Nayar, Kuldip, *Beyond the Lines: An Autobiography*, Roli Books, New Delhi, 2012.
[8]Sethi, Chitleen K., 'Rivalry between Sikhs & Nirankaris Is Almost a Century Old', *The Print*, 20 November 2018, https://tinyurl.com/4f62ut7r. Accessed on 24 November 2023.

radical mass leader even before the Congress adopted him. He was anointed as the fourteenth head of the Damdami Taksal by the thirteenth head, Guru Kartar Singh, who overlooked his own son to do so. He later died mysteriously in an accident and Bhindranwale became the leader of the Damdami Taksal. He was radical and religious, had a violent mind and often chose to carve out his own path—catering to his own interests that were different from the Congress's. One such example was when the reporters asked him about the creation of a separate Sikh country led by Sikh leaders. While he was willing to say that if the government made this offer, he would be in support of it, he wasn't willing to make it a primary demand in his religious sermons. He would only go so far as to say, '*Agar Bibi* [Indira] *Khalistan meri jholi mein daal degi toh mein manaa bhi nahi karunga.*'[9] This was a problem for the Congress because the demand was central to their mission in order to make the Hindu–Sikh divide a national issue that could be milked for political gains.[10] So, to solve this problem, in 1978, the Sanjay-led gang floated a radical religious Sikh organization called the Dal Khalsa, which would openly and outrightly demand Khalistan.[11] The evidence that this was the Congress's creation comes from the fact that Zail Singh, a senior Congress leader, paid the bill of ₹600 in Hotel Aroma, where Dal Khalsa's first meeting was held.[12]

On 6 August 1978, the Dal Khalsa held a press conference where it announced that their main objective was the establishment of an independent Sikh state. The Congress leadership is believed to have footed the bill for the aforementioned press conference as

---

[9]Sidhu, G.B.S., *The Khalistan Conspiracy: A Former RAW Officer Unravels the Path to 1984*, HarperCollins India, 2020.

[10]ANI News, 'EP-74| Unheard, Detailed Story of the Khalistan Conspiracy as Told by Former R&AW Official GBS Sidhu', *YouTube*, https://tinyurl.com/24925ewm. Accessed on 24 November 2023.

[11]Sidhu, G.B.S., *The Khalistan Conspiracy: A Former RAW Officer Unravels the Path to 1984*, HarperCollins India, 2020, pp. 37–8.

[12]Rana, Yudhvir, 'Dal Khalsa Slams Kuldeep Nayyar over His Statements in Autobiography', *The Times of India*, 11 July 2012, https://tinyurl.com/fjw4bzst. Accessed on 24 November 2023; Nayar, Kuldip, *Beyond the Lines: An Autobiography*, Roli Books, New Delhi, 2012.

well.[13] It has been reported widely that Zail Singh, who was made the union home minister in 1980 and the president of India in 1982, consistently maintained contact with the Dal Khalsa and often rang up the press too, urging them to publish stories of the Dal Khalsa on front pages.[14] So, two things happened simultaneously with Congress intervention—Bhindranwale was groomed and began to gain strength, and the Dal Khalsa soon became a powerful organization demanding Khalistan. Thus, over the following couple of years, Bhindranwale and the Dal Khalsa began to be correlated over the demand for Khalistan. It also became a popular belief that the Dal Khalsa was Bhindranwale's political party.

However, the fascination of Khalistan took time to catch on despite vigorous efforts by Bhindranwale and the Dal Khalsa. The youth of Punjab at the time were wealthy and content, and didn't really have any interest in religion sermons or agitations. Bhindranwale's militant approach didn't attract the masses either.[15] Punjab, which had been responsible for providing food security through the Green Revolution and was on its way to become an industrial powerhouse, was sadly on the turn of adverse events that would halt its growth. In 1980, the Sikhs in India as well as the diaspora in the US and Canada had no particular interest in the demand of Khalistan.[16]

In the general elections that followed the collapse of the Jana Sangh government, Bhindranwale campaigned for Congress leaders. While Indira claimed to have never met Bhindranwale, she campaigned for Congress leaders in Punjab alongside Bhindranwale, sharing the stage. One such occasion seems to have been the

---

[13]Sidhu, G.B.S., *The Khalistan Conspiracy: A Former RAW Officer Unravels the Path to 1984*, HarperCollins India, 2020; Nayar, Kuldip, *Beyond the Lines: An Autobiography*, Roli Books, New Delhi, 2012.

[14]Sidhu, G.B.S., *The Khalistan Conspiracy: A Former RAW Officer Unravels the Path to 1984*, HarperCollins India, 2020.

[15]Deshmukh, B.G., *From Poona to the Prime Minister's Office*, HarperCollins India, New Delhi, 2004; Sidhu, G.B.S., *The Khalistan Conspiracy: A Former RAW Officer Unravels the Path to 1984*, HarperCollins India, 2020.

[16]Ibid.

election tour of the Gurdaspur constituency in January 1980.[17] With plenty of evidence of her sharing stage with Bhindranwale and other senior leaders in regular touch with him, here is a quote illustrating Indira's misrepresentation of facts during an interview she gave to the BBC, when asked if her party had helped Bhindranwale come to prominence: 'Certainly not. I did not know him. I never knew him.'[18]

By bashing the local leaders of the Akali Dal, Bhindranwale began to attract massive public following and attention. His transformation from a radical sant to a prominent political force capable of dismissing governments was now complete.

Within months of returning to power, a new branch was creating in the Research and Analysis Wing (R&AW) called 'Sikh Extremism and its relationship to ISI'.[19] This was the first of several steps that followed, which would be taken by the Sanjay Gandhi gang to inflate the Khalistan demand, make it an issue of friction between the Sikhs and the Hindus in Punjab and Haryana, and allow the Congress to appear as saviours of Hindu sentiments. To ensure that the plan remained flawless, Bhindranwale would have to be projected as a monster in popular imagination, only after which Indira would have to dramatically slay him. However, all this had to be timed meticulously, so that maximum political capital could be extracted. Thus, to moderate the speed of events to their liking, they began to engage with the Opposition, the Akali Dal, which had been agitating for quite some time. They intended to engage the Akali Dal in multiple rounds of talks, seemingly to ensure adequate passage of time. They held over 26 rounds of talks with the Akalis just to make sure that problems did not find resolutions prematurely, ruining the chance of their political exploitation. But first, Bhindranwale had to be projected

[17]Tully, Mark and Satish Jacob, *Amritsar: Mrs Gandhi's Last Battle*, Rupa Publications, New Delhi, 2006, p. 61.

[18] The India Archive, 'Indira Gandhi - Interview - TV Eye – 1978', *Facebook*, 20 July 2016, https://tinyurl.com/55yb3b78. Accessed on 24 November 2023.

[19]Sidhu, G.B.S., *The Khalistan Conspiracy: A Former RAW Officer Unravels the Path to 1984*, HarperCollins India, 2020.

as so much of an evil element detrimental to the social fabric that even the Opposition would be compelled to endorse demands to exterminate him, at which point Indira would step in and oblige, reminding people of her carefully crafted Durga reputation—the saviour of the Hindus and of the integrity of India. Winning the general elections after emotionally charging the people of the country would be a cakewalk.

So, several questionable decisions followed. Violence significantly increased in Punjab, where Bhindranwale created a military of his own to kill anyone who came in his way or opposed his rise. As a result, repeated violent clashes broke out, and the idea of Khalistan also began to gain ground. To help this, Ganga Singh Dhillon, who had a personal abiding friendship with the then Pakistani premier Zia-ul-Haq, travelled to Punjab from the US in 1980 to deliver a lecture at a conference, where he declared that 'Sikhs are a separate nation' (a pertinent point to remember here would be that Sikhs were 2 per cent of the total population of India).[20] He also put forth a resolution during the conference stating that 'Sikhs be admitted as an associate member of the UN as they are not a part of Hindu mainstream and had a separate identity'.[21] It was also reported at the time that Zail Singh was in touch with Dhillon at the behest of his party bosses and that the latter was allowed into the country despite clear links with Pakistan.[22] Many more signs of Pakistani intelligence's involvement in exploiting the Punjab problem began to emerge. However, the Congress leadership couldn't care less.[23]

---

[20]Badhwar, Inderjit, 'I Don't Need Zia or the CIA to Tell Me to Do What I Must Do: Ganga Singh Dhillon', *India Today*, 31 October 2014, https://tinyurl.com/2cnuukma. Accessed on 24 November 2023.
[21]Sidhu, G.B.S., *The Khalistan Conspiracy: A Former RAW Officer Unravels the Path to 1984*, HarperCollins India, 2020.
[22]Sidhu, G.B.S., *The Khalistan Conspiracy: A Former RAW Officer Unravels the Path to 1984*, HarperCollins India, 2020; Badhwar, Inderjit, 'I Don't Need Zia or the CIA to Tell Me to Do What I Must Do: Ganga Singh Dhillon', *India Today*, 31 October 2014, https://tinyurl.com/2cnuukma. Accessed on 24 November 2023.
[23]Badhwar, Inderjit, 'I Don't Need Zia or the CIA to Tell Me to Do What I Must Do: Ganga Singh Dhillon', *India Today*, 31 October 2014, https://tinyurl.com/2cnuukma. Accessed on 24 November 2023.

The mission to the electoral win in 1984 was more important to them than long-term repercussions with regard to the security of the country. Till as late as August 1981, Indira continued to maintain that '[s]o far, Khalistan exists only in Canada and perhaps the USA also, but it does not mean that we would lower our guards and not exercise utmost vigilance.'[24] The R&AW was allowed to set up seven stations to monitor and manage the Khalistan issue posts with the Indian consulates and embassies abroad by the Ministry of External Affairs at breakneck speed within a matter of months, breaking the otherwise unbearably slow speed of approvals, thus indicating direct involvement of the PMO.[25]

Bhindranwale's militant army not only killed folks who opposed their ideology but also people in the media who were critical of him. It was believed that Lala Jagat Narain, owner of *Punjab Kesari* that ran negative pieces on Bhindranwale, was shot dead by the latter. This was evidenced by the first information report (FIR) filed after the murder in which Bhindranwale was named an accused. The police began a chase to arrest Bhindranwale, who was in Haryana, but he was continuously tipped off about the movements of the Punjab police and even helped by the Haryana CM Bhajan Lal, who, in fact, sent his car to escort Bhindranwale back to Mehta Chowk gurudwara in Punjab. Each time the Border Security Force tried to stop Bhindranwale, they received instructions from Union home minister Zail Singh's office to let him pass. To demonstrate some semblance of the law being followed, Bhindranwale was respectfully detained by the Punjab police, in a rest house near Ludhiana where he was interrogated for the sake of it and released in less than a month. Zail Singh later told Parliament that no incriminating evidence had been found against Bhindranwale and he was thus released. His arrest and release further raised his status as a man of supreme importance. In fact, the Dal Khalsa hijacked an Indian Airlines flight from Srinagar to Delhi, diverted it to

---

[24]Ibid.
[25]Sidhu, G.B.S., *The Khalistan Conspiracy: A Former RAW Officer Unravels the Path to 1984*, HarperCollins India, 2020.

Lahore and demanded Bhindranwale's release.[26]

As violence and unrest began to spread in Punjab, Indira needed to show that she was sympathetic to the needs of the electorate, and, hence, she allowed the former R&AW director and her close colleague R.N. Kao to lead the Special Frontier Force (SFF) commando operation to arrest Bhindranwale at either of his three known hideouts—Mehta Chowk, Guru Nanak Niwas and the Golden Temple complex. This not only pacified the people of Punjab and the Opposition but also gave an impression to the government agencies and officials that Indira was in the favour of detaining Bhindranwale. At the same time, negotiations between the Congress and the Akali Dal were still ongoing—the latter had resorted to assuaging popular sentiment by demanding a separate religious state for the Sikhs.[27]

With no solution in sight, people were losing faith in the ability of the Akali Dal to represent their interests effectively, which was to adopt a secessionist stance.[28] Bhindranwale amped up his involvement and took up the cause more aggressively in his sermons. At this point in 1982, he was roaming around with an army of armed men who made no effort to hide their weapons. Bhindranwale was followed by busloads of militants with armed men popping out of windows, standing on open jeeps and sitting on roofs of buses followed. When asked by journalist Kuldip Nayar as to why he was surrounded by so many armed men toting rifles and Sten guns, he had counter-questioned in local Punjabi dialect, 'Why do police carry guns?' To this, Nayar had said that the police represented authority, and Bhindranwale had responded, 'Let them ever challenge me, and I shall show them who has the authority.'[29]

---

[26]Ibid.

[27]Nayar, Kuldip, 'Operation Blue Star: How Congress Invented a Saint', *India Today*, 6 June 2018, https://tinyurl.com/425zkzd3. Accessed on 24 November 2023.

[28]Ibid.

[29]Nayar, Kuldip, *Beyond the Lines: An Autobiography*, Roli Books, New Delhi, 2012; Sidhu, G.B.S., *The Khalistan Conspiracy: A Former RAW Officer Unravels the Path to 1984*, HarperCollins India, 2020.

What this short exchange represents is the mentality of the man who enjoyed far too many privileges from the highest office of the country. So many were the number of privileges that all his misdeeds, no matter how gruesome, were overlooked as long as he sang the song they wanted him to sing. Little did he know that he was the bait and about to be slayed by the same people who gave him this freedom.

By 1983, Bhindranwale's reign of terror had become unbearable. He kept Hindus and moderate Sikhs in fear and any dissenting voices were swiftly killed. The Punjab police force was not allowed to act and neither was the CRPF. By then, Sanjay Gandhi had died and Rajiv had taken his place. The general elections were still over two years away, and Rajiv's team had to ensure that the Punjab potboiler remained hot but didn't cross the threshold of the Punjab polity's patience. If it did, Rajiv would be compelled to act prematurely, thus diminishing the Congress's political gains from their well-planned experiment. Disappointed with the centre's disinterest in resolving their issues, the Akalis created a voluntary corps of 1 lakh Sikhs called the 'marjiwares'—the do-or-die squad. While announcing the creation of the marjiwares, Akali head Longowal said, 'I want to tell Mrs Gandhi that our patience is getting exhausted. She should stop playing with fire. We will die like soldiers at the hands of the police. We will tolerate no further ruse till she stops playing Holi with our blood.'[30] Amidst this deep unrest, a Hindu police officer was killed by Bhindranwale's men, and there was allegedly a hit-list of men that Bhindranwale wanted to eliminate, which included Hindus and Sikhs alike. Since he was above the law by then, he carried out his gory activities without any fear, and pushed Punjab and Haryana further into fear. The nature of clashes turned communal with the killing of the Hindu police officer. Following that, a Hindu assistant superintendent of jails was beaten up by Bhindranwale's men in the Golden Temple

---

[30]Dhillon, Gurdarshan Singh, *Truth about Punjab: SGPC White Paper*, Shiromani Gurudwara Parbandhak Committee Amritsar, https://tinyurl.com/mryyvdar. Accessed on 24 November 2023.

and Hindu shops were looted. Indira announced Governor's rule in the state.

By end of 1983, Bhindranwale had moved to the Golden Temple complex and set up a fort with his army. From the langar roof of the Akal Takht, he began to hold durbars and delivered sermons that were mostly anti-Hindu in tone and content. The langar roof was an adjoining building to the Akal Thakt and his armed men would walk around the entire temple complex freely. The Akalis began to fear that Bhindranwale, who had now made the Golden Temple the base for all his activities, might eventually take over the gurudwara if there wasn't enough resistance.[31] They began to arrange huge morchas with thousands of volunteers and attendees in the Golden Temple complex. With him conducting his business from the complex and now the morchas, the Golden Temple complex became the fulcrum of all the political action.[32] His hate-filled sermons were taped and cassettes were made available freely in local shops for people to listen to. Within two weeks of governor's rule in Punjab, the Kashmir Mail train passing through Punjab was derailed, leading to the death of 19 passengers. Within weeks, another bus was hijacked and four Hindu passengers were shot dead. Meanwhile, after 26 rounds, when the talks between the Akalis and the Congress leadership failed, Hindus retaliated in Haryana and began to attack Sikhs in public transport, shops and gurudwaras. Communal clashes and killings had become commonplace. With this, the Nehru–Gandhi family and the gang had come a long way in achieving their mission. The monster that they had plotted for was created, and it was now time for Indira to come in and slay him, reinforcing her Ma Durga image in popular imagination.

By March 1984, on getting wind of an operation to capture him, Bhindranwale's armed men had taken vantage positions in nearby

[31]Nayar, Kuldip, 'Operation Blue Star: How Congress Invented a Saint', *India Today*, 6 June 2018, https://tinyurl.com/425zkzd3. Accessed on 24 November 2023.
[32]Ibid.

buildings and houses overlooking the complex. Under the watchful eyes of the officials of the Punjab government, ammunitions and arms were taken into the complex and gun positions were fortified. His close associate Major Gen. Singh also moved into the Akal Takht and began preparing defence strategies in case of an attack.

OPERATION BLUE STAR

Rameshwar Nath Kao, who had been entrusted the responsibility to capture Bhindranwale in 1982, had, by 1984, prepared a detailed plan with Director General of Security (DGS) R.T. Nagrani, which he proposed to Indira. It was called Operation Sundown.[33] As the head of R&AW for nine years from 1968 to 1977, he knew the capability of trained SFF commandos very well and proposed a 'snatch and grab' operation to capture Bhindranwale alive from the Golden Temple complex with the least amount of loss of lives and property as possible. The plan prepared by Nagrani was foolproof— commandos in helicopters would enter the Guru Nanak Niwas guesthouse near the Golden Temple and abduct the militant leader. The operation was so named because it was timed for past midnight when Bhindranwale and his guards would least expect it.[34]

The plan included two Mi-4 helicopters that would fly pretty low, carrying two teams of SFF commandos. They would then approach the spot where Bhindranwale gave his sermon from and just before the end of his sermon, when his security was lax, taking advantage of the situation, the two teams would rope down. Some commandos would rush towards and grab Bhindranwale while the others would neutralize the armed security guards who would be expected to fire on seeing the commandos. Some others would block Bhindranwale's access to the Golden Temple sanctum in case he made a run, and another group would take charge of the

---

[33]Sidhu, G.B.S., *The Khalistan Conspiracy: A Former RAW Officer Unravels the Path to 1984*, HarperCollins India, 2020, pp. 141–3.

[34]'The Untold Story before Operation Bluestar', *India Today*, 6 June 2019, https://tinyurl.com/55kbjbnf. Accessed on 24 November 2023.

bulletproof vehicles that would have arrived to take a captured Bhindranwale away. An SFF unit would take Bhindranwale outside the complex to the bulletproof vehicles that would be stationed right outside.[35]

However, during a briefing in early April 1984 at Indira's private office wing at 1 Akbar Road, adjoining her 1 Safdarjung Road residence, Indira turned down the plan, allegedly citing that she could afford loss of civilian lives.[36] This wasn't the first time that such an operation had been planned. In middle of 1982, Kao had been ready to capture Bhindranwale from his Mehta Chowk residence, but a R&AW officer in the guise of reporter had made an untimely visit, which had spooked Bhindranwale and led to his move to the Golden Temple complex. Had this operation been allowed, at most five commandos and about 60 civilians would have lost their lives as per G.B.S. Sidhu's estimates. Mr Sidhu also states that the reason Indira rejected this operation was that she didn't want Bhindranwale alive. If he was captured alive, he would disclose the secret that the gang of Congress leaders led by Sanjay and Rajiv were his handlers, and that certainly would not bode well for the family.[37] In the storm of Operation Blue Star that was about to follow, the meticulous details of Operation Sundown were carefully buried in RAW's secret archives, until they surfaced decades later in a set of declassified letters dating to February 1984, which revealed that Margaret Thatcher's government had helped India on 'a plan to remove Sikh extremists from the Golden Temple'.[38]

As press from India as well as the world had been directed to watch the action that Indira was to take to tackle the discontent in

[35]Sidhu, G.B.S., *The Khalistan Conspiracy: A Former RAW Officer Unravels the Path to 1984*, HarperCollins India, 2020.
[36]'The Untold Story before Operation Bluestar', *India Today*, 6 June 2019, https://tinyurl.com/55kbjbnf. Accessed on 24 November 2023.
[37]Sidhu, G.B.S., *The Khalistan Conspiracy: A Former RAW Officer Unravels the Path to 1984*, HarperCollins India, 2020.
[38]Nayar, Kuldip, 'Operation Blue Star: How Congress Invented a Saint', *India Today*, 6 June 2018, https://tinyurl.com/425zkzd3. Accessed on 24 November 2023.

Punjab and Haryana, it was time to make the final move, that is, bring a dramatic end to the problem that the Congress leadership had meticulously created under her guidance.

About 165 Hindus and Nirankaris had already been killed by Bhindranwale's extremist followers and over 410 had died during police encounters, riots, train derailments and other such incidents. The Congress had lost the state elections in Uttar Pradesh—a state that was considered its stronghold. In order to make political gains out of slaying Bhindranwale and consolidate those gains in time for the general elections, which were a few months away, in May 1984, Indira decided that the time to act was then. The initial plan was to siege and flush out, that is, use adequate force to prevent movement of people, food and weapons into the Golden Temple complex, thus forcing extremists to surrender.

Chief of Army Staff Gen. Arunkumar Shridhar Vaidya assured her that during such an operation, no damage to the gurudwara buildings, and especially to the Golden Temple complex, would be caused. While Indira was in agreement in the siege-and-flush plan, a few days after her discussion with Gen. Vaidya, the latter called on her again and informed her that a revised plan would have to be used where the army would have to make a quick entrance into the Golden Temple and take the terrorists by surprise. He was of the opinion that a gradual siege may result in more Sikhs gathering in the complex and terrorists taking refuge in the inner sanctum of Harmandir Sahib, from where it would be very difficult to remove them without damage to the sanctum.[39] A woman who had rejected Operation Sundown on the pretext of loss of civilian lives just a few months ago approved a heavily armed contingent to go into the Akal Takht, which was severely fortified with weapon-carrying Bhindranwale's Sikh extremists by then. While she had regular meetings with Sikh colleagues of the Congress and even met Zail Singh, now president of India and Commander-in-Chief of the Indian Armed Forces, she did not discuss her consent to

---

[39]Sidhu, G.B.S., *The Khalistan Conspiracy: A Former RAW Officer Unravels the Path to 1984*, HarperCollins India, 2020.

Operation Blue Star. Sardar Swaran Singh, on observing heavy troop movements, even warned her that under no circumstance should she approve sending the army inside the Golden Temple, as it would have devastating consequences for the future of Punjab and Sikhs. However, she lied to his face and replied, 'Sardar Sahib, how can you imagine that I would commit such a mistake?'[40] Perhaps she knew that she couldn't confide in any of the Sikh colleagues, as they would never support the destruction of their holiest site and perhaps sabotage the operation, ruining all her accumulated political gain.

Finally, on 2 June 1984, Indira addressed the people of India in the evening on All India Radio and recounted various efforts she and her government had been making to reach a peaceful settlement with the Akali leaders who were on the verge of a large agitation against her misrule. She said, '[L]et us join hands together and heal the wounds ... [D]on't shed blood, shed hatred.'[41] Shockingly, just hours later, her government announced that the army would undertake Operation Blue Star.

After clearing out 37 gurudwaras on the night of 3 June 1984, on 4 June, announcements were made on loudspeakers asking pilgrims inside the Golden Temple premises to leave. These announcements were not clearly audible and created more confusion in an already panicked complex. Only 129 people managed to come out of the temple area. There was unwillingness among Bhindranwale's militant army to surrender. At this point, it became clear that Bhindranwale would not go down without a fight. He was insistent on keeping his legacy alive and would rather die a legend, remembered as a martyr who succumbed while defending the Harmandir Sahib from Indira's army. The army bombed several outer structures of the complex and moved

[40]ANI News, 'EP-74| Unheard, Detailed Story of the Khalistan Conspiracy as Told by Former R&AW Official GBS Sidhu', *YouTube*, https://tinyurl.com/24925ewm. Accessed on 24 November 2023; Sidhu, G.B.S., *The Khalistan Conspiracy: A Former RAW Officer Unravels the Path to 1984*, HarperCollins India, 2020.
[41]@SikhRI, X (formerly Twitter), 3 June 2022, 2.30 a.m., https://tinyurl.com/s5a43n7d. Accessed on 24 November 2023.

tanks and armoured personnel vehicles on the road just outside the complex. After failing several times to enter the Akal Takht, Major Gen. Brar, who was leading the operation, requested Indira Gandhi for approval to use tanks. He received the approval at 7.00 a.m. on 5 June, and eight Vijayanta tanks were deployed. As a part of Operation Blue Star, the tanks fired 80 shells, devastating the Akal Takht, the holy shrine. Sikhs believe that the library that housed valuable manuscripts was set on fire deliberately by the army, but the Indira government later claimed that it caught fire accidently.[42] By evening, Major Gen. Brar gave orders to the men to storm inside the Akal Takht and shoot anyone who came in the way. On the morning of 7 June, bodies of Bhindranwale and his close associates Major Gen. Shahbeg Singh, Amrik Singh and Thara Singh were recovered in the basement. Bodies of Sikh pilgrims were piled alongside militants in garbage trucks and taken to the cremation ground. While the government's White Paper claimed that 83 army men, including four officers and 493 civilians were killed,[43] a journalist Brahma Chellaney, who managed to stay back in Punjab despite government orders for all press to leave the state, reported that over 1,200 civilians had died. The *London Times* carried his story on 14 June 1984.[44] Chellaney was charged with sedition and interrogated by the police for 35 hours. Due to the Supreme Court's intervention, his arrest was prevented. His passport was impounded and credentials not renewed by the Congress government. The passport was only returned due to international pressure in 1985.[45] Several eyewitness accounts claim that at least 1,500 dead bodies lay in the complex on the completion of the operation,[46] similar

---

[42]Singh, Surjit, 'The Missing Chapter of 1984: Book by Book, Sikh Reference Library Struggles to Restore Glory', *Hindustan Times*, 6 June 2018, https://tinyurl.com/4jjmb3ep. Accessed on 24 November 2023.

[43]'Operation Bluestar: The Untold Story: June 7, 1984', *Gateway to Sikhism*, https://tinyurl.com/8fzc6nsc. Accessed on 24 November 2023.

[44]Sidhu, G.B.S., *The Khalistan Conspiracy: A Former RAW Officer Unravels the Path to 1984*, HarperCollins India, 2020, p. 191.

[45]Ibid.

[46]Ibid.

to Chellaney's numbers.[47] The whole operation lasted nearly 56–60 hours from 4.00 a.m. on 4 June to about 4.00 p.m. on 6 June. Eyewitnesses have also reported that despite claims in the White Paper, the firing was almost incessant and continuous and had no constrains.[48] Interestingly, it was found that most of the arms used by Bhindranwale's men, including sophisticated ones, were procured within India.[49]

CONGRESS AVENGES INDIRA'S ASSASSINATION: THE 1984 SIKH MASSACRE

While Bhindranwale and his men were killed, bringing an end to a violent phase in Punjab and great relief to the majority population, several things went wrong with Operation Blue Star, which continue to hurt Sikh sentiments even today. Apart from destruction of the Akal Takht, it was the merciless attitude of the army. Even the chosen day to carry out the operation, which was the martyrdom day of Guru Arjan Dev, was wrong as a large number of pilgrims were in the temple. But for the Congress leaders running the operation from the PMO, the only thing that seemed to matter was the political capital they could extract from the mission. Sikhs have made large, positive contributions to the fabric of India, including, but not limited to, their dedicated fight against the British from the early days of the freedom struggle. Sikhs, not just in India, but all around the world were livid at the destruction of the Akal Takht.

As if this wasn't enough, another operation called Operation Woodrose was carried out all over Punjab immediately after Operation Blue Star from June to September 1984. Operation

---

[47]'Operation Bluestar: The Untold Story: June 7, 1984', *Gateway to Sikhism*, https://tinyurl.com/8fzc6nsc. Accessed on 24 November 2023.

[48]Ibid.

[49]Sidhu, G.B.S., *The Khalistan Conspiracy: A Former RAW Officer Unravels the Path to 1984*, HarperCollins India, 2020; ANI News, 'EP-74| Unheard, Detailed Story of the Khalistan Conspiracy as Told by Former R&AW Official GBS Sidhu', *YouTube*, https://tinyurl.com/24925ewm. Accessed on 24 November 2023.

Woodrose was a plan to eradicate Sikh militancy by going to every hamlet and town to capture suspected militants, which ended in the torture and murder of thousands of young innocent Sikhs.[50] The Indian Army, once again, used severe force against innocent civilians, employing tanks, artillery, helicopters and armoured vehicles.[51] It went from village to village, captured Sikh men, humiliated them in public and then killed or detained them. Accounts of the operation describe that women were also raped and forced to walk around naked on the streets.[52] It seems that the army really went after the young Sikhs, which led to mass murder of the youth in Punjab.[53] This was the final straw of tolerance for the Sikhs. Indira's hostility towards them got them incredibly enraged and vengeful.

The R&AW picked up intelligence that some Sikh extremists may avenge Operation Blue Star by assassinating Indira and recommended replacing the Sikh bodyguards on duty or at least ensure that only one Sikh guard was on duty at a given time. However, their recommendations were ignored by the PMO, and, on 31 October, about three months after Operation Blue Star, Indira was assassinated.[54] By 5.00 p.m., while Indira's body was at AIIMS and Rajiv had not yet been administered the oath of office, the Congress leaders and their goons were already dragging Sikhs out of their cars, scooters, shops, stabbing them and flinging them off bridges on railway lines.

Rajiv learned that Indira had been assassinated by her two Sikh bodyguards from Pranab Mukherjee. At that time, he was in Calcutta, delivering a speech during an election rally. Even as Pranab and Rajiv boarded a plane to return to Delhi around

---

[50]TLMUN Herald, '1984—The Truth That Was Never Told', *Medium*, 17 April 2022, https://tinyurl.com/bdfrex7d. Accessed on 24 November 2023.
[51]Ibid.
[52]Ibid.
[53]Ibid.
[54]ANI News, 'EP-74| Unheard, Detailed Story of the Khalistan Conspiracy as Told by Former R&AW Official GBS Sidhu', *YouTube*, https://tinyurl.com/24925ewm. Accessed on 24 November 2023

1.00 p.m., anti-Sikh riots began in Calcutta but were quickly controlled by the then West Bengal government led by Jyoti Basu (CPIM). Arun Nehru received Rajiv at the airport, and their car immediately went to AIIMS. Zail Singh was away on a state visit, and after Operation Blue Star, his relationship with the Nehru family had soured. In the car ride to AIIMS, Arun Nehru is believed to have recommended to Rajiv that the latter get administered the oath of office by the vice-president instead of waiting for Zail Singh to return. However, Rajiv waited for him to return. His plane landed at 5.00 p.m., and around 6.30 p.m., Rajiv was administered the oath of office as the next PM of India.[55] By that evening, Congress goons were moving around with voters' lists to identify Sikh homes and Congress leaders were supplying them with old tyres, kerosene, oil and other materials that were used to burn Sikhs alive.[56]

The PMO took security in its hands, overriding Home Minister P.V. Narasimha Rao, in order to overlook the violent anti-Sikh pogrom. Rao chose to stay silent and obey his party instead of carrying out his duty to protect *all* citizens. Cases of arson, mass killings and rapes in Sikh colonies like Sultanpuri and Trilokpuri became the order of the day. When targeted Sikhs made distress calls to police control rooms, their calls were ignored. At Tughlakabad railway station, goons massacred Sikhs in a train, killing over 70 of them, while the police simply watched.[57] Witnesses have described details of the massacre in telling, soul-shattering words:

> Frenzied gangs of young Hindu thugs, thirsty for vengeance,
> burned Sikh-owned stores to the ground, dragged Sikhs out
> of their homes, vehicles, and trains, then clubbed them to

---

[55]Sidhu, G.B.S., *The Khalistan Conspiracy: A Former RAW Officer Unravels the Path to 1984*, HarperCollins India, 2020, p. 210.

[56]Rao, Amiya, Aurobindo Ghose and N.D. Pancholi, *Truth about Delhi Violence: Report to the Nation*, Citizens for Democracy, 1985.

[57]'Cobrapost Sting: Government Didn't Allow Police to Act in 1984 Riots', *Biharprabha.Com*, 22 April 2014, https://tinyurl.com/mv3c2hdy. Accessed on 24 November 2023,

death or set them on fire before raging off in search of more victims just hours after the assassination. Witnesses watched in horror as crowds raped Sikh women, murdered Sikh men, and set fire to Sikh homes, businesses, and gurudwaras on the streets of New Delhi. According to eyewitness accounts, police enforcement and government officials took part in the atrocities by participating in the violence, urging civilians to take revenge, and arming the mobs.[58]

This violence spread all over the country and led to a large-scale state-sponsored Sikh genocide. Over 3,000 Sikhs were killed in New Delhi alone and more than 20,000 were killed over the country. Rajiv Gandhi, in his speech at the Boat Club in New Delhi on 19 November, merely a couple of weeks after the bloody massacre began, said, 'Some riots took place in the country following the murder of Indira ji. We know the people were very angry and for a few days it seemed that India had been shaken, but when a mighty tree falls, it is only natural that the earth around it does shake a little.'[59]

These were not just riots. The violence was a targeted, government-sponsored Sikh genocide. Time and again, over and over, Sikhs have been abused by the Congress. The Congress ecosystem followed up this bloody massacre by tweaking FIRs and ensuring that evidence was tampered, thus leading to delayed and denied justice.[60] Testimonies of witnesses were mostly rejected by judges to whom the cases were sent after investigation on the grounds of delay in filing FIRs or delay in recording witness statements.[61] The Justice Dhingra Committee, which was set up to inquire the cause of the Sikh riots, observed in its report that

[58]TLMUN Herald, '1984—The Truth That Was Never Told', *Medium*, 17 April 2022, https://tinyurl.com/bdfrex7d. Accessed on 24 November 2023.
[59]'Watch Rajiv Gandhi Make His Infamous "Big Tree Falls" Speech Justifying the 1984 Anti-Sikh Riots', *Scroll*, 20 November 2015, https://tinyurl.com/cn3bwf6m. Accessed on 24 November 2023.
[60]Sidhu, G.B.S., *The Khalistan Conspiracy: A Former RAW Officer Unravels the Path to 1984*, HarperCollins India, 2020.
[61]Ibid.

'[t]he whole effort of the police and administration seem to have been to hush up the criminal cases concerning riots.'[62]

Killings of thousands of innocent Sikhs led to a whole generation of them who were inherently angry. Most took refuge in Punjab, while the rest moved out of the country. In Punjab and abroad, angry Sikhs who had lost loved ones in the riots became disenchanted with the Hindu majority and the Indian government. They began to find solace and refuge in the idea of Khalistan, where they'd feel safe and secure. The Congress cannot absolve itself from the responsibility of turning India-loving Sikhs away from the country.

In fact, as we have also recently seen, during the protests against the Farm Bills in 2020, it has been alleged that the disenchanted Sikh elements and the Khalistanis were once again mobilized to create a violent atmosphere in an otherwise peaceful protest when they brought down the Indian flag hoisted at the Red Force and had clashes with the police. The Congress believes that every time it needs fuel against the Modi government, it can activate its Bhindranwale strategy. However, they now need to realize that a majority of the Sikhs are becoming alert to their machinations and this kind of gaslighting may not work for much longer.

---

[62]Mahapatra, Dhananjay, 'Congress Govt Showed No Interest in Nailing 1984 Rioters', *The Times of India*, 16 January 2020, https://tinyurl.com/3rj62fct. Accessed on 29 November 2023.

CONCLUSION:
THE STATE OF TODAY'S CONGRESS

The prime ministerial tenures of P.V. Narasimha Rao and Dr Manmohan Singh are marked with unchecked corruption. Narasimha Rao tried to bring in reforms due to the pressure from the World Bank and IMF. However, the family became quickly disenchanted with him, so much so that Sonia Gandhi even refused to grant her consent to open the gates of the Congress office to let in his dead body. Dr Manmohan Singh, on the other hand, ignored the rampant corruption and collusion of his party members with terrorist elements and preferred to stay silent.

In 2014, the Congress, for the very first time, fielded Rahul Gandhi as its PM candidate. Amateurish, reluctant and ill-informed, despite a strong machinery working to build him up, Rahul failed miserably when confronted with an overpowering candidate like Narendra Modi. In fact, so terrible has been his performance that he even lost his Amethi seat, which had been the Nehru family's stronghold, to the BJP's Smriti Irani in 2019. Since 2019, the Congress has stepped up its attacks on the Modi government, realizing that if they do not stop the Modi juggernaut, it may be decades before they are able to return to power or even retain the position of the primary Opposition party.

Using the same rule book as members of the family, the Congress instigates and fuels protests, which often take a violent and hateful turn before any major election. Rahul seems out of touch with ground reality and has systematically killed dissenting voices, even the well-intentioned ones, within the Congress party. Thus, what is left is a Congress that is run by Rahul and supported by his sister Priyanka Gandhi Vadra and some yes-men who surround them at all times. With piles of money having been exported out of the country for decades, Rahul and Priyanka depend on their international networks and family friends to tutor them and devise narratives and strategies to gain lost political ground. For this, the duo is willing to bend over backwards and engage in activities that may and already do hurt India and Indians.

Several good political minds in the Congress have either left the party due to Rahul's arrogance or chosen to retire from active politics. Think of the G23 leaders who wrote an open letter to the Congress leadership to hold democratic elections for various posts in the party. The family actively sabotaged the election process to ensure that their chosen yes-man occupies the chair of the party president, keeps it warm and is instructed rather than consulted. Multiple attempts of rebranding Rahul have been made so openly that now it has become a running joke as to which PR agency will bag the next multi-crore contract.

The problem lies in the fact that Rahul himself seems totally clueless about the history of his family and of the Congress party. He has made contrasting statements, clueless observations and disrespectful notes one too many times. Reading this book in detail will perhaps remind him of the '*nafrat ki dukaan*' legacy he comes from and of the fact that his party and family have repeatedly chosen politics over the blood of the Indian people. It is my opinion that India will keep rejecting him and his family for the foreseeable future due to their past and current misdeeds.

EPILOGUE:
INDIA, THAT IS, BHARAT

The destiny of independent India changed in 2014 when the Narendra Modi-led BJP government came to power. Typically, across the 75 years when the Congress rule had been interrupted, the longest a PM was able to retain office was for one full term, that is, Atal Bihari Vajpayee. All others, barring the Congress leaders, lost power, their governments disintegrating even before the completion of a full five-year term. It became natural for the Congress and its ecosystem to assume that a change in leadership from the Congress would only be temporary, considering it a small hiccup in the long road of India's destiny. The Nehru–Gandhi family began to think of India as its private property to adjudicate and exploit. Thus, when Narendra Modi not only completed his first term but also returned to power in 2019 with an even larger majority than 2014, the Opposition got disturbed. The attacks on the Modi government began to get more frequent, more aggressive and more international. As we see today, their entire narrative-building infrastructure is at work, constantly showing down the Modi government's achievements, underplaying India's incredible growth story over the past decade while simultaneously building Rahul as India's natural inheritor— the deserving prince.

Over the last decade, India's growth trajectory has been truly remarkable. We have become the fifth largest economy in the world as well as the fastest growing economy in the world, from the tenth position that we occupied before 2014. With the significant increase in the size of our economy, India has become a preferred destination for all major global companies to do business. The Indian consumer base, which is wealthier than it was in 2014, is now courted by global businesses. With a more aware, educated and skilled young demographic that has attained a sense of self-confidence, India has become a nation to be friends with. Whether it is pharmaceuticals or mobile phones, textiles or innovative technologies, manufacturing in India has become a preferred choice for several global corporations. India is now being called the bright spot in the world economy by the IMF—accompanying numbers, quarter after quarter, attest to the much-deserved title.

Due to this unprecedented growth, Modi's India asserts itself confidently in its bilateral and multilateral dealings. The Congress made major judgement errors in building and maintaining relations with the Western countries, becoming heavily dependent on Russia, hugely trusting of China, keeping a distance from the Middle East, nor caring about the Global South and refusing to help Israel. In comparison, Modi's foreign policy is one of multilateralism in its true spirit. He and his team have built strong bonds with Middle Eastern nations and Israel, made ties with Western countries stronger than they ever were, reduced dependence on any one country for defence equipment, become a voice of the Global South, engaged with the US much more than any previous government, kept China at bay and essentially destroyed Pakistan's standing in the international arena. With an India-first spirit, Modi's team seems to have an approach where it engages in nations with a multi-alignment principle. It understands that staying aloof, shut off and non-aligned does help us and in fact can be counterproductive to our long-term interests. Multi-alignment and multiple engagements with countries based on respecting mutual interests, as well as being on the side of peace, has gotten us very far in the last decade. With this renewed self-confidence, India has been able to push several multilateral resolutions from climate to health, become an integral part of several groupings like the QUAD and I2U2 and also is often invited for G7 dialogues to represent its perspectives. We don't shy away from calling out defunct systems within multilateral organizations, like the UN and the WHO, and proposing reform that will make them more responsive to the needs of today. The world now listens when India, under the leadership of PM Modi, talks.

With strong economic growth, Team Modi's policies have supplemented individual growth. With the adoption of technology for financial inclusion, Team Modi has essentially eliminated the possibility of corruption while also connecting Indians to government schemes and benefits that play a decisive role in eliminating poverty. With universal health coverage and the free food grain programme, over 80 crore Indians receive free food grains from the government every year. The sanitation drive ensured that crores of toilets were built. With basic needs of health, sanitation and food taken care of, families have the opportunity to spend on other important items such as educating their children or skilling family members, thus improving their individual standard of living. Infrastructure has been yet another trademark of the Modi government. Team Modi has doubled the number of airports just in 10 years from the number in 2014. The rail and road connectivity that the government has been able to build over the decade has been equally impressive.

In terms of terrorism and national security, India under PM Modi's leadership has maintained a zero-tolerance stance, ensuring that threats, whether internal or external, are immediately neutralized, with no sympathy or vested interests for antinational elements. The years before 2014 were marked with frequent bomb blasts, killings and extortions, making lives of Indians vulnerable each day. The Congress, which frequently nurses anti-national elements, needs to be questioned for lives that were lost. The India of the last decade has left the Congress-run India so far behind that it has become an existential crisis for the Congress to resurrect itself enough to even remain the principal opposition party, let alone return to power. The people of the country continue to choose progress over corruption, truth over manufactured lies, security over terrorism and growth over stagnation. In my opinion, the Congress's resurrection is improbable in the near future, if not impossible.

ACKNOWLEDGEMENTS

This book is a retelling of the events that occurred around the time of Independence and in the decades following it. I have referred to hundreds of sources to find accurate information. However, there are some books that gave me much needed direction from time to time. Much gratitude to the authors whose meticulous research helped me build this book. Some of these include: *The Shadow of the Great Game: The Untold Story of India's Partition* by Narendra Singh Sarila, Leonard Mosley's *The Last Days of the British Raj*, Iqbal Chand Malhotra and Maroof Raza's *Kashmir's Untold Story*, Brig. J.P. Dalvi's *Himalayan Blunder: The Curtain-Raiser to the Sino-Indian War of 1962*, Bruce Riedel's *JFK's Forgotten Crisis: Tibet, the CIA, and the Sino-Indian War*, Gautam Chikermane's *Reform Nation*, Taylor C. Sherman's *Nehru's India: A History in Seven Myths*, Sagarika Ghose's *Indira: India's Most Powerful Prime Minister,* Ramchandra Guha's *India after Gandhi: The History of the World's Largest Democracy*, memoirs of J.P. Goyal called *Saving India from Indira: Untold Story of the Emergency* and G.B.S. Sidhu's *The Khalistan Conspiracy: A Former R&AW Officer Unravels the Path.*

A book so difficult is impossible for one person to work on. In this case too, it has truly taken a village. I have many, many people to thank who came together selflessly to ensure that this piece of work comes out the way it is intended to. I am extremely grateful to the entire team at Rupa Publications, specifically to Kapish Mehra and Dibakar Ghosh. At Rupa, I have found reliable and trustworthy partners to make my writing come alive, over and over again.

Of course, without the support of my family and close ones, a work like this simply cannot be delivered. To them, I owe my most sincere thanks. There are several people I am unable to name and thank, but these silent supporters have unmatched contribution to this piece of work. They provided immense mentorship and support at crucial junctures in my life, and I am grateful for their support every day.

Finally, most importantly, my most heartfelt gratitude to PM Narendra Modi, who continues to inspire entire generations with his fiery and thought-provoking speeches—one of which being the inspiration behind this book.

INDEX

Made in the USA
Monee, IL
15 May 2026

4524cb09-afdd-40c8-91c7-bd988e452306R01